SECOND GENERATION MOBILE
AND WIRELESS NETWORKS

ISBN 0-13-621277-8

9 780136 212775

90000

Prentice Hall Series In
Advanced Communications Technologies

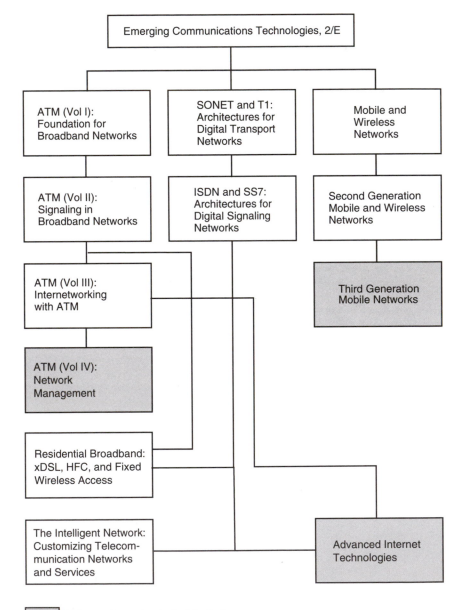

Emerging Communications Technologies, 2/E

ATM (Vol I):
Foundation for
Broadband Networks

SONET and T1:
Architectures for
Digital Transport
Networks

Mobile and
Wireless
Networks

ATM (Vol II):
Signaling in
Broadband Networks

ISDN and SS7:
Architectures for
Digital Signaling
Networks

Second Generation
Mobile and Wireless
Networks

ATM (Vol III):
Internetworking
with ATM

Third Generation
Mobile Networks

ATM (Vol IV):
Network
Management

Residential Broadband:
xDSL, HFC, and Fixed
Wireless Access

The Intelligent Network:
Customizing Telecom-
munication Networks
and Services

Advanced Internet
Technologies

Indicates future books in this Series

SECOND GENERATION MOBILE AND WIRELESS NETWORKS

UYLESS BLACK

Prentice Hall PTR
Upper Saddle River, New Jersey 07458
http://www.phptr.com

Library of Congress Cataloging-in-Publication Data

Black, Uyless D.
    Second generation mobile and wireless networks / Uyless Black.
      p. cm.
    Includes bibliographical references and index.
    ISBN 0-13-621277-8
    1. Wireless communication systems. I. Title.
TK5103.2.B5323 1999
621.382—dc21   98-29585
                                        CIP

Acquisitions editor: Mary Franz
Cover designer: Scott Weiss
Cover design director: Jerry Votta
Manufacturing manager: Alexis R. Heydt
Marketing manager: Miles Williams
Compositor/Production services: Pine Tree Composition, Inc.

Published by Prentice Hall PTR
Prentice-Hall, Inc.
A Simon & Schuster Company
Upper Saddle River, New Jersey 07458

Prentice Hall books are widely used by corporations and government
agencies for training, marketing, and resale.

The publisher offers discounts on this book when ordered in bulk
quantities. For more information contact:

        Corporate Sales Department
        Phone: 800-382-3419
        Fax: 201-236-7141
        E-mail: corpsales@prenhall.com

        Or write:

        Prentice Hall PTR
        Corp. Sales Dept.
        One Lake Street
        Upper Saddle River, New Jersey 07458

Printed in the United States of America
10 9 8 7 6 5 4 3 2

ISBN: 0-13-621277-8

Prentice-Hall International (UK) Limited, *London*
Prentice-Hall of Australia Pty. Limited, *Sydney*
Prentice-Hall Canada Inc., *Toronto*
Prentice-Hall Hispanoamericana, S.A., *Mexico*
Prentice-Hall of India Private Limited, *New Delhi*
Prentice-Hall of Japan, Inc., *Tokyo*
Simon & Schuster Asia Pte. Ltd., *Singapore*
Editora Prentice-Hall do Brasil, Ltda., *Rio de Janeiro*

There is a good chance that the reason you are reading this book is to clear-up the confusion that surrounds the technology called second generation mobile wireless systems. You are in good company. Almost everyone, except those who work with these systems day-to-day, are also confused. It is for this reason that the Tower of Babel is on the cover of this book.

As I was nearing the completion of this book, my editor called to remind me that I had not yet selected a "creature" for the cover. Until now, I have selected animals for the covers of this series' books, and have written in each book's preface an analogy of the creatures' communications skills to those of modern communications systems.

For this book, I have chosen the Tower of Babel based on the well known biblical story. Most of us know this story. According to Genesis, the ancient Babylonians decided to build a great city and "make a name for themselves" by building a tower in the city "whose top is in the heavens." God disrupted this work by confusing the languages of the workers and the tower could not be built.

The second generation mobile wireless systems being built today also exhibit a multitude of confusing "languages." For example, in a typical metropolitan area in North America, one might encounter several different conventions for one mobile phone to communicate with another. And, like the ancient Tower of Babel's workers, these modern toilers are not compatible. Examples are CDMA, GSM, IS-136, Wireless local loop, D-AMPS, and satellite PCS . . . with others, such as DECT, on the way.

While these systems unto themselves are understandable, some of them employ a jumble of overlapping and redundant terms in describing their communications behavior.

It sometimes seems as if the Tower of Babel has been reincarnated at the mobile base station.

It is my hope that this book will clear-up the "babel" surrounding the technology of second generation mobile wireless systems, and provide you with an understanding of how the technology operates and why the technology consists of so many different implementations.

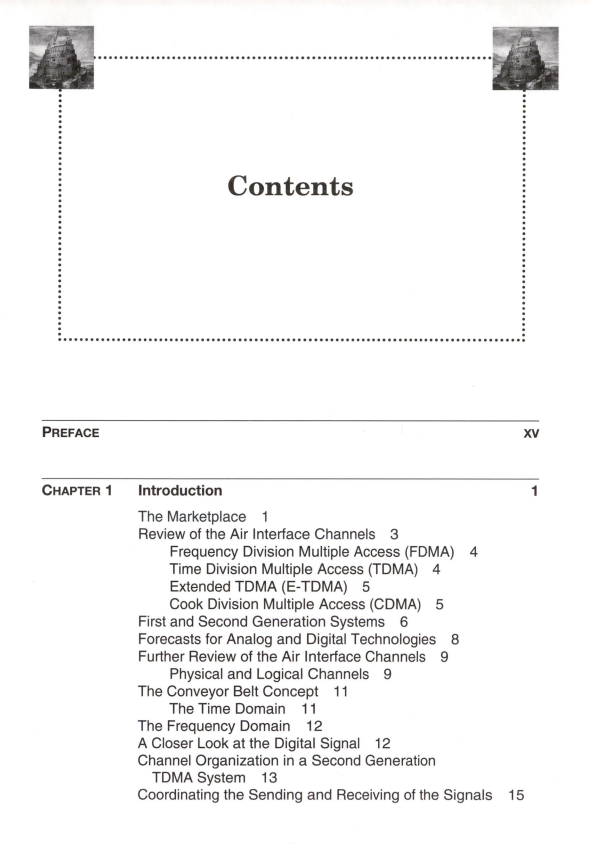

Contents

CHAPTER 2   **First Generation Systems**   **39**

CHAPTER 3   **Digital AMPS (D-AMPS): IS-54-B**   **55**

**CHAPTER 4   The Global System for Mobile
Communications (GSM)   77**

CHAPTER 5   IS-136   **125**

Abbreviations/Acronyms   349

Index   355

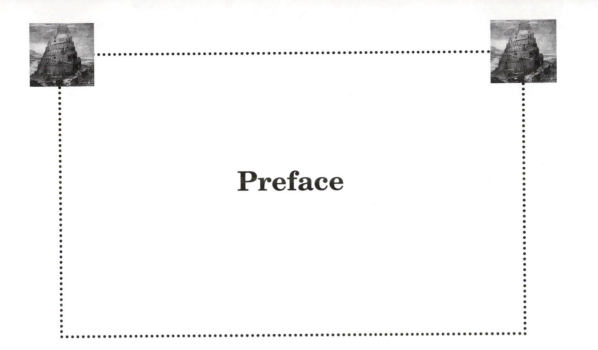

Preface

The information in this book represents an overview of the second generation mobile and wireless technologies. The specifications for these technologies number several thousands of pages. As I was doing research for this book, I had an opportunity to stack a hard copy rendition of some of the standards on a table. The stack was several feet high. I say several feet high because my stack did not include all the documents pertaining to the specifications. The reason I am explaining this aspect to the reader is to once again explain that my books are not meant to be used as a detailed design guide for your work. The intent is to provide you a bridge from these very detailed and technical specs to a general tutorial, which I hope will enable you to assimilate more efficiently the information in these detailed and voluminous standards.

You will learn as you read this book that many of the second generation mobile wireless systems have many similarities. Indeed, many of their operations perform the same functions, but with different procedures. For example, GSM, IS-136, and D-AMPS have methods to combat the noise and fading characteristics of the mobile wireless channel. But the IS-136 (for example) procedures to support these methods are different from GSM. In order to avoid simply repeating the description of each specification, which would serve no one's use, my approach is to explain the subject once, and make reference to it as appropriate.

ACKNOWLEDGMENTS

I would like to thank British Telecom (BT) for their contributions to this book. During my lectures in Europe the past couple years, several BT engineers offered their thoughts on GSM and third generation systems, which I have incorporated into these chapters.

Nortel has my thanks as well. Their designers at the Richardson, Texas lab were especially helpful to me on the subjects IS-136, IS-41, and their implementations of these technologies. Their inputs are always insightful and valuable.

Thanks also to my friends at Award Solutions in Richardson, Texas. They made major contributions to the IS-95 material.

Also, Joan Gillen helped me in my research efforts by her effective Internet browsing, and saved me many hours of "searching" with her prompt responses to my requests.

Of course, any errors or other problems in this book are mine.

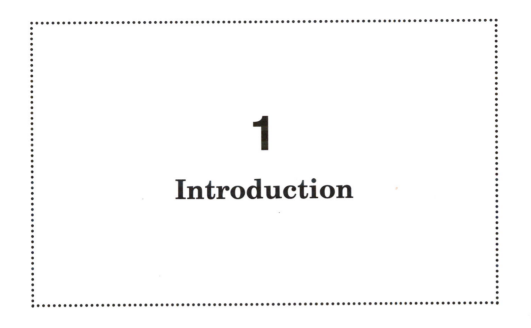

1
Introduction

This chapter reviews the basic concepts of a mobile wireless system. A classification scheme is provided that will be useful for tracking the second generation systems in later chapters. We take a look in a general way at the systems covered in this book, and examine some market projections on the deployment of second generation systems.

THE MARKETPLACE

One of the fastest growth areas in the telecommunications industry is the mobile cellular phone market. Since the late 1980s and early 1990s, the market has increased its growth rate each year. The recent growth in this industry is depicted in Figure 1–1, as well as the prediction for growth through the year 2001 (as compiled by Dataquest Inc. and published by the Wall Street Journal, September 11, 1997).

Figure 1–1a shows the worldwide cellular market, tabulated by the number of subscribers. Figure 1–1b shows the service revenue; that is, the income the cellular service providers receive from the cellular customers. Of course, the predictions on the future subscriber base and the service revenues, are just that—predictions. But many of the marketing forecasts on the growth of mobile, cellular technology have been inaccurate—they have been too conservative.

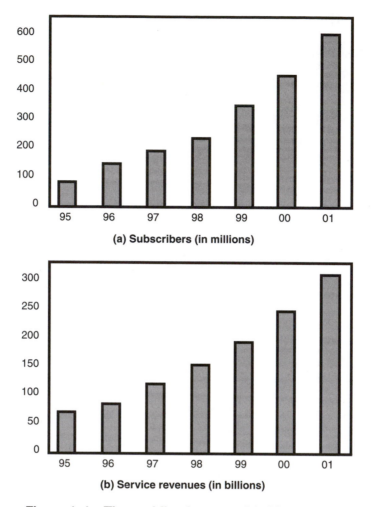

Figure 1–1   The mobile phone worldwide market.

Nonetheless, if these predictions hold true, in the next few years the mobile phone will become a common appliance in the homes of many families. Moreover, due to the relatively modest capital investments required to deploy a wireless system (in comparison to a wire-based alternative), much of this high growth is occurring in so-called third-world countries that do not have an abundance of capital in which to invest in their telecommunications infrastructure. Simply stated, we can look to the future and see that the mobile phone will play an increasing role in our professional and personal lives.

REVIEW OF THE AIR INTERFACE CHANNELS

It is assumed the reader of this book has a basic understanding of mobile wireless networks and the concepts of cells. Notwithstanding, this section provides an overview of some of these ideas to make sure several key concepts are understood. This diversion is to review air interfaces, the channels on these interfaces, and channel utilization techniques. We then use this information to compare first and second generation mobile wireless networks. Figure 1–2 will be a helpful reference during this discussion.

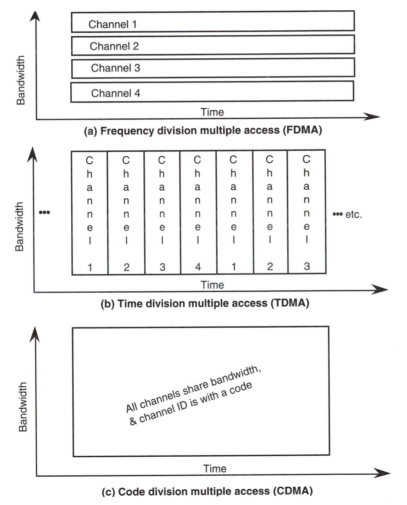

Figure 1–2   The channels at the air interface.

Frequency Division Multiple Access (FDMA)

First, frequency-division multiplexing divides the bandwidth of the air interface between the mobile station (MS) and the base station (BS) into multiple analog channels; each radio frequency (RF) channel occupies one part of a larger frequency spectrum (see Figure 1–2a). For example, some second generation systems divide a larger frequency spectrum of 15 MHz into multiple 200 kHz channels. This technique is called *frequency division multiple access* (FDMA). And as another example, some second generation systems divide a larger frequency spectrum of 10 MHz into multiple 30 kHz channels.

If two separate FDMA channels are available, one for each direction of transmission, the system is said to be operating in a *frequency division duplex* (FDD) mode, also known as *full-full duplex* (FFD).

Time Division Multiple Access (TDMA)

Time-division multiple access (TDMA) operates on an RF channel (for example, a 200 kHz RF channel), but divides this analog channel into time slots, which contain digital traffic (see Figure 2–2b).

With TDMA, a user is given a digital time slot, and the slots are rotated among the users on a periodic basis. For example, user A might be assigned time slot 1 on a specific 200 kHz RF channel, user B could be assigned time slot 4 on the same RF channel, and so on. Each user is assured of having these slots available at a known time, which means the user's mobile station knows the exact time to send (and stop sending) traffic.

Bits, bytes, or blocks of voice or data from the user application are multiplexed together and interleaved into the slots. The slots are combined together to form TDMA frames, and it is these frames that are sent onto the single radio frequency (RF) carrier.

As stated earlier, the digital TDMA signals are modulated onto an analog carrier (an FDMA channel). Therefore, a TDMA system is a combination of FDMA and TDMA. In contrast, a pure FDMA interface does not divide the RF channel into slots, but dedicates each RF channel to one user. FDMA is strictly an analog-based air interface.

In some TDMA systems, a channel-sharing technique called *time division duplex* (TDD) is used on the air interface. With this approach, one frequency is used for both directions between two stations and each station takes turns using the channel—first the mobile station uses the RF channel, then the base station uses it, and so on.

TDD is also known by two other rather self-descriptive names: flip-flop and ping-pong. Essentially, TDD is a half-duplex system that gives the illusion of full-duplex operations, because the channel is flip-flopped quite rapidly. For example, one system flips the direction of transmission every 5 ms—so quickly that two persons engaged in a normal conversation cannot discern that they are not given a dedicated channel in each direction.

Extended TDMA (E-TDMA)

A conventional TDM system wastes the bandwidth of the communications link for certain applications because the time slots are often unused. Vacant slots occur when an idle user terminal has nothing to transmit in its slot; for example, during a pause in a conversation on the phone. To address this problem, a different technique called *statistical TDM* (STDM) multiplexing dynamically allocates the time slots among active user terminals. Dedicated time slots (TDMs) are not provided for each mobile phone on the channel. Consequently, an idle terminal time does not waste the RF channel capacity, because its slots can be borrowed by another active user (someone who is talking, or perhaps a data application that is sending e-mail).

This technique has been around for a number of years, and is now being employed in the new versions of second generation systems. It is known as *extended TDMA* (E-TDMA).

Code Division Multiple Access (CDMA)

The third major channel sharing technique is called *code division multiple access* (CDMA), depicted in Figure 1–2c. This technology does not divide the time spectrum nor the frequency spectrum into pieces. Rather, CDMA places all users onto the same frequency spectrum at the same time. Thus, the conventional concepts of TDMA and FDMA are not used in CDMA.[1]

---

[1] We will see that CDMA does use take advantage of FDMA and TDMA techniques. To clarify briefly here, the FDMA approach is taken by dividing a large bandwidth (typically 10 MHz) into FDMA channels. Then, CDMA takes a large chunk of this bandwidth (about 1.23 MHz), and places all users onto this spectrum. The remainder of the spectrum may be used for conventional FDMA or TDMA operations. For the CDMA aspect, even though all users are using the same spectrum, their transmissions are often divided into time slots for purposes control and efficiency.

This concept uses a technique developed many years ago called *spread spectrum,* which means traffic is transmitted (spread) over the entire spectrum (typically across a wide bandwidth of 1.23 MHz). Each user is identified on the channel with a unique code. This code is used at the transmitting site to encode the traffic and it may also be used to spread it across the frequency spectrum. At the receiver, the code is used to extract the user's traffic.

In concept, CDMA is intended to provide more capacity than FDMA or TDMA as well as allow a graceful degradation of the channel performance as more users enter a cell and use the spectrum. The nature of the coding is such that each user's coded signals result in an approximate even number of binary 1s and 0s in the signal. As a consequence, the combined signals (without decoding) are perceived as noise. As more users enter a cell and use the spectrum, the network informs each user to reduce the mobile station's transmission power, which means all users on the channel are acting in deference to each other.

In actual practice, CDMA is quite complex and some of the concepts, while attractive on paper, are difficult to implement. Notwithstanding, the technology provides very high quality with cells that are not densely populated and offers more capacity than an FDMA system of comparable bandwidth.

With this overview behind us, we now focus on what are known as first and second generation mobile wireless systems and begin an analysis of the main subject of this book, second generation mobile wireless systems.

FIRST AND SECOND GENERATION SYSTEMS

The main difference between a first generation and second generation mobile wireless system is that a first generation system uses analog signaling (FDMA) for the user traffic on the air interface and a second generation system uses digital signaling (with TDMA or CDMA channel sharing) for the user traffic. Both second generation techniques modulate the user traffic over an analog radio frequency (RF) channel. For second generation systems, the voice signals are converted to digital bits through an analog-to-digital (A/D) process, and then imposed (modulated) onto an RF carrier. For first generation systems, the voice signal is not converted to digital signals, but modulated directly onto the RF channel.

The second major difference stems from the first. Since second generation systems digitize the user traffic (as well as non-user traffic, such as control signaling), it is a relatively simple matter to encrypt the digital bits to provide privacy and security for the mobile network customers. The signals cannot be intercepted and interpreted by unauthorized parties (at least with the current systems, not yet). First generation systems do not encrypt the traffic, and the voice images are sent "in the clear." They are subject to interception, and many instances have occurred in which the cellular user's identification numbers have been picked off the air and used to make illegal calls. This problem does not occur in a secure digital encrypted system.

The third major difference also stems from the first. Since the second generation systems use digital technology, it is possible to apply digitally based error detection and error correction procedures to the bit streams. The result can lead to very clear signals with little or no noise on the channel. For example, the bits of the user signal are repeated and interleaved (spread out in time) before being sent across the RF channel. This practice makes the transmission more robust and combats the noise and fading effects that occur on the channel.

Of course, the actual quality of the voice image depends upon the specific analog-to-digital method, the amount of compression of the bits, and the error control methods. Some systems perform extensive compression on the voice signal, and their signals are perceived by some customers as "hollow" or "tinny".[2]

A fourth distinction is how the traffic channels (the channels that carry the user's traffic) are employed. In conventional analog systems, the RF channel is allocated to one user; in a digital system, the RF channel is allocated to more than one user, and each user's traffic is identified with time slots or codes. This distinction allows for the implementation of another attractive feature: the allocation of bandwidth for user traffic only when the user needs the bandwidth. Two terms are used to convey this idea. The term *dedicated mode* refers to a mobile station that has been assigned a traffic channel (TCH). The term *idle mode* refers to a mobile station that has not had a TCH assigned (dedicated) to it.

Dedicated and idle modes are common throughout modern mobile and wireless systems. The practice permits the use of control channels to keep the mobile station and network informed about each other when the user of the mobile station has turned the mobile station on but is not using it. Consequently, the precious bandwidth of the air interface is not

---

[2]These systems are being replaced by enhanced voice coders (vocoders), and will likely be obsolete in several years. See Appendix 1A for more information on this subject.

committed to the reservation of resources for user traffic when there is no user traffic to be sent. At the same time, the idle mode permits resources to be assigned to the user when needed and keeps the network informed about the mobile station.

Some people state that there is a fifth major difference: First generation systems use lower frequencies on the air interface (around 800 to 900 MHz), and second generation systems use frequencies in the range of about 1800 to 2000 MHz. Therefore, the physical nature of the signals differs significantly since the higher frequency systems send signals with very short wavelengths, which translates into a less robust signal. The short waves are attenuated by foliage, atmospheric conditions, and so on.

This fifth distinction is not entirely correct. As discussed in later chapters, many systems in place today are using the lower frequencies and "retrofitting" the digital technology onto these channels. Therefore, this approach produces the advantages of digitization that were just discussed, and at the same time, allows the use of the ubiquitous first generation infrastructure.

FORECASTS FOR ANALOG AND DIGITAL TECHNOLOGIES

Predictions for use of analog and digital wireless services vary, depending upon who is doing the predicting. Table 1–1 represents a study conducted by EMCI on the mobile phone sales from 1995, projected out to the year 2000.

Most predictions into the next century hold that analog systems will still be around. At this writing, they are still a pervasive technology, and even though digital systems have more to offer, analog systems have a lot going for them. The vendors recognize that they must still maintain investments in analog, because some of their customers wish to keep their analog handsets, and as just mentioned, the analog-based infra-

Table 1–1   Ongoing North American Use and Projections of Analog and Digital Mobile Phone Sales

	1995	1996	1998	2000
Analog	35.1m	43.5m	54.6m	50m
Digital	0.94m	2.4m	13.8m	35.6m
Analog as % of total	97%	95%	80%	58%

m = million

structure is widely deployed. Additionally, new analog-based products require a modest investment (TDMA over existing FDMA systems, for example), whereas a new digital system requires a significant capital investment. In the United States, the world's largest single cellular market, the deployments of the second generation systems have experienced some difficulties.

However, pure analog systems will eventually disappear, and the predictions of most analysts foretell analog technology moving to obsolescence. Indeed, other forecasts show analog based systems moving into obsolescence sooner than 2000.

FURTHER REVIEW OF THE AIR INTERFACE CHANNELS

We discussed earlier that the air interface operates on radio frequencies (RF), which are assigned in each country by a government regulatory agency. The frequencies are used in different ways, depending upon the specific mobile wireless technology. Figure 1–3a shows the approach taken with first generation systems. Separate physical channels are reserved for control operations and ongoing user traffic. Furthermore, two separate channels are used for the control and user traffic, one for the downlink (forward channel) from the network to the mobile station, and one for the uplink (reverse channel) from the mobile station to the network.

The newer systems discussed in this book use the method shown in Figure 1–3b. In this configuration, the control channels (CCHs) and user traffic channels (TCHs) share the same RF channel. Through the use of TDMA techniques, these channels use reserved time slots on the physical channel. Alternately, with CDMA operations, each user and control channel is identified with unique codes.

Physical and Logical Channels

The term *channel* is used in a variety of ways in the telecommunications industry. In the broadest sense, it is used to describe the transport media between two machines. In a narrower sense, it is used to describe either the physical media (such as a wire or RF medium) or the arrangement of the signals on the physical wire or RF medium.

In second generation mobile wireless systems, most of the industry uses the term logical channel to describe a part (slot, frame, packet, cell,

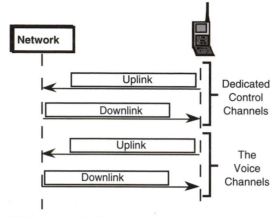

(a) Seperate physical channels for traffic and control

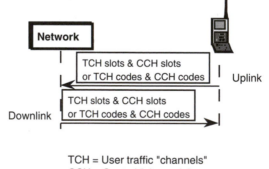

TCH = User traffic "channels"
CCH = Control "channels"

(b) Same physical channels for traffic and control

Figure 1–3   Channels at the air interface.

etc.) of the physical channel. However, some of the second generation mobile wireless specifications tend to blur this unambiguous distinction.

For example, some of the descriptions of the air interface describe eight physical channels existing on one 200 kHz physical carrier. This definition implies that the physical burst of energy (the burst period that creates the slot) is a physical channel. Consequently, this definition assumes physical channels running on other physical channels, a distinction I find confusing in relation to general practice in the industry. Nonetheless, these are the terms used in some of the specifications, and we will deal with them accordingly.

Then, what is a logical channel in these systems? The logical channel defines what is happening inside the slot; that is to say, how it is coded and what its functions are. So, a slot might carry user traffic—it would be called a traffic channel. Or, it might carry signaling traffic, and it is then called a control channel. Further distinctions are made as to the type of traffic channels and the type of control channels. That is to say, the slots are coded in a variety of ways to manifest themselves as different types of logical channels.

Thus, a burst of electromagnetic energy on the RF carrier is a physical channel, and the nature of the burst, identified with binary 1s and 0s, constitutes a logical channel.

THE CONVEYOR BELT CONCEPT

The Time Domain

With any mobile interface that uses channel slots, the slots can vary in the information they contain. Some slots will transport user traffic, and others will contain control traffic, such as roaming information, mobile station pages, a variety of synchronization information, and so on.

Some of the second generation systems provide the network administrator with options in how these slots appear on the air interface: how often they are present and how they exist in conjunction with other slots. These options give the administrator more flexibility in tailoring the mobile system to specific cell sizes and traffic patterns.

The system must provide a means for the mobile station to know the function and contents of each received slot. As we shall see later, during an initial handshake between the mobile station and the network, the mobile station is provided with data from the network that enables it to know about each slot on the air interface. This important ability is aided by the conveyor belt concept.

The slots sent and received across the air interface are periodic—they repeat themselves. In effect, they resemble a conveyor belt that goes around and around, but always in a predictable manner.

To extend the analogy, let's paint the conveyor belt with a set of stripes, each being a different color. The colors are periodic, so if one is told that the next stripe on the conveyor belt is blue, it is easy to know that the color stripe after blue stripe will be yellow, and the next red, and so on—*if* one is informed about the repeating pattern of the stripes. Once we know about the position and identity of the stripe (color) we know the position and identity of all the stripes on the conveyor belt, because they are repeated time after time. These stripes symbolize the slots on the air interface.

The process just described is known in the mobile wireless systems as *synchronization*. Subsequent chapters will elaborate on time synchronization and the use of the conveyor belt analogy to explain aspects of synchronizing in the "time domain."

THE FREQUENCY DOMAIN

At the risk of oversimplifying some complex concepts, I am going to extend the conveyor belt analogy further. Before accepting the slots on the conveyor belt, it is important that the conveyor belt itself is actually working and moving the slots around and around. Think of the conveyor belt as the RF channel. If it is of poor quality and has inconsistent performance, the paint stripes may not be transported in a concise fashion—or perhaps not at all.

Therefore, in a mobile wireless system, the mobile station can pick and choose the best conveyor belt (RF channel) to receive its information. It scans through a set of RF channels, finds a good one, and locks onto it. Thus it synchronizes in the "frequency domain." Then it looks for the special slots to obtain its "time domain" information.

A CLOSER LOOK AT THE DIGITAL SIGNAL

We have learned that a digital transmitter impresses digital signals onto the RF carrier. Traffic is burst onto the channel at specific periods, in this example (Figure 1–4a) from the Global System for Mobile Communications (GSM) technology, each burst lasts 0.577 ms. Up to eight mobile stations are assigned to a communications channel of 200 kHz bandwidth. Thereafter, their bursts are controlled such that each station knows when to send its burst onto the channel. In this manner, the eight users do not interfere with each other. The bursts shown in this figure are also called time slots.

In order to prevent a TDMA burst from interfering with the burst from another slot, the cellular specifications define the amplitude and time requirements for the signal. Figure 1–4b shows the requirements for a burst as defined in the GSM specifications. The transmitter in this example must switch its signal on in 28 µs, and then send its information

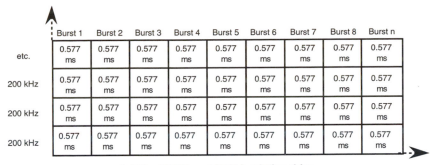

(a) The FDMA and TDMA relationships

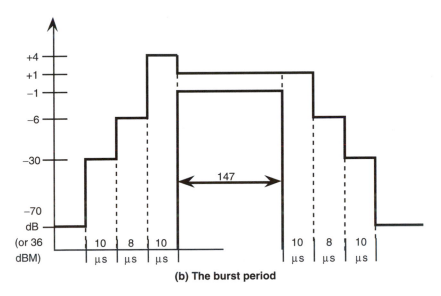

(b) The burst period

Figure 1–4   Examples of the digital signals.

for 542.76 μs, which permits the sending of 147 bits during this burst. It then has 28 μs to turn off its transmitter. A guard time on each side of the 542.76 μs burst requires that the signal must be below –70 dB.

CHANNEL ORGANIZATION IN A SECOND GENERATION TDMA SYSTEM

We will use TDMA to explain other aspects of second generation air interfaces (Figure 1–5). The frames sent back and forth between the network (the network component is called the base station [BS], explained

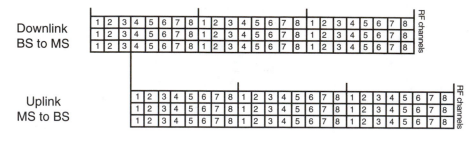

Downlink
BS to MS

Uplink
MS to BS

(a) Staggering on the downlink and uplink channels

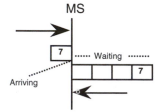

(b) As viewed by the mobile station (MS)

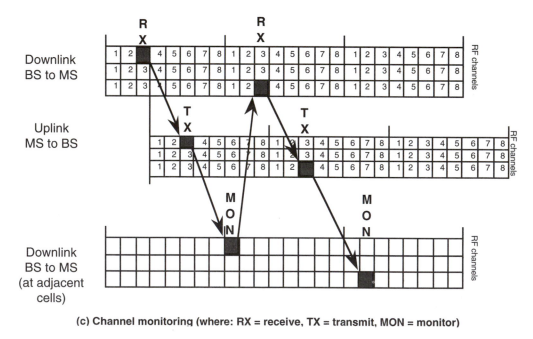

Downlink
BS to MS

Uplink
MS to BS

Downlink
BS to MS
(at adjacent
cells)

(c) Channel monitoring (where: RX = receive, TX = transmit, MON = monitor)

Figure 1–5   Staggering the frame transmissions.

in more detail shortly) and the mobile station (MS) are sent in a staggered fashion. As Figure 1–5a shows, the frames are staggered by three time slots. The uplink (MS to BS) is delayed in relation to the downlink (BS to MS).

This concept is used on many systems that have only one physical RF channel, but it is also used with air interfaces with two RF channels (an uplink and downlink channel). For the former, staggering provides full duplex operations on one channel, called *time division duplex* (TDD). For the latter, even though the systems use two channel pairs, the staggering of the frames is still employed. This approach means that the MS can avoid the requirement to transmit and receive at the same time, which translates into less complex and expensive receivers. This approach obviates a duplexer (a duplexer permits two-way simultaneous transmissions), which is a cumbersome device and draws lots of power. This approach is one example of the advantages of using digital signals (and slots) in contrast to the first generation analog systems, in which the transceivers are duplexers.

Figure 1–5b shows another view, from the perspective of the MS. It is receiving slot 3 of a frame and is waiting three time slots to send out its slot 3.

As shown in Figure 1–5c, during periods when the MS is not sending (TX) or receiving (RX) its slot, it monitors (MON) other channels in adjacent cells. The MS informs the network about these other channels, and if it finds one that is of better quality than the one it is "camped on," it can ask the network for a handover operation to the higher-quality RF channel.[3]

COORDINATING THE SENDING AND RECEIVING OF THE SIGNALS

The mobile stations operating on the same frequency are different distances from the base station. As a result of this situation, the bursts from the mobile stations exhibit different delays and amounts of signal loss. As depicted in Figure 1–6a, it is possible that the mobile stations' time slots may overlap, especially in adjacent time slots, when they ar-

---

[3]The term *handover* is used in some countries; in others, the term *handoff* is used. These terms are used synonymously in this book.

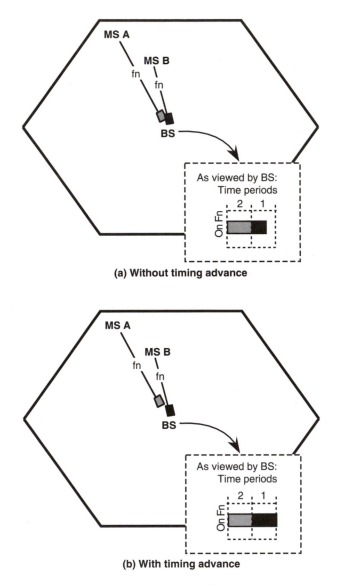

Figure 1–6   Delay differences.

rive at the base station's receiver. Furthermore, the longer the distance the signal must travel, the more it will decay in power (attenuation).

These potential problems are solved if the base station and mobile stations are able to (a) control, in a very precise manner, when the mobile stations transmit their bursts, and (b) control the power levels of the transmissions.

To synchronize the sending of the bursts, the base station uses a control channel to direct the timing of the mobile stations' transmissions. By monitoring the mobile stations' transmissions to it, the base station determines which stations should have their bursts synchronized (or not synchronized further), as depicted in Figure 1–6. This concept is called a timing advance.

At this same time, the base station also informs each mobile station what its transmit power level is to be. Mobile stations further away from the base station must use higher power levels than those closer. With this approach, all the slots have about the same power level when they reach the base station.

As shown in Figure 1–7, the base station measures the reception of the signal from the mobile station relative to what it expects based on a zero distance, under static conditions, with zero timing advance. Stated another way, the base station measures the reception of the mobile station's signal as if the mobile station were adjacent and attached to the base station. As part of these monitoring activities, the base station sends to each mobile station a *timing advance* (TA) message, based on the measured round trip propagation delay of the signal (BS to MS to BS). The mobile station must then adjust (advance) its timing by this amount.

This part of the chapter has explained some of the unique aspects of digital mobile systems. It is evident that the technology requires precise synchronization operations in order for the information to be received correctly at the mobile and base stations. The examples have focused on

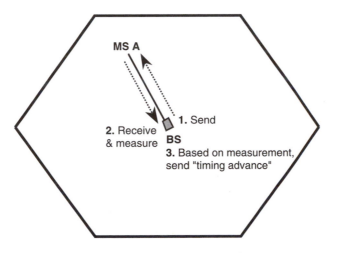

Figure 1–7   Synchronizing the time slots.

TDMA air interfaces. CDMA uses similar techniques, but with different types of timing operations, a subject that is explored in later chapters.

TAXONOMY OF MOBILE WIRELESS SYSTEMS

The subject of second generation mobile wireless systems can be quite confusing to a newcomer. This problem stems from the fact that several second generation systems are being deployed throughout the world, and some of these systems are identified with different names. Moreover, some of these names describe the same basic air interface technology, but with a different rendition of the technology.

To take one example, consider the TDMA technology. In the United States, more than one TDMA system has been deployed in the past few years. Several of these systems operate with 8 TDMA slots in a frame, while one system uses a 3-slot approach. Some TDMA systems operate on an 800 MHz carrier, and others operate on a 1900 MHz carrier. A second point of confusion arises from the fact that some systems use the same terms to describe different types of RF operations.

Let us clear up these perplexing issues in this section by using Figure 1–8 as a principal reference point. The figure represents a taxonomy of the major wireless mobile systems in operation today.

The Improved Mobile Telephone Service (IMTS) is an old analog technology and is included here to give you an idea of the evolution of the mobile wireless technology. IMTS served as the launching point for the first generation mobile wireless systems that originated in the early 1980s.

The analog-based systems (called first generation systems in this book) are still prevalent and will be in the marketplace for a number of years. They are shown in this figure as the Advanced Mobile Phone System (AMPS) and the Total Access Communications System (TACS). AMPS and TACS are two examples of first generation systems; others have been deployed as well. AMPS is the most widely used first generation system in the world and is the North American implementation.

However, the digital-based second generation systems are now more widely used than the first generation technologies. The remainder of the systems in this figure are digital-based, except for IS-41, which supports analog or digital air interfaces (more on IS-41 shortly).

The so-called cordless telephony (CT) technology was originally a "closed" system. The mobile station operated within a fixed area and did not connect to the public telephone network. For example, a factory, uni-

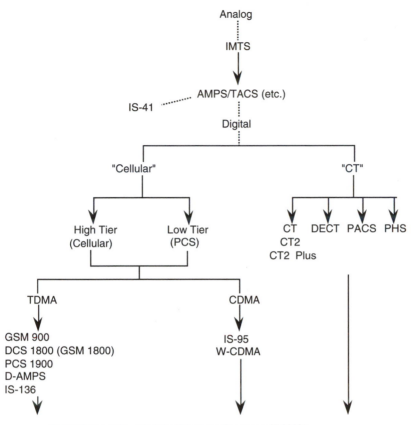

Third Generation Mobile Wireless Systems (TGMS)

AMPS	Advanced mobile phone system
CDMA	Code division multiple access
CT	Cordless telephony
D-AMPS	Digital AMPS
DCS 1800	Digital cellular system (renamed to GSM 1800)
DECT	Digital European Cordless Telephone
GSM	Global system for mobile communications
IMTS	Improved mobile telephone service
IS-41	Interim standard 41
PACS	Personal access communications system
PCS	Personal communications system
PHS	Personal handyphone system
TACS	Total access communications system
TDMA	Time division multiple access
W-CDMA	Wideband CDMA

Figure 1–8   A taxonomy of mobile wireless systems.

versity, or an industrial campus might install a private CT system for use within the confines of the specific enterprise. The mobile phone was not taken home when the employee left work, because it could not be used elsewhere.

I have been using the past tense in the description of CT, because the more recent CT implementations are dual mode, in that they can operate with the private mobile wireless system, as well as a public system, such as AMPS. So, the term CT does not mean that it is a closed system. The distinction between cellular and CT is blurring, and in the future, the distinction between CT and other mobile wireless systems will likely fade away.

CT is experiencing mixed success in the marketplace. As the Global System for Mobile Communications (GSM), IS-136, and CDMA-based systems continue to grow, the future of CT is uncertain. But DECT (Digital European Cordless Telephony) appears to be on the road to success, so there are exceptions to my statements.

Why So Many TDMA Interfaces?

The reader may wonder why there are so many TDMA specifications shown in Figure 1–8. (And most of the CT systems shown in the figure use TDMA techniques as well.) The answer is that different standards groups and other organizations have promoted them, and each represents the views of that respective group of designers. Most of them are similar, but none of them are compatible. A brief diversion is needed here to explain in more detail why so many technologies exist for the second generation mobile wireless air interface.

In the United States and Canada, the regulatory bodies have been reluctant to impose one standard for the air interface (as was the case with the FCC in the United States requiring AMPS for all first generation systems). This approach has lead to a "Tower of Babel" (discussed in the preface to this book) in that incompatibility of equipment is commonplace. The key question is does this incompatibility matter? The answer is both yes and no.

The yes part of the answer stems from the fact that a mobile user who travels to another city may not be able to make a call in that city because his or her mobile phone's air interface is not supported in that city. The alternative for the user is to subscribe to another service and buy another phone or wait for the availability of dual mode phones. The dual mode phones are more complex and more expensive to build. In addition, some critics state that the proliferation of multiple standards leads to a fragmented industry and slows the growth of the technology.

The no part of the answer stems from the fact that much of the capability of the dual mode phones can be implemented with hardware (application specific integrated circuitry, ASIC) at a relatively modest cost. Moreover, by not establishing one standard, the regulatory authorities keep the competitive marketplace open and encourage additional research and development to abet an embryonic technology.

An example of this philosophy is the Federal Communications Commission (FCC) taking a hands-off approach in dictating the air interface for second generation systems in the United States. The CDMA technology has been the prime beneficiary of this approach.

The GSM 900 specification forms the basis for Digital Cellular System 1800 (DCS 1800, recently renamed GSM 1800) and the Personal Communications System 1900 (PCS 1900). Because GSM 900, GSM 1800, and PCS 1900 are quite similar, they are covered in the same chapter in this book.

The IS-136 specification is considered a U.S. standard and was developed largely in the United States by U.S. vendors. It is a direct competitor to the GSM TDMA systems (and, of course, to other second generation systems, such as IS-95).

IS-95 is the accepted standard for the CDMA air interface. As of this writing, there are no competitive CDMA interfaces to IS-95.

The term Digital AMPS (D-AMPS) refers to IS-54-B, which defines a hybrid first generation and second generation air interface. The D-AMPS mobile station operates in a dual mode fashion. It can support the conventional analog AMPS operation. Alternately, if the cell in which the mobile station is located uses some of the AMPS RF channels in a TDMA mode of operation, the mobile station can adjust its "behavior" to take advantage of the more efficient TDMA mode and tune to an RF channel that supports TDMA.

The IS-41 specification is not used at the air interface, but is employed by the network to manage the overall activities of the mobile stations, such as roaming, location updates, and authentication procedures. Figure 1–8 shows its association with AMPS, but IS-41 is versatile enough to support IS-136, IS-95, and other air interfaces.

IS-41 is not used in many parts of the world. Instead, a similar "network" protocol is used, known as the Mobile Application Part (MAP). The best known and most widely used MAP is defined as part of the GSM specification. But a rose by any other name is still a rose and IS-41 is indeed a MAP. As we will see later in this book, due to the prevalence of GSM's MAP and IS-41, systems have been deployed to interwork these protocols. For example, gateways have been constructed to allow the interaction of North American networks (that use IS-41) with European networks (that use GSM's MAP).

For the foreseeable future, it is likely that some handsets will offer dual mode services; that is, handsets that support different air interfaces. This situation is especially true for U.S. networks, since the second generation systems of TDMA and CDMA are both being deployed in many cities in the United States.

But dual mode second generation phones are not yet in the marketplace. Presently, first generation dual mode systems are available for AMPS/TDMA and AMPS/CDMA air interfaces. When powered up, a dual mode phone searches for the presence of a second generation procedure operating in the cell in which the mobile station is located. If the second generation system is not available, the mobile station will attempt to log on and connect with a first generation system.

Yet another term should be defined here: dual band systems. A *dual band* mobile station is capable of operating in the 800 MHz band or in the 1900 MHz band. These mobile phones have not yet seen commercial use, but as the newer 1900 MHz systems are more widely employed, they must co-exist with the earlier 800 MHz systems in the same geographical locations. So, it is certainly possible that a market will emerge for dual-mode/dual-band mobile stations.

Use Caution When Utilizing Some Terms

Be aware that a practice by some vendors and service providers is to use the following terms to describe these specifications:

- TDMA: IS-136 and/or Digital AMPS (D-AMPS, IS-54-B)
- GSM: GSM 900, GSM 1800, and PCS 1900
- CDMA: IS-95
- PCS: Any second generation system

This classification scheme is not correct, since the GSM-based technologies use TDMA channel operations at the air interface. Furthermore, some books and articles in technical journals use the term Personal Communications System (PCS) 1900 in a more generic sense: to describe the spectrum space (1900 MHz) used by a TDMA or CDMA system, such as GSM for TDMA and IS-95 for CDMA. In Europe the term personal communications network (PCN) is used in place of the North American term PCS.

To complicate matters further, the term PCS is sometimes applied to what are known as low-tier systems, which are systems that use small cells. In contrast, a high-tier system is one that uses large cells (and may only describe AMPS cells). The terms low-tier and high-tier are not used in most parts of the world; I have come across them only in the United States.

As you can see, the terminology can befuddle a newcomer. So, a word of caution: When you are having a discourse with someone about second generation mobile wireless systems, make sure these terms are understood.

The bottom of Figure 1–8 depicts efforts underway to develop third generation mobile wireless systems (TGMS). This effort, coordinated in Europe, is to combine many of the disparate technologies (such as paging, earth-based PCS, satellite PCS, etc.) into one technology and operate these technologies with one user handset. It will be a number of years before TGMS reaches the consumer, and the subject must wait for another book to describe it, although Chapter 10 in this book provides a general description of TGMS.

A REVIEW OF THE MAJOR COMPONENTS IN THE MOBILE WIRELESS NETWORK

To make certain the terms used in subsequent chapters are understood, this part of the chapter reviews the major components in a mobile wireless system. These components are found in one fashion or another in all the second generation systems that are explained in this book.

Figure 1–9 shows a typical topology for a cellular mobile radio system. The principal components of this system are the mobile switching center (MSC), the cell and its base transceiver station (BTS) (also called a base station, or BS), a base station controller (BSC), a mobile unit, the mobile station (MS), and several databases. The BTS (or BS) is also known as the land station in some literature.

The mobile station contains the mobile transceiver that is installed in an automobile, truck, portable telephone, and so on. It contains a frequency-agile machine that allows the mobile station to tune to a particular frequency designated for it to use by the network.

The cell site contains the base station (BS), which manages the air interface between the mobile station and the BS. By receiving signals and directions from the MSC, the BS sends and receives traffic to/from the mobile station. The BS is also responsible for power control operations on the air interface. These overall tasks are known as radio resource (RR) management.

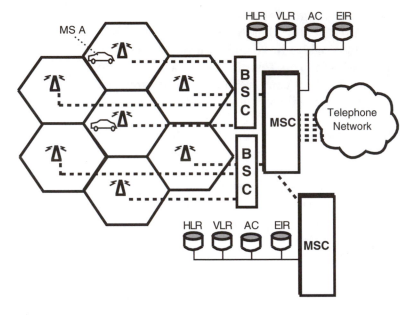

where:

AC   Access control, or authentication center
EIR   Equipment identity register
HLR   Home location register
MS   Mobile station
MSC   Mobile switching center
VLR   Visitor location register

Figure 1–9   Mobile wireless arrangement.

The MSC is the control element for the mobile wireless network. It is responsible for switching the calls to the cells, providing for backup, interfacing with telephone networks, monitoring traffic for charging activities, performing testing and diagnostic services, and overall network management. The MSC communicates with the MS through the base station or the base station controller.

The call management (setting up and tearing down the call) operations are coordinated at the MSC (and not the BS). These operations are called connection management (CM) functions.

Certain functions are delegated to the BS or BSC, such as radio resource management, link diagnostics, link setups, and so on. But the MSC knows about most of these activities, even though it might not be performing all of them.

Another component is employed in most second generation systems, the base station controller (BSC). Its main task is to offload functions from the MSC. The BSs are controlled by the BSCs. They are responsible for handover operations of the calls as well as controlling the power signals and frequency administration between the BSs and MSs; that is, radio resource (RR) management. The BS and BSC may be co-located, the BSC may be stand alone (usually the case), the BSC may be located at the mobile services switching center MSC, or it may not be used.

Two databases (at least) are used in all mobile systems: (a) the home location register (HLR) and (b) the visitor location register (VLR). Each subscriber belongs to one HLR, which is associated with a cellular operator (the commercial network provider). The HLR keeps track of a subscriber's location, and it also stores information about the subscriber (accounting information, subscribed services, etc.).

The VLR keeps track of visiting subscribers that are operating in the specific VLR's serving system. The location of a user (in Figure 1–9, mobile station A) is known by the subscriber A's HLR and the visited VLR exchanging information with each other. The VLR must inform the subscriber's HLR when the subscriber logs on to its system, and in turn, the HLR will update its records, indicating that the subscriber is now located at this particular location. During the logon process, the HLR will also send to the visited VLR information about the subscriber.

The HLR and VLR are attached to an MSC, and their overall operations are known as mobility management (MM), because they are responsible for keeping track of the location of the mobile station.

The authentication control (AC) (also called access control) database contains authentication and encryption information on each subscriber. The AC interacts with the HLR and VLR to provide these services.

The fourth database is the equipment identity register (EIR). It contains information on the MS equipment, such as the identification of the manufacturer of the MS, conformance testing information, and the identifier of the factory that assembled the MS.

Although I have discussed these four databases as separate entities, they may reside in the same physical file at an MSC. The actual deployment of the databases in a data base management system is implementation-specific.

CONNECTION MANAGEMENT (CM) OPERATIONS

All mobile wireless systems employ connection management (CM) operations, which are used to set up, manage, and clear down a call between the MS and another party. Most systems use similar CM techniques. Figure 1–10 shows a telephone user placing a call through the

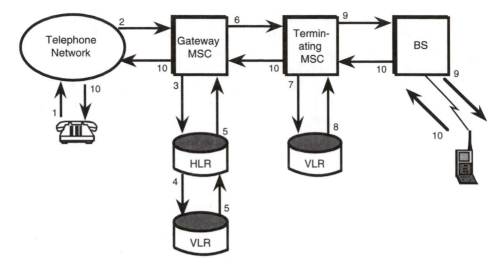

Figure 1–10   Example of connection management (CM) operations.

public telephone network to the mobile station by accessing the network in event 1. The call is routed to a gateway MSC (event 2). The identity and location of a designated gateway MSC are a matter of arrangements that are established among the various telephony and mobile network service providers. The called party telephone number is used to route the call to the gateway MSC.

This MSC examines the dialed digits and determines that it cannot route the call further. Therefore, in event 3, it interrogates the called user's home location register (HLR). In turn, the HLR interrogates the visitor location register (VLR) that is currently serving the user (event 4). In effect, the HLR is asking the VLR, "Is the called party still in your service area? If so, please provide me with the routing information to the called party's mobile station."

In event 5, the VLR returns routing information to the HLR, which passes it back to the gateway MSC. Based on this routing information, the gateway MSC routes the call to the terminating MSC (event 6). The terminating MSC then queries the VLR to match the incoming call with the identity of the receiving subscriber (events 7 and 8). In event 9, the terminating MSC sends the BS a paging request, which relays the page to the subscriber and the call is completed (event 10).

By the way, not all these events are classified as connection management operations. Events 3, 4, 5, 7, and 8 support the connection management services but fall into the classification of mobility management, discussed next.

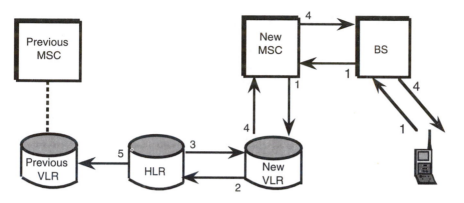

Figure 1–11   Mobility management (MM) operations.

MOBILITY MANAGEMENT (MM) OPERATIONS

Figure 1–11 shows an example of how a cellular subscriber can roam from cell-to-cell and how the system keeps a record of the subscriber's location, a function called mobility management (MM). Upon the mobile station crossing a certain boundary, it sends a location update request (event 1), which contains its identification, to the BS. In second generation systems, the mobile station monitors channels in other cells. If it detects a control channel in another cell that meets specific power and quality criteria, it notifies its serving base station by sending it a location update message.

This message is then routed to the new VLR. The new VLR has no information about the entry for this user (because the user has moved recently into its area). The new VLR sends the query message to the user's home location register (event 2). This message includes the identity of the user as well as the identity of the new VLR that sent the message. In event 3, the HLR stores the subscriber's new location at the new VLR and then downline loads the user's subscription information (calling origination and termination services, and authentication parameters) to the new VLR. Upon receiving this information, the new VLR sends the acknowledgment of the location update through the new MSC to the MSC, and back to the originating mobile user (event 4).[4] Finally, in event 5, the

---

[4]Remember that the VLR is attached to an MSC, and the operations between the MSC and VLR may not be "visible" with MAP messages. Since the VLR is a database, the communications between the MSC and the VLR occur with database management messages.

HLR sends a location cancellation message to the old VLR to clear the subscriber's data from its database.

The mobile subscriber must be known only to one VLR at a time. In this example, when the subscriber has roamed to another area (another cell), the HLR has had to be updated.

It can be seen that the HLR is the master of the subscriber database and therefore coordinates changes to the VLRs as the subscriber roams through the cells. Notwithstanding, in some situations, the new VLR will communicate first with the old VLR, then the HLR. These situations are described in the appropriate chapters.

USE OF IDENTIFIERS

Figure 1–12 shows an example of how identifiers are used with the HLR and VLR to support a call to a mobile station. In event 1, the called party number is relayed to a gateway MSC (GMSC). This number is used to access a table to correlate the number with the subscriber's HLR. In event 2, the gateway MSC sends a query to the HLR that contains the called party number or an internal number used by the network operator. Next, the HLR examines its records to find where the called subscriber is located. It sends a query to the visited MSC/VLR and may use the dialed number or a number internal to the network in this query (event 3). The MSC/VLR receives the query and sends back routing instructions that are contained in a routing number. This operation is depicted as event 4 in Figure 1–12. Next and in event 5, the HLR forwards the routing information to the gateway MSC, which uses this routing information to route the call directly to the MSC that is servicing the subscriber (event 6). In event 7, the MSC routes the call to the proper BSC, then the BS (event 8) and, finally in event 9, the call is sent to the called subscriber.

PREVALENT PROTOCOLS USED IN THE SECOND GENERATION SYSTEM

The overall operations between the MS, through the BSs, BSCs, MSCs, and the telephone network, entail a wide variety of operations. Figure 1–13 shows some of the prominent protocols and interfaces that are used by most mobile wireless networks.

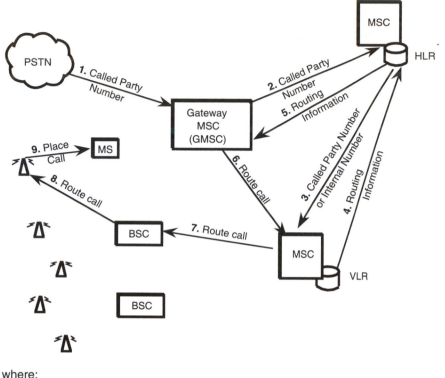

where:
GMSC   Gateway MSC
HLR   Home location register
MSC   Mobile switching center
PSTN   Public switched telephone network
VLR   Visitor location register

Figure 1–12   The complete picture.

In many systems, variations of signaling system number 7 (SS7) and the integrated services digital network (ISDN) are used between the mobile system and the telephone system. ISDN is not executed at some of these components, but its messages may be passed through them to certain machines that are designated to process them. For the reader who is not familiar with ISDN and SS7 (and you should have at least a rudimentary understanding of them), please refer to a book in this series *ISDN and SS7: Architecture for Digital Signaling Networks* on these technologies.

The mobile application part (MAP) protocols are used to support overall mobility management (MM) operations in the system, such as roaming, location updating, and so on. They do not participate directly in

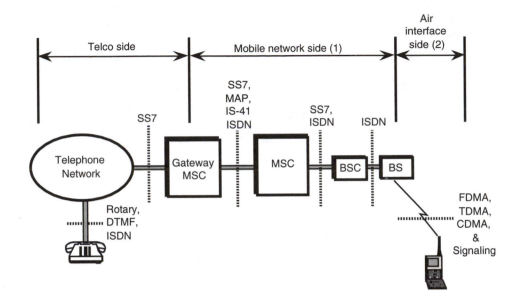

Notes:
  (1) These combinations vary, depending upon specific standards
  (2) Signaling is some variation of an OSI L_3 protocol

where:
  BS   Base station (base transceiver station)
  BSC   Base station controller
  CDMA   Code division multiple access
  DTMF   Dual tone multiple frequency
  FDMA   Frequency division multiple access
  IS-41   Interim standard 41
  ISDN   Integrated service digital network
  MAP   Mobile application part
  MSC   Mobile switching center
  SS7   Signaling system number 7
  Telco   Telephone company
  TDMA   Time division multiple access

Figure 1–13 Protocol/interface placements in a typical system.

connection management (CM), which is left to SS7 and ISDN (or similar systems), but MAP does support these operations.

As stated earlier, IS-41 is widely used in North America. It defines operations on the network side of a cellular system (it executes MAPs). It is a partner to various air interfaces, in that it manages the cellular operations from the base station back to various control stations, location registers, and the fixed-wire exchanges. It is designed to operate between MSCs.

One or a combination of three technologies are used at the air interface: (a) frequency division multiple access (FDMA), time division multiple access (TDMA), and (c) code division multiple access (CDMA). In addition to these physical layer operations, the air interface must have some means to perform connection management (CM), mobility management (MM), and radio resource management (RR). For this job, signaling protocols and a variety of other protocols are executed across the FDMA, TDMA, or CDMA wireless link to set up, tear down connections, handle mobility management functions, as well as radio resource management tasks.

TYPICAL OPERATIONS ACROSS THE AIR INTERFACE

The second generation air interface is organized around groupings of operations. Although not all the systems described in this book explicitly categorize their air interface operations as described here, they do indeed utilize these operations. I have written this section to describe both CDMA and TDMA air interfaces.

The air interface operations are further organized into the procedures shown in Figure 1–14. The first component entails system acquisition, which means the mobile station is powered on and searches for a control channel. Upon finding this channel, the mobile station receives a variety of identifiers and operating parameters. This component also includes the acquisition of timing instructions in a CDMA system.

After the initial system acquisition, the mobile station can enter an idle state and roam through an operator's system. If a call is made to the mobile station, the network initiates a paging request to locate a mobile station in order to establish the connection, as shown in Figure 1–15. The operation entails the network sending a paging request message to the mobile station and the mobile station returning a paging response. As part of this operation, the mobile station is provided sufficient information to know what control channel to use for further activity, such as authentication.

On the other hand, the mobile station can also originate a call. In this situation, the mobile station sends a channel request message that is conveyed on a defined access control channel. The network examines this message. If it is well formed and without problems and a channel is available, it responds with an immediate assignment message. The im-

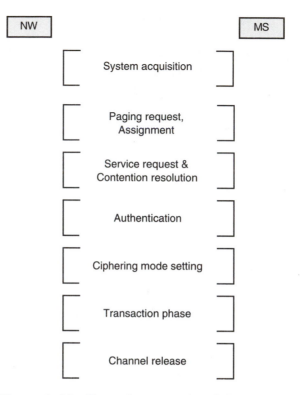

Figure 1–14   Procedures on the air interface.

mediate assignment message directs the mobile station to seize a specific dedicated channel, which is identified in the message.

After the completion of the initial paging request, the mobile station may send several messages as part of the service request and contention resolution operation. Figure 1–16 shows the mobile station issuing the well-known layer 2 Set Asynchronous Balanced Mode (SABM) frame to the network and the network responding with an unnumbered acknowledgment (UA). The SABM frame contains in the information field a layer 3 service request message. Typically, the service request message deals with: (a) connection management, (b) location updating, (c) exchanging identifiers, and (d) a paging response. In essence, this service request message informs the network which service the mobile station is requesting.

The UA frame contains the same information as the SABM frame. The mobile station compares the UA message with the one it sent in the SABM frame (which it has stored). If they do not match, the mobile station leaves the channel. This operation resolves contentions where mo-

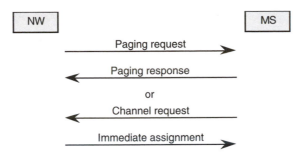

Figure 1–15 The paging and immediate assignment procedures.

bile stations have accessed the same access slot and one has succeeded. A random reference number is used for this operation, so each MS sends a different random reference number.

A fairly wide array of options are available to the mobile station by virtue of being able to send different messages in the SABM frame. Whatever the messages sent, the purpose of the service request and contention resolution procedure is to send nonconfidential information to the network that is used by the RR and MM functions of the network. It is also used to identify the network user without jeopardizing the security of the user's identity.

As stated earlier, this procedure is also used to support contention resolution by providing a process to resolve a situation where more than one mobile station tries to seize a channel that is allocated during the immediate assignment procedure. While this situation may be rare, it could occur if the mobile stations try to use the same random reference number at the same time during a random access. The contention is resolved by the network including in its UA frame the same information field as the one it received in the SABM transmission. The mobile station can then compare what it sent with what it receives to determine if a problem has occurred. If contention occurs, the mobile station can try again.

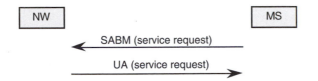

Figure 1–16 Service request and contention resolution procedure.

Authentication is used to validate the identity of the mobile station user. As shown in Figure 1–17, the authentication operation is initiated when the network sends an authentication request message to the mobile station. In addition, this procedure also provides the mobile station with information regarding ciphering keys. It is a network option as to whether authentication is employed. If it is employed, the mobile station must return a authentication response message, which contains the validation of the user's identity.

As just stated, another option used by the network is ciphering. Its purpose is to instruct the mobile station if ciphering is to be employed during the transmission process and what ciphering algorithm is to be used. This operation is achieved by the network sending the cipher mode command message to the mobile station, which responds with a cipher mode complete message. These operations are illustrated in the bottom part of Figure 1–17.

After all these bootstrapping operations have occurred between the network and mobile station, a variety of procedures are executed to send traffic back and forth across the air interface. These procedures are broadly classified as the "transaction phase" in Figure 1–14. For example, a mobile station may roam into another service area, and the procedures just explained are repeated. As another example, the mobile station may receive an e-mail message, and so on.

To conclude this brief overview, Figure 1–18 shows the operation for the channel release, which consists of a channel release message sent by

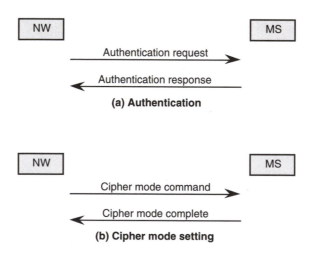

Figure 1–17   Authentication and ciphering.

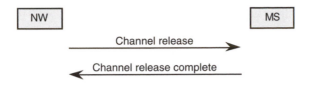

Figure 1–18   Channel release.

the network to the mobile station and the response from the mobile station with a channel release complete message. The result of this operation is the freeing of any radio resources that had been allocated for this connection that now become available for reallocation by the network.

THE SPECTRUM SPACE FOR THE SECOND GENERATION SYSTEMS

In the Omnibus Budget Act of 1993, the U.S. Congress authorized several auctions of the electromagnetic frequency spectrum in the United States. Figure 1–19 and Table 1–2 show this frequency allocation plan. The auctions began in 1994 and continued into 1998. Most of the interest centered on the PCS auctions, but auctions also were held in the interactive video and data (IVDS) area.

On June 9, 1994, the FCC allocated the PCS spectrum into the 1850–1990 MHz band, with 1910–1930 MHz allocated for unlicensed PCS systems. As shown in Table 1–2, blocks A, B, and C are allocated

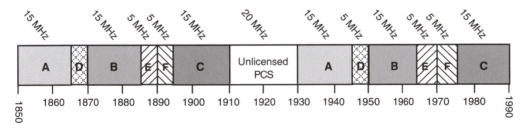

Notes:
   Blocks A, B based on Rand McNally's Major Trading Areas (MTA)
   Blocks C, D, E, F based on Rand McNally's Basic Trading Areas (BTA)
   Unlicensed PCS is nationwide

Figure 1–19   The spectrum allocation plan.

Table 1–2 Allocation and Licenses

Frequency Block	Amount of Spectrum	Geographic Scope	Frequency Range (MHz)	Number of Licenses
A	30 MHz	MTA	1850–1865/1930–1945	51
B	30 MHz	MTA	1870–1885/1950–1965	51
C	30 MHz	BTA	1895–1910/1975–1990	493
D	10 MHz	BTA	1865–1870/1945–1950	493
E	10 MHz	BTA	1885–1890/1965–1970	493
F	10 MHz	BTA	1890–1895/1970–1975	493
Unlicensed	20 MHz	Nationwide	1910–1930	—

30 MHz, blocks D, E, and F are allocated 10 MHz. The A and B blocks are licensed for the 51 major trading areas (MTAs). The C, D, E, and F blocks are licensed for the basic trading areas (BTAs). The A–F blocks have been sold to those operators that have tendered the highest bid to the FCC. These auctions, the granting of licenses, and the subsequent deployment of commercial systems led to many of the systems described in this book.

SUMMARY

A second generation mobile wireless system uses digital signaling (on TDMA or CDMA physical channels) for the user traffic. With digital signaling, the signals cannot be easily intercepted and interpreted and can be subjected to error correction operations and encryption functions.

This chapter also introduced the second generation specifications, and emphasized (and cautioned the reader) that some of the terms associated with the new mobile wireless systems are subject to more than one interpretation.

The stage is set for a more thorough analysis at second generation mobile wireless systems. The next chapter examines the major aspects of first generation systems. I include this chapter because it will prove useful to compare first generation systems to second generation systems, and some of the second generation systems (especially in North America) use parts of the first generation technology and procedures.

APPENDIX 1A   PROGRESS IN DIGITIZING THE VOICE SIGNAL

The techniques for digitizing (and compressing) the voice signal are described in many texts and papers. This book explains these operations in regard to the air interface.

Most of the original mobile wireless vocoders produce a compressed voice signal of 13 kbit/s, known as *full-rate*. As of this writing, efforts are well underway to migrate to a *half-rate* scheme to make more effective use of the limited bandwidth at the air interface. The half-rate bit rate varies and may not be exactly half the full-rate. But the new vocoders operate at about one-half the original coder's full rate. For example, one vocoder operates a 8 kbit/s.

With improved techniques, we will witness deployments in 1999 of voice rates of 7.2 kbit/s and even 4.8 kbit/s systems. In tests conducted by the Telecommunications Industry Association (TIA) a 4.8 kbit/s speech coder built by Digital Voice Systems, Inc. (DVI is on www.dsiinc.com) was rated of a higher quality than an ITU-T G.729 8 kbit/s vocoder.[5] I call these vocoders half/half-rate vocoders.

The 13 kbit/s and 8 kbit/s vocoders divide a speech signal into segments and determine if each segment is a periodic (voiced) signal or a silence/noise (unvoiced) signal. The coders use linear prediction with a single determination about the presence or absence of the voice signal.

The DSI 4.8 kbit/s coder divides each segment of speech into distinct frequency bands and makes a voice/unvoiced (V/UV) decision for each frequency band. The excitation signal for a particular speech segment can be a mixture of periodic (voiced) and noise-like (unvoiced) energy. This modeling of the excitation signal allows the speech model to generate higher quality speech than conventional speech models.

Linear prediction based speech coders do not yield high quality speech (or robustness-to-background noise) without the addition of a prediction residual. The prediction residual can be viewed as an error signal that corrects for inaccuracies in the linear prediction model. Elimination of this residual, as is done in a government standard 2.4 kbit/s system, results in a mechanical quality in the speech. Consequently, all linear predictive speech coders discussed in this book transmit a residual.

The primary difference between these systems is the manner in which they accomplish this task. The typical method used in linear predictive speech coding at rates below 8 kbit/s is to divide the residual into

---

[5]This discussion is based on DVIs vocoder, which is being deployed in the Iridium Satellite PCS system (see Chapter 8).

small pieces or vectors and to then search through a codebook to find the code vector that is the closest match. Searching through a reasonably sized codebook is a computationally complex task. Furthermore, a particular codebook is designed to operate at a fixed data rate and is not easily scalable to other data rates.

The half/half-rate coders are not based upon linear prediction. They use a multiband excitation speech model to produce high quality speech without the need for a residual signal. They maintain speech intelligibility and naturalness at rates as low as 2.4 kbit/s. In addition, the speech coders do not require the use of codebooks. Consequently, the system requires fewer computations than the linear techniques.

2

First Generation Systems

T his chapter provides a description of first generation mobile wireless systems with emphasis on the Advanced Mobile Phone System (AMPS). An account is provided of frequency allocations for AMPS control and traffic channels. We also examine the registration procedures, calling operations, as well as roaming and handoff operations. Emphasis is also placed on those aspects of AMPS that have been "ported" to the second generation systems.

AMPS ARCHITECTURE

The Advanced Mobile Phone System is a first generation mobile wireless system being used in the United States and many other countries. AMPS is designed to support voice telephone traffic and uses 30 kHz channels on the air interface between the mobile station (MS) and the base station (BS).[1] Figure 2–1 shows the AMPS configuration.

AMPS was conceived by Bell Labs in the late 1970s and early 1980s to overcome some of the deficiencies of older mobile wireless systems,

---

[1]Several AMPS documents use the term *land station* for the base station. This chapter uses both terms synonymously.

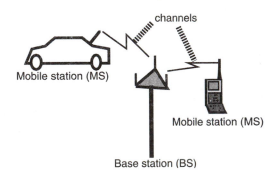

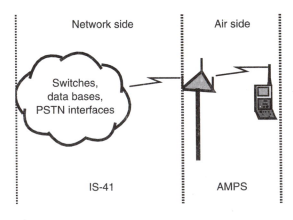

Figure 2–1 The Advanced Mobile Phone System (AMPS).

principally to use the spectrum space more effectively. Consequently, AMPS was designed around the concepts of cells to allow the reuse of radio frequencies. The 3 kHz voice signal is modulated onto the 30 kHz RF channel using analog signaling techniques.

The AMPS air interface (radio interface) is published as EIA/TIA-553 by the Electronics Industries Association and the Telecommunications Industry Association. As depicted in Figure 2–2, a complementary specification on the network side is IS-41, which handles mobility management operations. IS-41 was written originally to support just AMPS air interfaces, but it has been upgraded and modified and now supports other interfaces as well, such as IS-136 and IS-95.

AMPS is a relatively old technology, but it remains one of the dominant systems in the industry. The AMPS infrastructure is found throughout North America (and other parts of the world). Even with the development of new technologies, AMPS continues to hold a piece of the market, and many newer systems continue to use much of the AMPS

where:
    PSTN   Public switched telephone network

Figure 2–2 Relationship of AMPS and IS-41.

technology then add additional (new technology) operations onto the AMPS channels.

For example, Digital AMPS (D-AMPS), described in Chapter 3, uses the AMPS air interface, but modifies some of the analog 30 kHz channels by dividing them into 10 kHz channels. D-AMPS also digitizes the voice images on these channels. D-AMPS continues to use the conventional AMPS analog control channels, with options on how the traffic channels are used (30 kHz analog, or three TDMA digital slots sharing the 30 kHz channel).

IS-136 goes one step further. The initial deployments of IS-136 use the AMPS frequency spectrum and a number of AMPS protocol procedures, but displace the AMPS analog control channels with digital control channels. Future IS-136 systems will upband to the 1.9 GHz spectrum.

AMPS DEVELOPMENT

In the late 1970s, the FCC allocated spectrum space for AMPS in the 800 MHz spectrum and issued licenses for test systems in Chicago and Washington, DC. The tests were followed shortly thereafter by the construction of commercial systems, and the first system was brought on-line in 1983. In a few short years, AMPS was available in all the major cities in the United States. These events were the fruition of extensive research and development conducted by the Bell System in the 1960s and 1970s.

The 800 MHz spectrum was chosen because of the limited spectrum space available at the lower frequencies. TV and FM systems operate at the lower frequencies with FM operating around 100 MHz and the TV systems operating from the range of 41–960 MHz. Other systems such as air-to-ground systems and maritime services also operate in the lower frequency ranges.

In addition, the choice of the 800 MHz band was dictated by the fact that using higher frequencies (for example, in the 2 GHz range) are subject to severe information loss due to weather conditions (such as rain), multipath fading, and unacceptable propagation path loss. Since error correction techniques (trellis coding, bit repetition, and bit interleaving) were in their infancy, it made sense to use a low frequency medium. Low frequency signals exhibit longer waveforms and are more impervious to these impairments.

With some exceptions, the 800 MHz band was not being utilized. Even though parts of this spectrum space were originally assigned to educational TV stations, some of the load that would have probably been assigned to these stations was assumed to be allocated to cable TV services.

Nonetheless, 800 MHz was certainly a compromise because technology had improved by the late 1970s and early 1980s. At that time, it was possible to provide high-quality services beyond this limited bandwidth, but not to the extent we see now with the second generation systems.

AMPS FREQUENCY ALLOCATIONS

Table 2–1 shows the resultant channel numbers and frequencies for AMPS. Each base station's transmit and receive channel is separated by 45 MHz. A total of 416 channels are allocated for the customer's traffic channels and control channels. The traffic channels (TCH) are used for the user calls. Band A is allocated to one service provider (operator) in a geographical area and uses channels 1-312. Band B is allocated for the second operator and has channels 355-666 allocated. So, each operator has 312 voice channels at its disposal.

Table 2–1   Channel Numbers and Frequencies

System	MHz	Number of Channels	Boundary Channel Number	Transmitter Center Frequency, MHz	
				Mobile	Land
Not used		1	(990)	(824.010)	(869.010)
A″[1]	1	33	991	824.040	869.040
			1023	825.000	870.000
A2	10	333	1	825.030	870.030
			333	834.990	879.990
B2	10	333	334	835.020	880.020
			666	844.980	889.980
A′[1,3]	1.5	50	667	845.010	890.010
			717	846.480	891.480
B′[1,3]	2.5	83	718	846.510	889.510
			799	848.970	883.970

[1]Added later. Sometimes referred to as extended AMPS (EAMPS).
[2]Channel 1-666 have a 20 MHz range.
[3]May use optional 5 MHz.

The control channels are used by the mobile and base stations to set up and clear calls and exchange other network management and provisioning messages. Both bands contain 21 control channels for a total of 42 channels. Band A uses channels 313–333 for control signaling, and band B uses channels 334–354.

The cellular operator is free to use the control channels in any manner deemed appropriate. A logical way to approach the allocation of the control channels is to group them to control the voice channels (remember, if the total channels available equal 333, it means that 312 voice channels and 21 control channels are available). Therefore, each control channel can be associated with a group of voice channels. In this scenario, each set of voice channels can be grouped into about 16 channels with each group associated with a control channel.

AMPS IDENTIFIERS

Three identification numbers are used in AMPS: (a) the mobile station's electronic serial number (ESN), (b) the mobile operator's system identification (SID) number, and (c) the mobile station's mobile identification number (MIN).

The FCC requires an ESN to be used for each mobile station in service in the cellular system. The ESN is a 32-bit binary number that uniquely identifies a cellular unit. The ESN for a mobile station is set up by the mobile unit manufacturer at its factory and is not supposed to be easily altered. It is burned into ROM so that circuitry providing the number is secure and any attempt to change the serial number is supposed to make the mobile unit unusable.

The format of the ESN is shown in Figure 2–3. The manufacturer's code (MFR) is an 8-bit field that is assigned by the FCC to each manufacturer of mobile equipment. Bits 18–23 are reserved for later use and are set to all zeros. Bits 0–17 are assigned by the manufacturer. The idea is that when a manufacturer uses all its serial number space, it can obtain another MFR code number from the FCC, which allocates the next sequential number within the reserved block.

Figure 2–3 The electronic serial number (ESN).

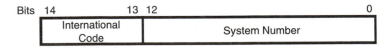

Figure 2–4   The system identification number (SID).

System identification numbers (SIDs) are 15-bit binary numbers that are assigned to cellular systems (Figure 2–4). Each cellular operator is identified by a unique SID number. The mobile station in the cell must transmit the SID to a base station so the cellular receiver can determine the system through which they are communicating. An additional purpose of the SID is to determine if the two stations (mobile and fixed) are working within the same system or if they are in a roaming situation. The FCC assigns one SID to each cellular system and these systems may transmit only their assigned SIDs (or another SID, if this other group so permits).

The third identifier is the mobile identification number (MIN). It is a 34-bit number that is derived from the mobile station's 10-digit telephone number. The specification refers to MIN1 (24 bits that correspond to the 7-digit directory number) and MIN2 (10 bits that correspond to the 3-digit area code). TIA/EIA-533 provides several simple conversion algorithms that describe the conversion process.

THE STATION CLASS MARK (SCM)

The station class mark (SCM) information is used for a number of purposes. For one purpose, it contains information about the mobile station's maximum effective radiated power (ERP) that the station can deliver, as depicted in Table 2–2. The SCM also provides information on: possible use of continuous/discontinuous (DTX) transmission characteristics, and the mobile station's bandwidth utilization. Discontinuous transmission (DTX) describes the ability of a station to change its transmission power level between two power level states during a conversation that is occurring on the voice channel.

TRAFFIC AND CONTROL CHANNELS

Figure 2–5 depicts how the traffic and control channels are used between the base station and mobile station. Twenty-one channels are available for control purposes. When a mobile station is not engaged in a

Table 2–2 Mobile Station Nominal Power Levels

Mobile Station Power Level (PL)	Mobile Attenuation Code (MAC)	Nominal ERP (dBW) for Mobile Station Power Class Function		
		I	II	III
0	000	6	2	−2
1	001	2	2	−2
2	010	−2	−2	−2
3	011	−6	−6	−6
4	100	−10	−10	−10
5	101	−14	−14	−14
6	110	−18	−18	−18
7	111	−22	−22	−22

conversation, it must monitor designated control channels. It tunes to and locks onto the strongest channel to receive a variety of control information. In addition, control information can be sent on the voice channels under certain conditions, which are explained later.

The *forward control channel* (FOCC) is a continuous data stream sent from the base station to the mobile station. A data stream on the *re-*

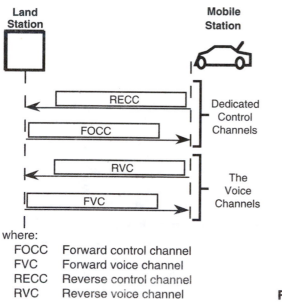

where:
FOCC   Forward control channel
FVC   Forward voice channel
RECC   Reverse control channel
RVC   Reverse voice channel

Figure 2–5   The AMPS channels.

verse control channel (RECC) is sent from the mobile station to the base station. Both channels operate at 10 kbit/s.

The FOCC is a time division multiplexed (TDM) channel in which three data streams are multiplexed together. The information streams are called stream A, stream B, and the busy-idle stream. Streams A and B are identified with the least significant bit (LSB) of the mobile station's MIN, where a 0 signifies stream A and a 1 signifies stream B. The busy-idle stream indicates the current status of the reverse control channel. It is used to indicate if a mobile station is currently using the channel. This procedure is necessary because the reverse control channel can be used by more than one mobile station. Thus, the busy-idle stream reduces the possibilities of message collision on the RECC.

The voice conversation takes place on the forward voice channel (FVC) and the reverse voice channel (RVC). These channels are selected by the network and assigned to the mobile station during a call origination or call termination. Using the FOCC, the base station informs the mobile station which RVC to use for the call. The mobile then switches (tunes) to this channel. The base station will also switch to the appropriate FVC for the call.

AMPS FEATURES

AMPS uses both data messages and frequency tones for its control signaling. This part of the chapter examines these messages and tones.

The Supervisory Audio Tone (SAT)

There are two supervisory audio tones employed on the air interface: the *supervisory audio tone* (SAT) and the *signaling tone* (ST). The SAT is used to determine link continuity between the base station and the mobile station. It is sent on the traffic channels (TCHs) and enables the mobile and base stations to stay informed about the transmit capabilities of each other. The base station adds this tone on each forward voice channel (FVC) prior to the modulation of the signal. The mobile station uses this same tone on its reverse voice channel (RVC) to the base station. As a general practice, SAT determination is performed at least every 250 ms. Three SAT signals are currently defined: 5970 Hz, 6000 Hz, and 6030 Hz.

When a SAT is transponded to the base station from the mobile station on a new voice channel, the base station knows that the mobile station has confirmed its "arrival" on the new channel, and the handoff was successful. The mobile station finds out which SAT it is to expect by a field in a message sent on the FOCC called the SAT color code (SCC):

SAT Frequency	SCC Code
5970 Hz	00
6000 Hz	01
6030 Hz	10

The Signaling Tone (ST)

The second signal used on the AMPS interface is the *signaling tone* (ST). It is used to perform four operations. The request to send signal is used during an ongoing conversation to allow the user to input more data on the keypad. Typically, the user inputs data, presses the send button on the handset, and the 400 ms request to send signal is sent to the network.

The alert signal is a continuous signal that is sent on the RVC after the mobile station has been alerted. It is sent until the called is answered, after which it is removed.

The disconnect signal is used by the mobile station to indicate the termination of the call. It is sent over the RVC and its duration is 1.8 seconds.

Finally, the handoff confirmation signal is sent by the mobile user after it receives a message from the network for a handoff operation. Its duration is 50 ms.

INITIALIZATION PROCEDURES

The initialization procedures between the mobile station and the base station are depicted in Figure 2–6. Upon the mobile station being activated (power up), it enters a task called receive system parameters. This task involves the mobile station configuring parameters to use cellular provider system A or B (event 1).

In event 2, the mobile station scans the 21 dedicated control channels to receive overhead messages. The term "overhead" is not a generic term, but describes a specific type of control message. If all goes well, a channel is selected within 3 seconds. It will continue to scan until it finds an acceptable channel. Also, during this process, the mobile station enters the Enable Status (preferred system is A) on Disable Status (pre-

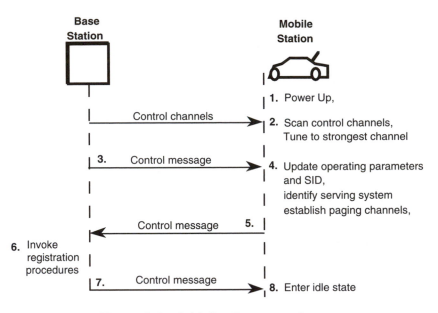

Figure 2–6   Initialization procedures.

ferred system is B). The operations allow the mobile station to receive the SID of the serving system.

Next, in event 3, the mobile station receives a system parameter message on the control channel. As shown in event 4, the contents in this message provide the information needed for the mobile station to update any parameters that were received in the previous overhead messages, if any had been received from a previous initialization. In addition, the mobile station compares its home SID (home identification of the mobile station) to the SID in the message, which identifies the serving system. If the two are not equal, the mobile station knows it is in another serving area and sets parameters to enable roaming operations to take place.

The mobile station must also identify itself to the network. In event 5 it uses the RECC to send its MIN, ESN, and SID. These parameters are examined by the MSC (and its VLR) to determine the roaming status of the station, depicted in event 6. In event 7, the base station sends a final control message to the mobile unit to verify the initialization parameters.

After these tasks have been performed successfully, the MS enters into an idle state (event 8). During the idle state, the mobile station is hardly idle; it performs ongoing tasks at least every 46.3 ms to keep the mobile and base stations synchronized with each other, and to keep the network aware of the mobile station's mobility status.

EXAMPLES OF AMPS OPERATIONS

Mobile Station Originates a Call

Figure 2–7 shows how a mobile station originates a call to its base station. Through the use of the reverse control channel (RECC), the mobile station in event 1 sends the base station an origination message. This message contains the mobile station's MIN, ESN, and the phone number of the called party. In addition, the message contains the appropriate order and order qualification codes described earlier. In event 2, the base station receives this information and passes it to the network side for further processing through the MSCs via IS-41. In event 3, the base station forwards a control message back to the mobile station that also contains the channel number that is to be used for the voice call as well as the order (ORDER) and order qualification code (ORDQ) fields. The ORDER field is coded to describe the type of message that is being transmitted—for example, an origination message. The ORDQ informa-

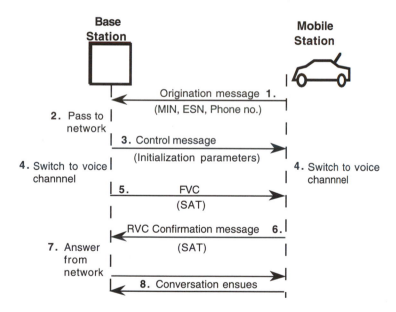

where:
ESN Electronic serial number
FVC Forward voice channel
MIN Coding of the mobile station's phone number
RVC Reverse voice channel
SAT Supervisory audio tone

Figure 2–7 The mobile station originates a call.

tion contains a power level parameter and a parameter to aid in registration procedures. The message also contains the set color code (SCC) that designates the SAT frequency that is to be used.

At this time (in event 4), the land and mobile stations switch from the control channels to the voice channels. In event 5, the base station sends a forward voice channel (FVC) control message with the SAT signal. In event 6, the mobile station confirms the channel continuity through a reverse voice channel (RVC) SAT signal. Thereafter, the mobile station awaits completion of the call, which occurs with the result coming from the network in event 7. Then, in event 8, conversation ensues on the channels.

Mobile Station Receives a Call

Figure 2–8 shows the operations involved when a call is originated from either a fixed or mobile telephone unit to a mobile station. In event 1, the identification of the mobile station is passed to the base station

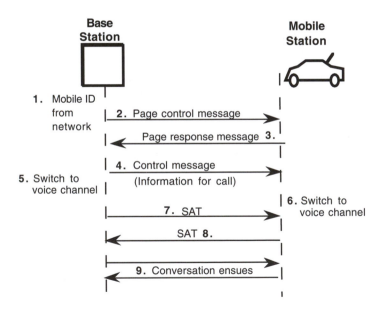

where:
    ESN   Electronic serial number
    FVC   Forward voice channel
    MIN   Coding of the mobile station's phone number
    RVC   Reverse voice channel
    SAT   Supervisory audio tone

Figure 2–8   The mobile station receives a call.

from IS-41. In event 2, the information in the IS-41 message is mapped into a page control message and the additional information MIN, SCC, ORDER, ORDQ is added. In addition, the channel number (CHAN) is placed in the message to instruct the mobile station as to which traffic channel it is to use for the connection. The mobile station responds (in event 3) by returning its MIN, ESN, ORDER, and ORDQ fields in the page response message.

The receipt of this message at the base station invokes the control message shown in event 4. The control message contains the SCC field, which informs the mobile station about the frequency to be used on the channel identified in the field (CHAN). In events 5 and 6, the operations are switched to the voice channels. In event 7, the base station sends a SAT, and the mobile station responds with a confirmation shown in event 8. After this handshake occurs, the traffic channel is then opened as shown in event 9.

Operations on the Network Side

Figure 2–9 adds the operations on the network side to show how the network reacts to the mobile station's operations, in this example, a mobile-originated call. The operations on the air interface have been de-scribed in earlier material. On the network side, the messages exchanged between the base station, the MSC, and the public switched telephone network (PSTN) are a combination of IS-41 and signaling system number 7 (SS7) messages.[2] More than one operation is depicted as event 6 be-cause the exact sequence in which these events occur varies, depending upon the network. Notice that I have grouped the mobile station's BS and MSC together in this figure. The reason is that the operations be-tween the BS and the MSC are vendor-specific. As noted in footnote 2, this situation will change when IS-634 enters into the industry.

On the network side, the operations shown as events 6, 9, 12, and 17 usually occur with SS7's ISDN user part protocol (ISUP) or the telephone user part (TUP) protocol. Events 2 and 4 are IS-41 messages, described in Chapter 7. Also, notice the use of the alert signaling tone (ST) in event 10, and the 1.8 sec. disconnect ST in event 16.

---

[2]IS-41 is defined to operate between MSCs. In recognition of these facts, IS-634 is being developed by the standards groups. It is designed to support a 800 MHz air inter-face and defines the operations between the BS and MSC. As of this writing, IS-634 was nearing completion.

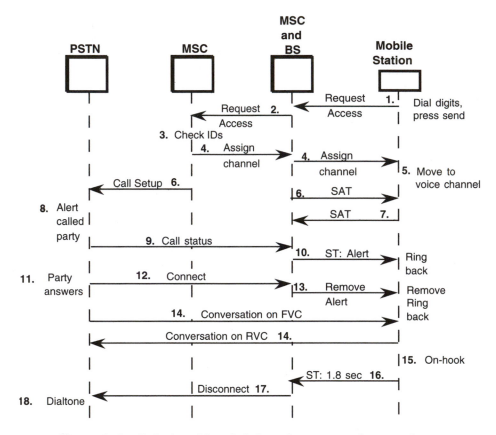

Figure 2–9   **Relationship of air interface operations and network operations.**

Handoff Operations

A handoff operation occurs when a mobile station moves to another cell, as depicted in Figure 2–10. It involves a mobile switching center (MSC) interworking with two or more base stations; two are shown in this figure. Base station 1 is handling the call for the mobile station (event 1). It notices the mobile station's transmission is decreasing in power (event 2). It sends a handoff measurement request message to its MSC (event 3). The MSC can request a number of base stations to report on their reception of the mobile station's signal. In this example, it requests that base station 2 monitor and report back its results (events 4, 5, and 6).

The MSC decides that base station 2 is the best choice to take over the call, so it allocates a traffic channel (TCH) to this station and the station acknowledges (events 7 and 8). Next, the MSC sends a handoff order

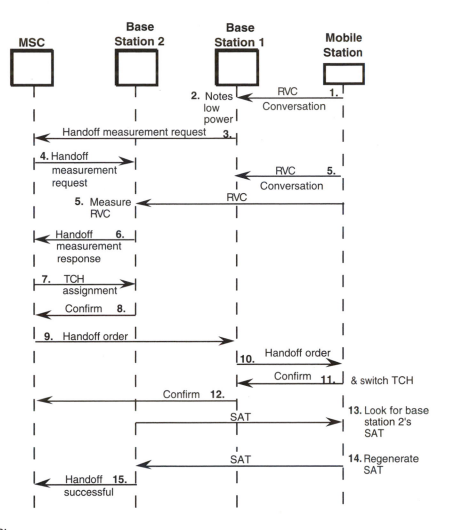

Figure 2–10   A handoff operation.

Notes:
- Event 10 occurs on old FVC, and event 11 occurs on old RVC
- The confirm is a ST of 50 ms

message to base station 1, which sends a similar message to the mobile unit (events 9 and 10). The message in event 10 informs the mobile station of the new channel assignment, as well as the power level to be used in the new cell. With the confirmations (events 11 and 12), the mobile station receives base station 2's SAT and regenerates this SAT back to the base station (events 13 and 14). This continuity check is sufficient for base station 2 to confirm the handoff (event 15) to the MSC.

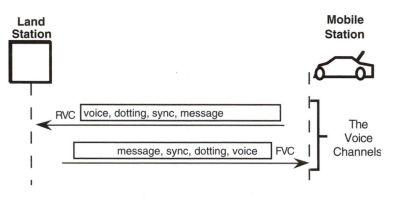

Figure 2–11   Voice channel signaling.

BLANK AND BURST OPERATIONS

The voice channels (RVC and FVC) also carry digital signaling messages in addition to the analog voice traffic. The voice signals are inhibited when a message is sent. The message is sent with a frequency shift key (FSK) signal at 10 kbit/s. This concept is called blank-and-burst, (Figure 2–11).

To inform the receiver that digital messages are forthcoming, the sender first transmits a 101-bit sequence, which is called the *dotting sequence*. The receiver detects this signal and prepares to receive the message. The receiver then looks for a synchronization field, which precedes the message. The messages are repeated to ensure they arrive safely.

SUMMARY

The Advanced Mobile Phone System (AMPS) is a first generation mobile wireless system. AMPS is based on analog transmissions using FDMA. It does not employ voice digitization or encryption operations. A number of the AMPS features such as the 30 kHz channels and the electronic serial numbers are used in second generation systems such as IS-54-B (D-AMPS), IS-95, and IS-136. But the trend in the new systems is to migrate away from the analog aspects of AMPS, such as the analog voice traffic and frequency-based signaling tones. As you read the following chapters, the AMPS technology may appear to be primitive. In hindsight, it is, but it has served the industry well and was considered to be a very advanced technology when it was conceived.

3

Digital AMPS (D-AMPS): IS-54-B

T his chapter describes Digital AMPS (D-AMPS), a hybrid air interface that uses both first generation and second generation technology and has been published as IS-54-B. The rationale for developing D-AMPS is explained and the concept of dual mode operations is introduced. D-AMPS's TDMA operations are analyzed, as well as the messages used to control operations on the air interface.

The reader should have a basic understanding of AMPS before reading this chapter. See Chapter 2 in the this book and the book in this series titled *Mobile and Wireless Networks*.

RATIONALE FOR D-AMPS

D-AMPS was introduced in North America in the early 1990s to overcome some of the limitations of the original AMPS technology. Since that time, it has found its way into several other countries around the world, and even though its user base is limited, it continues to grow.

Because of the co-channel interference ratio exhibited in AMPS technology, its capacity is quite limited when compared to some other technologies. In addition, the 30 kHz channel assigned to each user represents excess capacity for that user. With the use of new technology, it is possible to reduce the amount of bandwidth assigned to a user.

D-AMPS represents a hybrid approach in which the current AMPS bandwidth is used as well as many of the ongoing AMPS procedures. The hybrid aspect of AMPS comes into play when the second generation TDMA technology is placed on the AMPS traffic channels. In essence, D-AMPS is classified as a dual-mode operation in that both traditional analog AMPS (FDMA) and Digital D-AMPS (TDMA) services are available in the same network.

This dual mode operation is quite attractive to cellular providers because it allows them to migrate to digital services on an evolutionary basis. The use of D-AMPS permits mobile stations to co-exist with either analog or digital technology in the AMPS frequency band. The approach also permits the use of the current AMPS physical plant, such as base stations, with minor alterations to hardware.

In a typical D-AMPS operating environment, certain 30 kHz channels are allocated for traditional analog AMPS traffic and others are allocated for TDMA traffic. While migrating these channels to digital technology results in the loss of analog capacity for those mobile users who have a traditional AMPS mobile station, the overall end result is the increase in capacity because each 30 kHz AMPS channel is time division multiplexed to carry three subscribers' signals. As an example, assume a cell can support 40 physical analog channels and one of these channels employs digital TDMA operations only. Obviously, the result is the loss of one analog channel dedicated to one AMPS user. But the gain is three digital channels for three users who employ digital signaling.

REVIEW OF SOME AMPS CONCEPTS AND OPERATIONS

Before proceeding further, it is a good idea to pause and explain several basic AMPS concepts and operations that are used in IS-54-B, some with additions. The approach is to give a brief definition or description of each.

- Digital verification color code (DVCC): An 8-bit code sent by the base station to the mobile station in initialization messages, such as a handoff message. It is stored at the mobile station and later used to check the CDVCC, discussed next.

- Coded digital verification color code (CDVCC): A 12-bit code (containing the 8-bit DVCC and 4 protection bits) sent in each slot to and from mobile stations and base stations to indicate the correct data (rather than co-channel data) is being received; that is, to distinguish the current traffic channel from traffic co-channels.
- Discontinuous transmission (DTX): An operation in which the mobile station switches between two transmit power levels.
- Mobile station attenuation code (MAC): Consists of VMAC, the voice mobile attenuation code, and DMAC, the digital mobile attenuation code. The purpose of the MAC is to give direction to the mobile station about the power level it is to use on a new traffic or voice channel.

THE D-AMPS HANDSHAKE

IS-54-B is the specification defining dual mode operation. One of its principal goals is to ensure that the existing base of traditional AMPS mobile stations and base stations do not have to be changed. Consequently, IS-54-B defines the use of (a) analog traffic channels, (b) digital traffic channels, and (c) analog control channels. All channel bandwidths and frequency allocations remain identical to the AMPS specification.

The mobile station is responsible for the following actions (see Figure 3–1):

- It initially accesses the network with a traditional AMPS analog control channel, shown in events 1–4.
- In event 5, the mobile station signals if it is capable of dual mode operations (that is, capable of using a digital traffic channel).
- If available, the network allocates a digital traffic channel. The mobile station is informed of the frequency to be employed for the traffic channel as well as the time slot to be used on the channel.
  In turn, the mobile station tunes to the traffic channel and proper time slot for the exchange of traffic (events 6, 7, and 8 in the middle of the figure).
- If the digital traffic channels are not available due to previous allocations, the base station informs the mobile station of this situation by sending to the mobile station a channel frequency assignment pertaining to a conventional AMPS analog traffic channel (shown in events 6, 7, and 8 at the bottom of the figure).

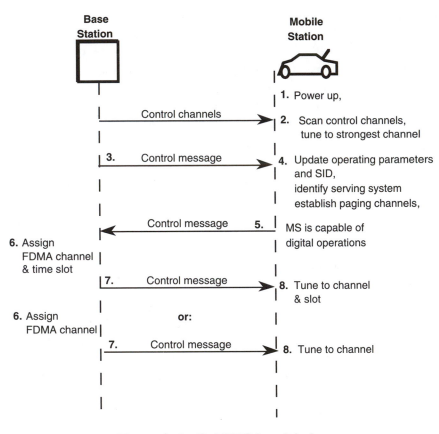

Figure 3–1   D-AMPS handshake.

FRAME STRUCTURE

IS-54-B uses time division multiple access (TDMA) frames consisting of six slots, as shown in Figure 3–2. The frames are 40 ms in length and are transmitted in the uplink and downlink directions on the air interface. Each user uses two of the six slots in the frame. One frame is 1944 bits, and with a duration of 40 ms, 25 frames per second are transmitted on the channel. Thus, three users can share a physical channel utilizing the full six slots. One user uses slots 1 and 4, the second user uses slots 2 and 5, and the third user uses slots 3 and 6. This approach is called full-rate. It is planned that D-AMPS will eventually support six users per channel, which is called half-rate.

As with many mobile systems, the uplink and downlink frames are staggered by a certain number of time slots. For D-AMPS, the staggering

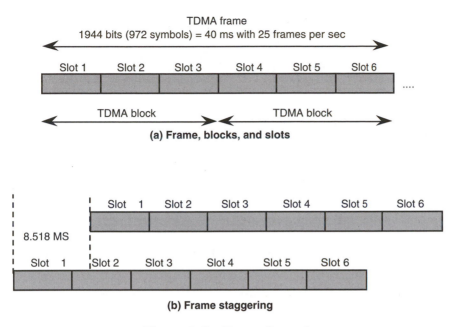

Figure 3–2   Frame format.

is 8.518 ms. This concept is a variation of time division duplexing (TDD). Its attraction is that the mobile station does not have to send and receive at the same time, which allows the mobile station to operate in a half-duplex mode instead of full duplex. Duplex operations require expensive hardware and consume considerable power.

D-AMPS uses a $\frac{\pi}{4}$ shifted, differentially encoded quadrature phase shift keying (DQPSK) modulation scheme. With differential encoding, symbols are sent as relative phase changes and not absolute phases. Each $\frac{\pi}{4}$ symbol carries 2 bits of information. For the mobile station, the offset between the reverse and forward frame timing (with no timing advance, explained later) is one time slot plus 45 symbols (207 symbol periods). The slot is 162 symbols in length, 45 + 162 = 207 symbol periods.

REDEFINING THE AMPS CHANNELS

The AMPS channels described in Chapter 2 are still used, but the content and formats for the 30 kHz channels are changed. The traffic channel is that portion of the digital information sent from the BS to the MS or from the MS to the BS and can contain both signaling and user information. The organization of the traffic channel is shown in Figure 3–3.

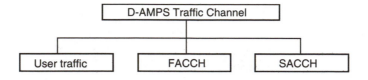

where:
  FACCH   Fast associated control channel
  SACCH   Slow associated control channel

Figure 3–3   The D-AMPS traffic channel.

The channel definitions for D-AMPS are as follows:

- Forward analog control channel (FOCC): BS-to-MS control channel (same as AMPS)
- Forward analog voice channel (FVC): BS-to-MS voice channel (same as AMPS)
- Forward digital traffic channel (FDTC): BS-to-MS digital user and control channel (consists of FACCH and SDCCH)
- Reverse analog control channel (RECC): BS-to-MS control channel (same as AMPS)
- Reverse analog voice channel (RVC): MS-to-BS voice channel (same as AMPS)
- Reverse digital traffic channel (RDTC): MS-to-BS digital user and control channel (consists of FACCH and SDCCH)

The fast associated control channel (FACCH) is used for signaling purposes. It cannot be used simultaneously with user information. The FACCH is a *blank-and-burst* operation in which the traffic channel frame's primary traffic is preempted by signaling traffic (preemption is performed on a frame-by-frame basis). The slow associated control channel (SACCH) is a continuous channel also used for signaling. It is not subject to the blank-and-burst operations, because of a fixed number of bits all reserved for the SACCH in each TDMA slot.

IS-54-B defines two different slot organizations for digital traffic. The slots are shown in Figure 3–4 and are also called signals in some literature. The digital traffic channel (DTC) employs two channels that are used to supervise call setup and tear down and manage the ongoing call. These channels are called the fast associated control channel (FACCH) and the slow associated control channel (SACCH), just discussed.

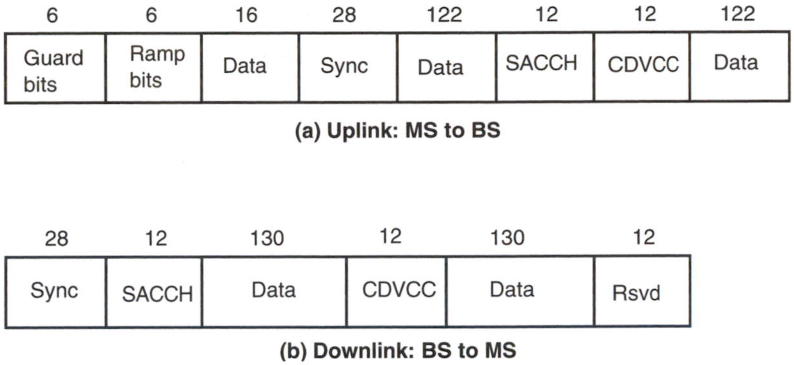

6	6	16	28	122	12	12	122
Guard bits	Ramp bits	Data	Sync	Data	SACCH	CDVCC	Data

(a) Uplink: MS to BS

28	12	130	12	130	12
Sync	SACCH	Data	CDVCC	Data	Rsvd

(b) Downlink: BS to MS

Figure 3–4   Uplink and downlink slots.

- Guard bits: Used on uplink to compensate for different distances and timing variations between the MS and BS. Guard time is 3 symbols in duration.
- Ramp bits: Allow some time for the build-up (power ramp up) of the RF signal. Ramp time is 3 symbols in duration.
- Data: The traffic (voice) that was explained earlier. Signaling traffic may be placed in the data field in the event of heavy signaling traffic. This traffic is called the fast associated control channel (FACCH).
- Sync: Used for equalizer training and for discerning the correct time alignment on the slot. Its sync sequences are the same as IS-136.
- SACCH: The slow associated control channel, used as a signaling and control channel.
- CDVCC: The coded digital voice color code, used like the AMPS SAT for co-channel identification. It contains the 8-bit DVCC and 4 protection bits. It is sent in each uplink and downlink slot and is used to detect (a) correct reception or (b) co-channel interference. The same CDVCC can be used for all BS and MS transmissions in the same cell (or cell sector).

TIME ALIGNMENT

D-AMPS uses the time alignment process discussed in Chapter 1 (see Figure 1–6). The misalignment of arriving slots is detected at the base station by detecting errors in arriving slots. The base station then sends a time alignment message to the mobile stations to correct the time alignment. This message is discussed later in the chapter.

The Shortened Burst Slot

The shortened burst slot, shown in Figure 3–5, is used for calculating the distance of the mobile station to the base station. It aligns the MS and BS in the time domain and avoids collisions at the base station between the mobile station's slot (burst) and a neighbor mobile station's slot.

At certain times it is necessary for a mobile station while operating on a digital traffic channel to transmit during its slot interval a sequence 324 bits long, defined as a shortened burst, in order to avoid collisions at the base station between the mobile station's burst and the burst of a neighboring slot. The collision of neighboring bursts is due to the mobile station not having the proper time alignment information in relation to its distance from the base station.

The mobile station receives directions from the base station and moves to a traffic channel. The mobile station first synchronizes to the forward traffic channel, then transmits at the standard offset reference position the shortened burst message. The mobile station continues to transmit this message at the standard offset reference position until it receives a time alignment message from the base station or the mobile station is directed to stop transmission. If the mobile station receives a time alignment message, it adjusts its transmission timing and transmits during the next available slot a time-aligned full duration slot burst.

A mobile handoff message contains estimated time alignment information. For smaller cells, this estimated time alignment information is

G1	R S D S D V S D W S D X S D Y S	G2

where:
    G1:   3 symbol length guard time
    R: 3 symbol length ramp time
    S: 14 symbol length sync words
    D: 6 symbol length CDVCC
    G2:   22 symbol length guard time
    V = 0000
    V = 00000000
    V = 000000000000
    V = 0000000000000000

Figure 3–5   The shortened burst slot.

used to adjust the mobile station transmit timing. For sector-to-sector handoff, the estimated time alignment information will also be used to adjust the mobile station transmit timing. The estimated time alignment information may not be accurate enough to avoid burst collisions at the base station.

Analog-to-digital and digital-to-digital handoff messages contain a shortened burst indicator (SBI). This field indicates to the mobile station which of the following three handoff conditions exist:

1. Handoff to a small diameter cell
2. Handoff within a sector of a cell
3. Handoff to a large diameter cell

The format of the shortened burst slot is shown in Figure 3–5. The composition of the shortened burst message contains sufficient information to achieve time alignment at the base station after the detection of two or more sync words. The symbol interval between any two sync words is unique to the two detected sync words.

VOICE AND CHANNEL CODING

Voice Coding

The pattern of a speech signal is defined in 20 durations called speech segments. The segments are compared against a table of values (a codebook). The entry in the table that is closest to the actual value is used as the transmitted value instead of the longer PCM block. Figure 3–6 shows the approach, which is called *Vector-Sum Excited Linear Predictive Coding* (VSLEP).

The D-AMPS vocoder compresses each 20 ms speech segment into 159 bits, which are placed into a slot in the frame. Since 25 frames are transmitted each second and 2 slots are used in each frame, the compressed speech is 7950 bit/s.

Channel Coding

After the speech is coded, the channel coding operation takes over. It uses three operations to combat transmission impairments on the RF channel:

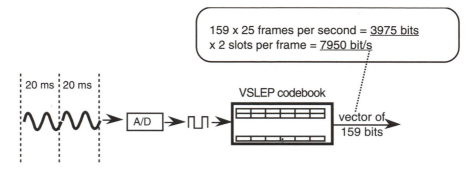

Figure 3–6   Functional view of Vector-Sum Excited Linear Predictive Coding (VSLEP).

1. A cyclic redundance check (CRC) operation on the most significant bits of the speech coder.
2. A convolutional coder to protect the more important (and vulnerable) bits of the speech stream.
3. The interleaving of the data over two time slots to mitigate the effects of Rayleigh fading.

However, the bandwidth requirements for the 7950 speech signal are 13 kbit/s. The 159 bits have other bits added to them, as shown in Figure 3–7. The original 159 bits are divided into 77 class 1 bits and 82 class 2 bits. The idea is to offer more protection to the more significant bits in the vector. These bits are the class 1 bits and receive two forms of protection: the 12 most significant bits are taken through a 7-bit CRC operation, and all 77 bits are processed through a convolutional encoder that recodes each bit with 2 bits. The result is a 178-bit output from the convolutional coder. These bits and the class 2 bits are subjected to a ciphering function, then placed into the two slots in the frame through the slot interleaver.

The resultant bit rate is 13,000 bit/s since: 260 bits per frame × 25 frames per second = 6500 bits × 2 slots per frame = 13,000 bit/s.

The 5050 bits of overhead (38.8% of the 13 kbit/s signal) may seem to be high, but it is necessary to ensure a high-quality signal. The actual overhead is higher, since a slot is 364 bits, which consists of other control bits, discussed later. So, a 159 traffic rate in a 364 bit slot translates to 49.1% for user traffic and 50.9% for overhead.

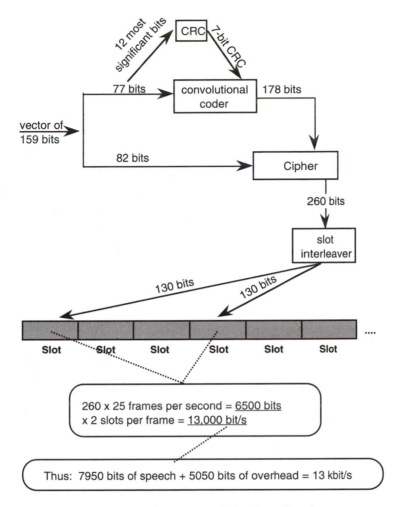

Figure 3–7   Coding and slot interleaving.

MOBILE-ASSISTED HANDOFF (MAHO)

Unlike AMPS, in which the mobile station does not participate or make decisions about handoff, IS-54-B defines the mobile-assisted handoff (MAHO), which is used to make the handoff process more efficient and faster. In this situation, the mobile station measures the quality of the forward traffic channel in relation to other channels emanating from other base stations (see Figure 3–8). It performs these operations during idle times when not involved in sending or receiving traffic (Figure 3–8a). The measurements taken by the mobile station are sent back to the base

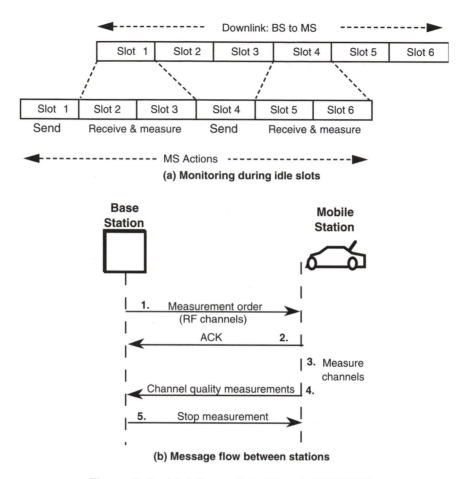

Figure 3–8   Mobile-assisted handoff (MAHO).

station. In turn, the base station uses this information to decide if hand-off is to be implemented. This modification to the traditional AMPS operation reduces signaling substantially because neighboring cells do not have to measure the channel of the mobile station.

IS-54-B is designed to support analog handoff or digital handoff as well as variations of analog-to-digital or digital-to-digital handoffs. Even though the mobile station participates more in handoff decisions than it did in the conventional AMPS, the operation is still controlled initially by the base station by directing the mobile station to send measurement messages back to the network (see Figure 3–8b). The message tells the mobile station which channels are to be monitored, measured, and reported upon.

USE OF AMPS OPERATIONS

D-AMPS continues the use of many AMPS operations. They are listed here. The reader can refer to Chapter 2 of this book and the prerequisite book in this series titled *Mobile and Wireless Networks*.

- Supervisory audio tone (SAT)
- Signaling tone (ST)
- Coded digital verification color code (CDVCC), a variation of AMPS digital color code (DCC)
- AMPS use words in the messages

SECURITY PROCEDURES

Since D-AMPS utilizes digital transmissions, it can avail itself of digital encryption. This operation is covered in the IS-41 section (Chapter 7).

D-AMPS MESSAGES

Most of the second generation mobile wireless systems use a variation of ISDN protocols for signaling purposes. D-AMPS uses some of the features of ISDN's layer 3 protocol, Q.931. Of course, significant changes are made to Q.931, but the basic nature of the protocol remains the same. In this section, the reverse digital traffic channel (RDTC) and forward digital traffic channel (FDTC) messages are explained. These messages are sent on the FACCH and SACCH channels.

All messages take the form shown in Figure 3–9. The protocol discriminator is set to 00. The message type value is coded to identify the

Protocol discriminator
Message type
Information elements (fixed, variable, mandatory, optional)

Figure 3–9 Formats for messages on FACCH and SACCH channels.

type of message, such as a CONNECT and RELEASE messages. Next, the information elements contain the fields of the message, some of which are mandatory and some are optional. In the ensuing discussion of the D-AMPS messages and operations, I make no further mentions of the protocol discriminator and message types fields; be aware that they reside in each message.

FDTC Messages

Table 3–1 lists the messages used on the FDTC, and this part of the chapter describes the functions of the messages. The approach taken here is to amplify previous explanations in this chapter as well as describe other aspects of D-AMPS operations. Be aware that several of the messages described in this section are acknowledged by the mobile station's MOBILE ACK message.

Table 3–1   The FDTC Messages

Messages	Channel Used
ALERT WITH INFO	FACCH
MEASUREMENT ORDER	FACCH
STOP MEASUREMENT ORDER	FACCH/SACCH
HANDOFF	FACCH
PHYSICAL LAYER CONTROL	FACCH/SACCH
RELEASE	FACCH
BASE STATION ACK	FACCH
MAINTENANCE	FACCH
AUDIT	SACCH
LOCAL CONTROL	SACCH
FLASH WITH INFO ACK	FACCH
SEND BURST DTMF ACK	FACCH
SEND CONTINUOUS DTMF ACK	FACCH
FLASH WITH INFO	FACCH
PARAMETER UPDATE	FACCH
STATUS REQUEST	FACCH
BASE STATION CHALLENGE ORDER CONFIRMATION	FACCH
SSD UPDATE ORDER	FACCH
UNIQUE CHALLENGE ORDER	FACCH

The ALERT WITH INFO message is issued to the mobile station when a call is to be terminated to that mobile station. The message contains the information elements of: signal (which is network-specific information) and the calling party number. This message is acknowledged from the mobile station with the MOBILE ACK message.

The MEASUREMENT ORDER message is sent to the mobile station to instruct it to begin the measurement of channels and the reporting of these measurements. The message contains the RF channel information element, which identifies 0–12 RF channels that are to be measured. This operation is illustrated in Figures 3–10 and 3–11.

In Figure 3–10 event 1, the MEASUREMENT ORDER message is sent to the mobile station, which acknowledges the message in event 2 with the MEASUREMENT ORDER ACK message. The mobile station commences to measure the designated channels in event 3. Periodically, the mobile station reports on the results of the measurements by sending a CHANNEL QUALITY message (discussed in the next section and shown as event 4). The received signal strength (RSSI) and the bit error rate (BER) are the key information elements in this message and they are described in the following section dealing with the mobile station's messages. At the base station's discretion, it sends a STOP MEASUREMENT ORDER message (event 5) to direct the mobile station to stop its measurement monitoring.

Figure 3–11 provides an example of how the slots are monitored by the mobile station. The example assumes the mobile station is assigned

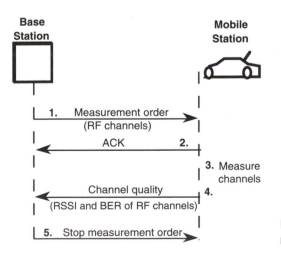

Figure 3–10 Example of channel monitoring.

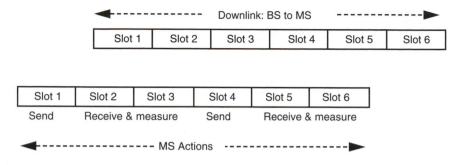

Figure 3–11   How the slots and channels are measured.

to slots 1 and 3. When it is sending on these slots, it cannot monitor. However, during time slots 2, 3, 5, and 6, it tunes to the designated RF channels, receives and measures them. Once again, more information is provided in the next section of this chapter.

The STOP MEASUREMENT ORDER message informs the mobile station that it is to terminate the channel quality measurements and reporting operations. This message is acknowledged from the mobile station with the MOBILE ACK message.

The HANDOFF message is used by the network to inform the mobile station to move from one traffic channel to another. The message contains:

- The RF channel information element contains the designation of the channel number ranging from 1–1023. The convention for identifying the channel number is to use N to identify the center frequency in MHz corresponding to the channel number:

Transmit side	Channel Number	Center Frequency (MHz)
Mobile station	$1 \leq N \leq 799$	$0.030\, N + 825.000$
	$990 \leq N \leq 1023$	$0.030\, (N - 1023) + 825.000$
Base station	$1 \leq N \leq 799$	$0.030\, N + 870.000$
	$990 \leq N \leq 1023$	$0.030\, (N - 1023) + 870.000$

- The rate information element is the designation of full-rate or half-rate channel.
- The timeslot indicator information element indicates the assigned time slot of the designated traffic channel. It is coded as follows: analog channel [000], time slot 1 [001], time slot 2 [010], time slot 3 [011], time slot 4 [100], time slot 5 [101], time slot 6 [110], reserved [111].

- The time alignment information element contains the standard offset reference (SOR). This information is used by the mobile station to time align the reverse frame on the reverse channel with the forward frame on the forward channel. With a "standard" operation, the offset between the reverse and forward frame is one time slot plus 45 symbols (207 symbol periods). Therefore, time slot 1 of a specific frame in the forward direction occurs 207 symbol periods after time slot 1 of the associated frame in the reverse direction (with no timing advance). This concept is called the SOR. So, the timing alignment value indicates a timing offset from the SOR.

- This information element is the color code SAT/DVCC and is coded in accordance with conventional AMPS specifications.

- The DMAC/VMAC information element is the designation of the power level to be used on the new channel and is coded in accordance with conventional AMPS specifications.

- The shortened burst information element is an indication if the mobile station is to use a shortened burst initially. This operation is described in the next section of this chapter.

- The voice privacy mode and message encryption mode information elements deal with operations covered in Chapter 7.

The PHYSICAL LAYER CONTROL message is used to control the physical layer operations at the mobile station. The message contains information elements to control output power level, time alignments, notation if DTX is allowed, and the delay interval compensation mode.

The RELEASE message is used by the network to inform the mobile station that the current call is terminated. This message is acknowledged from the mobile station with the MOBILE ACK message.

The BASE STATION ACK message is used to acknowledge the CONNECT message, RELEASE message, and the STATUS message.

The MAINTENANCE message is sent by the network to check the operation of the mobile station. This message is acknowledged from the mobile station with the MOBILE ACK message.

The AUDIT message is sent by the network to determine if a mobile station is active in the system. This message is acknowledged from the mobile station with the MOBILE ACK message.

The LOCAL CONTROL message is sent to customize the operations of a mobile station. The nature of the customization is not defined in the specification. This message is acknowledged from the mobile station with the MOBILE ACK message.

The FLASH WITH INFO ACK message acknowledges the FLASH WITH INFO ORDER message sent from the mobile station. This message indicates that the mobile user wishes to invoke a special service, which is network specific.

The SEND BURST DTMF ACK message and SEND CONTINUOUS DTMF ACK message acknowledge their counterparts, which are discussed in the next section.

The FLASH WITH INFO message plays the same role when sent by the network as it does when sent by the mobile station and these functions are described in the next section.

The PARAMETER UPDATE message is sent to the mobile station to instruct it to update parameters that are used in the authentication process (the internal call history parameter). See Chapter 7 for authentication procedures.

The STATUS REQUEST message is a query to the mobile station to ask for its status or to inform the mobile station that the network has unilaterally decided to change its voice privacy mode. Also, this message can be used to confirm the mobile station's request for a change in the voice privacy mode.

The remainder of the base station messages pertain to authentication and encryption operations and are explained in Chapter 7. A brief summary of the messages are provided here. First, the BASE STATION CHALLENGE ORDER CONFIRMATION message is sent in response to the mobile station's BASE STATION CHALLENGE ORDER message and contains the authentication algorithm's outputs (AUTHBS). The SSD UPDATE ORDER message is used by the network to instruct the mobile station to execute the authentication algorithm. This message contains the RANDSSD information element. The UNIQUE CHALLENGE ORDER message is used by the network to instruct the mobile station to execute the authentication algorithm. The message contains the RANDU information element.

RDTC Messages

Table 3–2 lists the messages used on the RDTC, and this part of the chapter describes the functions of the messages. Some of the operations associated with the messages have been explained earlier in this chapter, so the approach here is to amplify previous explanations as well as describe other aspects of D-AMPS operations.

Table 3–2   The RDTC Messages

Messages	Channel Used
CONNECT	FACCH
MEASUREMENT ORDER ACK	FACCH
CHANNEL QUALITY MESSAGE 1	FACCH/SACCH
CHANNEL QUALITY MESSAGE 2	FACCH/SACCH
RELEASE	FACCH
MOBILE ACK	FACCH/SACCH
FLASH WITH INFO	FACCH
FLASH WITH INFO ACK	FACCH
SEND BURST DTMF	FACCH
SEND CONTINUOUS DTMF	FACCH
PHYSICAL LAYER CONTROL ACK	FACCH/SACCH
STATUS	FACCH
PARAMETER UPDATE ACK	FACCH
SSD UPDATE ORDER CONFIRMATION	FACCH
BASE STATION CHALLENGE ORDER	FACCH
UNIQUE CHALLENGE ORDER CONFIRMATION	FACCH

The CONNECT message is sent by the mobile station to the network to indicate the answering of a call by the mobile phone user. This message contains no information elements beyond the required header.

The MEASUREMENT ORDER ACK indicates to the network that the mobile station has started the channel quality measurement operation. Recall that the network can direct the mobile station to monitor other channels in other cells or sectors. Upon receiving an order, the mobile station begins the monitoring process, and returns this message, which contains a list of the RF channels (or channel) that it is monitoring.

After the mobile station has begun the monitoring process, it sends to the base station CHANNEL QUALITY messages. The CHANNEL QUALITY MESSAGE 1 reports on RF channels 1–6 and CHANNEL QUALITY MESSAGE 2 reports on channels 7–12. The mobile station knows which of the channels to measure by receiving its instructions from the network in the MEASUREMENT ORDER message, which is described in the previous section on base station messages.

The mobile station's monitoring operations entail returning two important information elements in the CHANNEL QUALITY messages:

Table 3–3   RSSI Values

Bits	RSSI Value
00000	–113 dBm or less
00001	–111 dBm
00010	–109 dBm
00011	–107 dBm
–	–
11110	–53 dBm
11111	–51 dBm or greater

(a) the received signal strength (RSSI) and (b) the bit error rate (BER). RSSI values are returned on all monitored channels, whereas the BER value is returned for the current channel only. The channel strength is reported in the message with a 5-bit field, as shown in Table 3–3. The BER information is reported in with a 3-bit field as shown in Table 3–4.

The mobile station implements similar procedures to capture both RSSI and BER. It monitors each 40 ms frame and performs an averaging process on 25 successive frames. The results are reported back to the base station.

The RELEASE message is sent to inform the network that a currently established call has been terminated. The message contains a release reason parameter which obviously describes the reason for the release.

The MOBILE ACK message is sent by the mobile station in response to receiving several types of messages from the network. Once again, these messages were described in the previous section, but for our purposes here the MOBILE ACK acknowledges the following messages:

Table 3–4   BER Values

Bits	BER Value
000	< 0.01
001	0.01 to less than 0.1
010	0.1 to less than 0.5
011	0.5 to less than 1.0
100	1.0 to less than 2.0
101	2.0 to less than 4.0
110	4.0 to less than 8.0
111	≥ 8.0

ACK Message Type	ACK Channel
ALERT WITH INFO	FACCH
STOP MEASUREMENT ORDER	FACCH/SACCH
RELEASE	FACCH
MAINTENANCE	FACCH
AUDIT	FACCH/SACCH
LOCAL CONTROL	FACCH/SACCH
HANDOFF	FACCH

The FLASH WITH INFO message is sent to the network when a mobile station user wishes to invoke a special service. The special service is just that, special, and depends on what added features the network provides. The message contains a request number that is used by the receiver to send back an acknowledgment containing the same number. It also contains a field called the *key pad facility*, which contains the numbers and characters entered by the mobile station user via its telephone keypad or some other terminal. These numbers and characters identify the type of service (or other information) that is being requested. The FLASH WITH INFO ACK message acknowledges FLASH WITH INFO messages.

The SEND BURST DTMF message is used by the mobile station to request that dual-tone multiple frequencies be sent on the land line. The message contains a digit field that defines which digits are to be sent.

Likewise, the SEND CONTINUOUS DTMF message requests the network to send continuous DTMF tones on the land line. The sending of a DTMF tone is stopped when a null digit is sent.

The PHYSICAL LAYER CONTROL ACK message is used to acknowledge the network's PHYSICAL LAYER CONTROL message, described in the previous section. For this discussion, this message must contain all the information elements that are present in the message that it is acknowledging.

The STATUS message can be used as a reply to the STATUS REQUEST message sent by the mobile station or as a spontaneous message sent by the mobile station. For the latter operation, this message is used to indicate a change in the status of the mobile station. The message contains the ESN of the mobile station, the mobile station's call mode, as well as terminal information (which contains the model number of the mobile station, the firmware release issued by the mobile station manufacturer, the manufacturer's code, as well as the IS-54 version number), the mobile station's encryption mode and voice privacy mode.

The PARAMETER UPDATE ACK message ACKs the PARAMETER UPDATE message sent by the network.

The remaining messages are related to security operations and are explained in Chapter 7. I provide a brief description here. The SSD UPDATE ORDER CONFIRMATION message is sent by the mobile station to indicate the success or failure of the SSD update procedure. The BASE STATION CHALLENGE ORDER message is sent by the mobile station to convey the random number RANDBS used in the SSD update procedure. The UNIQUE CHALLENGE ORDER CONFIRMATION message is also part of the ongoing security operations and contains the response to the UNIQUE CHALLENGE ORDER message sent by the network. It contains the AUTHU information element, which is the output of the authentication algorithm produced in response to the UNIQUE CHALLENGE ORDER message.

SUMMARY

Digital AMPS (D-AMPS) is a hybrid air interface that uses both first generation and second generation technology. It is published as IS-54-B. D-AMPS was introduced in North America in the early 1990s to overcome some of the limitations of the original AMPS technology and to exploit the use of digital technology. The D-AMPS dual mode operation is attractive because it allows network operators to migrate to digital services on an evolutionary basis. It has found its way into several other countries around the world and even though its user base is limited, it continues to grow.

4

The Global System for Mobile Communications (GSM)

This chapter describes the Global System for Mobile Communications (GSM) network, a system developed in Europe and now present in the Americas, Africa, Australia, and Asia. The components and services of the GSM network are examined, as well as the GSM interfaces and layers. The GSM functional planes, identifiers, and MAP protocols are also explored. In addition, the relationships of GSM 900, GSM 1800/ GSM 1800, and PCS 1900 are described.

It is noteworthy that the North American rendition of GSM uses the exact same air interface frame and slot structure as the European GSM specification and, with some very minor differences, the addresses and identifiers are the same. Therefore, the discussion of the physical TDMA channels and the GSM identifiers in this chapter will not distinguish between the European and U.S. GSM versions.

DEVELOPMENT OF GSM

The GSM/DCS (Global System for Mobile Communications/Digital Cellular System) was initiated by the European Commission (EC) by adapting, in June 1987, a Recommendation and Directive for the Council of Ministers. The aim of this document was to eliminate the incompatibility of mobile wireless systems and to create a European-wide communications system structure. The aim was also used to accelerate the efforts of individual countries to develop a European-wide digital cellular system. As discussed in Chapter 1, the United States regulatory bodies did not take this approach and decided to let the marketplace determine the "winner." With no specific technology declared a winner, the U.S. market is replete with incompatible systems.

GSM is the foundation for the Digital Cellular System 1800 (DCS 1800), and the Personal Communications System 1900 (PCS 1900), as shown in Figure 4–1a. GSM 900 is the original system that was first implemented in Europe in the early to mid-1980s. DCS 1800 is an up-banded version of GSM 900. PCS 1900 is also based on GSM and is the North American version. It is quite similar to GSM, with only minor differences. In 1997, DCS 1800 was renamed GSM 1800, and this latter name is used in this chapter.

Since GSM 900, GSM 1800, and PCS 1900 are almost identical, this book uses the GSM specification as the model. Where differences exist, I point them out to the reader.

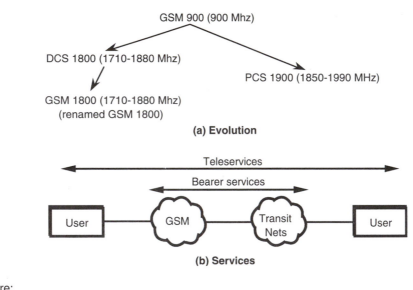

where:

   DCS   Digital Cellular System
   GSM   Global System for Mobile Communications
   PCS   Personal Communications System

Figure 4–1   GSM 900, GSM 1800, PCS 1900.

As shown in Figure 4–1b, GSM services are divided into bearer services and teleservices, which are part of the OSI (Open Systems Interconnection) Model. Bearer services represent the lower three layers of the model and include the services provided by the network to the user. Bearer services support the telephony call through the network, as well as several data services, such as asynchronous and synchronous operations, and packet mode access (access through GSM to a conventional packet network).

Examples of teleservices are conventional telephone services and emergency calls. Another example is short messages service (SMS), which is the incorporation of a paging function into the GSM handset. Other examples of teleservices are supplementary services, which include features such as call forwarding, call waiting, and call holding.

RELATIONSHIPS OF GSM AND PCS 1900

As stated earlier in this chapter, the North American rendition of the European GSM specification is quite similar to the original standards. Indeed, many parts of the North American specification simply cite a GSM document. Table 4–1 provides a cross-reference check of the North American GSM and the European GSM.

As of this writing, the North American GSM is also called PCS 1900, but the term PCS 1900 is also used in other contexts. One context is the description of any system that uses the 1900 MHz spectrum. Therefore, this context could include other air interface technologies such as IS-136 or IS-95. The term GSM was not used to any extent in North America until 1997 because of some rather silly "not invented here" attitudes exhibited by some Americans.

The North American specification is still under development and is published as TIA NA PN3389 (issued by the Telecommunications Industries Association). When it is completed, it will be published as Specification J-STD-007.

GSM TOPOLOGY AND ARCHITECTURE

The GSM topology and architecture is shown in Figure 4–2. The interface with the mobile station (MS) is provided through the base transceiver station (BTS). These two components operate with a range of radio

Table 4–1   North American (NA) Rendition of GSM

NA	Description	GSM
Volume 0	General description of network	01.02 & 01.04
Volume 1	Description of physical layer of air interface	05.01–05.10
Volume 2	Air interface signaling	04 series
Part 1	Layer 1 (physical) & Layer 2 (media access) signaling	04.01–04.06
Part 2	Layer 3 signaling	04.07 & 04.08
Part 3	Layer 3 supplementary services	04.10, 04.80–04.86, 04.88 & 04.90
Part 4	Layer 3 other aspects	04.11–04.13, 04.21
Volume 3	Speech coding	06 series
Volume 4	Terminal adapters	07 series, 04.22 & 08.20
Volume 5	Man machine interface & security aspects	02.09, 02.17, 03.20, 11.11
Part 1	Security & encryption	
Part 2	User interface module (UIM)	
Part 3	Man machine interface (MMI)	
Volume 6	Operations, administration, & maintenance	12.03 & T1M1.5/93–001/R6
Volume 7	Annex: normative & informative material	02.30, 02.40, 03.14, 03.22, 03.41, 03.38
Part 1	Functions of MS in idle mode	
Part 2	Procedure for call progress indications	
Part 3	Dual tone multi-frequency signaling (DTMF)	
Part 4	Alphabet & language-specific information	
Part 5	Short message service cell broadcast (SMSCB)	

Note: NA PN 3389 is under review, to be published as: J-STD-007.

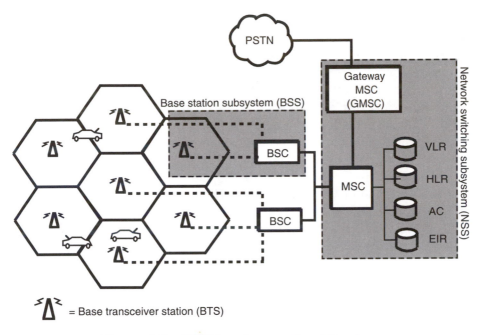

Figure 4–2 GSM topology and architecture.

channels across an air interface. The BTS acts as the interface of the MS to the GSM network.

The *mobile station* (MS) is the mobile unit operated by the customer. It operates on the air interface and may include various functions such as terminal equipment (TE) and terminal adapters (TA). More information on these operations is provided later.

The *base station system* (BSS) is functionally divided into the base station controller (BSC) and a radio transmitting/receiving function operated by the base transceiver station (BTS). The BSS is a composite term to describe the functions of the BSC and BTS and provides the physical equipment to provide radio coverage in at least one cell but typically in multiple cells. The BSS contains the necessary hardware and software to communicate directly with the MS.

The BTSs are controlled by the base station controllers (BSCs). They are responsible for handover operations of the calls as well as controlling the power signals and frequency administration between the BTSs and MSs. The BSC is quite intelligent, and much of the ongoing "house keeping" activities between the BTS and the MS are performed by the BSC. The BTS and BSC may be co-located, or the BSC may be located at the mobile services switching center (MSC), which is discussed next.

The *mobile switching center* (MSC) is the central controller of the mobile network. It holds information pertaining to the location of the subscriber and the information on the radio resources employed at the air interface. It keeps track of the information that is needed for hand-over operations as well as registration procedures when the user initially logs onto the network. The MSC is also responsible for interworking with the public switched telephone network (PSTN), and in this regard, it has functions that are germane to the telephone system. These functions are known as interworking functions (IWF). The actual implementation of the IWF operations with the telephone network depends on the type of network—the type of telephone network operating in a particular country and geographical area.

An MSC with interfaces to the telephone network is called a gateway MSC (or GMSC). It is a complete telephone exchange, with capabilities for relaying calls between the fixed public switched telephone network (PSTN) and the cellular network.

GSM uses two databases called the *home location register* (HLR) and *visitor location register* (VLR) to store permanent and temporary information about each GSM subscriber that belongs to an area controlled by an MSC. Each HLR correlates a subscriber to its area. The HLR provides identifying information on the user, its home subscription base, and any supplementary services provided to the user, such as call forwarding. The HLR also keeps information on the location of its "home" subscribers; that is, in which VLR a subscriber is registered.

The VLR stores information about subscribers in its particular area. It contains information on whether mobile stations are switched on or off and if any of the supplementary services have been activated or deactivated. The VLR is used extensively during the call establishment and authentication procedures. The idea is to use the VLR for these operations in order to reduce traffic to/from the HLR.

The HLR is the primary entity used when a call originates from the public telephone network. The VLR is the primary entity used when the call originates from the mobile station. Even though a subscriber may be in its own home area, both the VLR and HLR are used in order to keep matters consistent.

In addition, two other major components are part of GSM. The authentication center (AC or AUC) is associated with the HLR and is used to protect each subscriber from unauthorized access or from use of a subscription by unauthorized personnel. It also is used for authentication operations when a subscriber registers with the network.

The equipment identity register (EIR) is used for the registration of the type of equipment that exists at the mobile station. It can also provide for security features such as blocking calls that have been determined to emanate from stolen mobile stations, as well as preventing certain stations from using the network that have not been approved by the network vendor.

Finally, supplementary services can be provided during the call such as call forwarding, call holding, etc. It is the obligation of the HLR to downline load these parameters to the VLR during the registration procedure.

GSM INTERFACES

Four interfaces are defined in the GSM structure, as shown in Figure 4–3. Two mandatory interfaces are the Um interface and the A interface. The Um interface is the air interface between the mobile station and the BTS. The A interface exists between the mobile services switching center (MSC) and the base station system (BSS). A third interface,

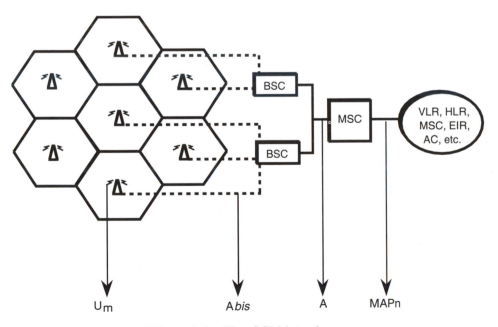

Figure 4–3 The GSM interfaces.

called A bis, defines operations between the BSS and the BTS. It was developed after the A interface was defined and thus was named A bis. Some vendors do not use the A bis standard in their equipment.

The mobile application part (MAP) defines the operations between the MSC and the telephone network as well as the MSC, the HLR, the VLR, and the EIR. MAP is an extension to ITU-T's Common Channel Signaling System 7 (SS7), in that it uses many SS7 features. But MAP is a separate set of protocols that operate over the SS7 protocol stack.

GSM is designed to permit functional partitioning. The major partitioning occurs at the A interface. One side of the interface deals with the MSC, HLR, and VLR operations and the other side of the interface deals with the BSS and air operations.

The Air Interface

The air interface (the Um interface) uses a combination of frequency division multiple access (FDMA) and time division multiple access (TDMA) techniques (see Figure 4–4). The original GSM system operated

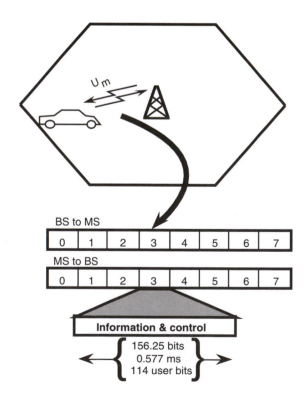

Figure 4–4   The U$_m$ interface.

in the 900 MHz range with 890 to 915 MHz allocated for the mobile station-to-base station transmissions and the 935 to 960 MHz allocated for the base station-to-mobile station transmissions. The GSM 1800 now uses channel spectrum space from 1710 to 1785 MHz and 1805 to 1880 MHz, therefore increasing the capacity in bandwidth of GSM 1800 over that of GSM 900.

124 channel pairs operate at full duplex (FDX) with the uplink and downlink allocated with different carrier frequencies. For example, one channel is allocated to the 935.2 carrier and another channel is allocated to the 890.2 carrier. Thereafter, these FDM channels use TDMA. TDMA slots are allocated with 8 slots to a frame and include information and control bits. Each individual slot comprises 156.25 bits with a slot time of .577 ms. However, the user only receives 114 bits from this slot. The remaining bits are used for synchronization and other control functions.

The instance of one particular time slot (such as slot number 3) in each frame makes up one physical channel and is shown in the bottom of this figure. This means that the physical channel uses one slot every 4.615 ms. Note that the same structure exists both on the uplink and downlink channels. In addition, the signals are separated into 124 channel pairs with a 200 kHz spacing to prevent channel interference.

The GSM Layers

As shown in Figure 4–5, the GSM architecture is based on the Open Systems Interconnection (OSI) Model. As such, it uses layered protocols, service definitions, service access points (SAPs), and the concepts of encapsulation and decapsulation. This figure shows the layers (consisting of protocols and physical connections) that exist at each interface. It is evident that GSM borrows heavily from ISDN and SS7.

Unfortunately, the GSM standards do not provide much information on GSM's overall architecture, and in some instances the standards do not provide a name for the protocol. In other instances, one name is used to describe a number of protocols operating at different interfaces. Figure 4–5 is an accurate representation of the GSM layers, but I have added the generic names to the description of GSM's architecture to aid in our dialogue. For example, the term Q.931+ is used to indicate the use of Q.931 with modifications.

Q.931 is an ISDN layer 3 protocol. In GSM, a modified version of Q.931 is used to set up, negotiate, and tear down a connection between the mobile station and the network. The link access procedure (LAP) has

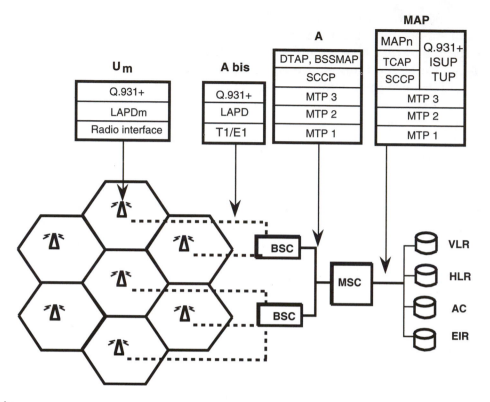

where:

BSSMAP	BSS Management Part (BSC–MSC)
DTAP	Direct transfer application part (MS–MSC)
LAP	Link access procedure, D
LAPDm	LAPD for mobile
MAP	Mobile application part
MTP	Message transfer part
SCCP	Signaling connection control part
TCAP	Transaction capabilities application part

Figure 4–5   The GSM layers.

three versions, LAPDm (LAPD for a mobile link), LAPD (link access procedure for the D channel), and MTP level 2. Their function is to ensure the safe delivery of traffic across the physical channel.

The signaling connection control part (SCCP), message transfer part (MTP), and transaction capabilities application part (TCAP) are derived from the SS7 standard.

THE MOBILE APPLICATION PART (MAP)

Different procedures are used between the GSM network components and are identified with MAP-n, where n is the specific MAP procedure (Figure 4–6). Unfortunately, the GSM standards are not consistent in providing a name for each of these interfaces, so I have grouped them under the name MAP. This figure shows the specific MAP-n protocols and where they operate. Also, the PCS 1900 specifications use the same MAP interfaces, but PCS 1900 also defines MAP-H.

Interface Designation	Between
B	MSC-VLR
C	MSC-HLR
D	HLR-VLR
E	MSC-MSC
F	MSC-EIR
G	VLR-VLR
H	AC-HLR (varies between GSM and PCS 1900)
I	User application protocol and HLR (not defined in PCS 1900)

MAP-E is one of the more extensive mobile access part protocols in the GSM suite. It governs the operations between MSCs. Its principal operations revolve around the overall control and management of the mobile network. In conjunction with the VLR and HLR, it promotes mobile station—intersystem station roaming. It also is responsible for the GSM short message service.

MAP-C operates between MSCs and HLRs. It is not executed if the HLR is co-located at the MSC. Furthermore, while this picture shows the HLR as an "stand-alone" icon representing a database, in practice it is attached to an MSC. Therefore, its execution takes place when a "foreign" MSC needs to interrogate a "non-attached" HLR that is attached to yet another MSC. Its principal responsibilities entail providing home subscriber information to those parts of the mobile network through which the home subscriber is roaming. This information includes call origination and call termination privileges, accounting information, as well as authentication and encryption keys.

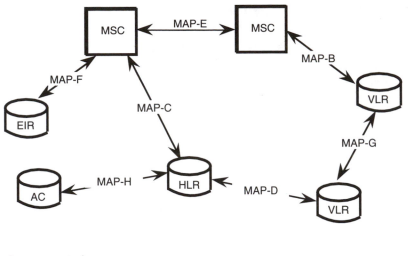

where:
    AC   Access control
    EIR   Equipment identity register
    HLR   Home location register
    MAP   Mobile applications part
    MSC   Mobile switching center
    VLR   Visitor location register

Figure 4–6   The MAP interfaces.

MAP-B is executed between an MSC and a VLR. Like the HLR just discussed, the VLR is actually attached to an MSC. Consequently MAP-B is invoked when a foreign MSC needs to interrogate a non-attached VLR. In practice, MAP-B is rarely executed in a system because the VLR is usually integrated into the MSC. We mention it in passing for continuity.

MAP-D is frequently used and provides the interface between an HLR and a VLR. Once again, MAP-D is invoked when a VLR or HLR needs to communicate with a non-attached VLR/HLR. In practice, the VLR and HLR are usually both attached to an MSC. Consequently, the MAP-D protocol is used to exchange information between non-attached HLRs/VLRs.

The principal operations supported by MAP-D entail the querying of the HLR by the VLR to obtain the profile of a home subscriber. Some limited call control features exist in MAP-D. In addition, MAP-D is invoked when the VLR needs security information about a subscriber resident at the HLR.

MAP-F's operations are straightforward and support the exchange of the international mobile station equipment identity (IMEI) value between the equipment identity register (EIR) and an MSC.

MAP-G operates between VLRs. Its invocation depends on specific circumstances, but its overall function is to provide a means to exchange information between two VLRs to support roaming and handoff operations. Under certain conditions, a VLR will interrogate another VLR to obtain identity and subscriber information on a newly arriving mobile station. Later, we will learn the specific circumstances in which MAP-G is invoked.

THE FUNCTIONAL PLANES

Figure 4–7 shows one of the more important aspects of the GSM architecture, the functional planes. These planes are used to describe the detailed operations of the GSM communications at the physical sites, and across the interfaces.

Five planes are present in GSM and shown in Figure 4–7. The reader may wonder what happened to the OSI layers. They are still present. A good way to view the functional planes is that they include the functions of some of the protocols described earlier, and they also include functions that are not described in the those protocols. For example, Q.931 can be found in some of the operations of the communication man-

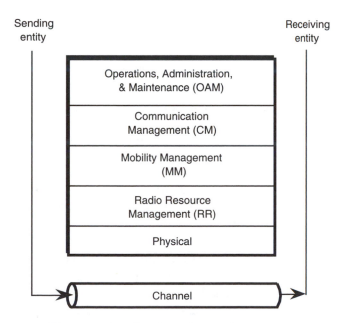

Figure 4–7   The functional planes.

agement (CM) plane, yet other operations in this plane are not described in the Q.931 specification. Some writers place these planes at the OSI network layer (layer 3), but many of the operations deal with layers 1 and 2 of the OSI Model. Parts of GSM machines are obviously concerned with transmission and reception of signals, which of course refers to the physical plane.

The radio resource management (RR) plane provides the RF support and is concerned with establishing and releasing connections between the mobile station and the network. Some of the major operations of RR include the assignment and release of channels, managing channel changes during handovers across cells, setting cipher mode operations, receiving status reports from the mobile station, changing frequencies, and managing frequency hopping.

The mobility management (MM) plane is responsible for the subscriber databases (such as subscriber location data). It operates on the MSC/HLR and MSC/VLR. Some of the major operations of MM include the registration of the mobile station, verifying the user with the EIR, checking which services the mobile station is allowed or not allowed to use, and most of the operations pertaining to location management with the HLR and VLRs.

The communication management (CM) plane is responsible for setting up and tearing down calls. The operations are quite similar to ISDN layer 3 operations.

Finally, the operations, administration, and maintenance (OAM) plane deals with network management functions, such as monitoring activities, configuration operations, and so on.

The Functional Planes and the Layers

Figure 4–8 shows the relationships of the functional planes to the layers as well as the interfaces. The GSM functional planes and layer relationships are quite involved and this figure should be used as a general model since the planes and layers are not integrated quite as cleanly as this picture illustrates. Notwithstanding, the figure is accurate from the standpoint of the conceptual placement of the planes in relation to the layers and interfaces.

As a general design goal, the radio resource (RR) operations are confined to the MS, BS, and BSC. In turn, most of the mobility management (MM) operations are executed between the MS and the MSC. The CM (connection management) operations begin and terminate at the MS/MSC. The BS and BSC act as pass-through entities for the CM operations.

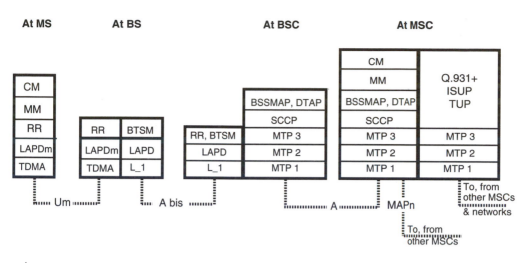

where:

CM	Connection management
MM	Mobility management
RR	Radio resource management
LAPDm	Link access procedure, d channel, for mobile
TDMA	Time division multiple access
BTSM	BTS management
BSSMAP	Base station subsystem management application part
DTAP	Direct transfer application part
MTP	Message transfer part
SCCP	Signaling connection control part
ISUP	ISDN user part
TUP	Telephone user part
MSC	Mobile switching center
MAP	Mobile applications part

Figure 4–8   Functional planes and layers.

The base transceiver station management (BTSM) is used to transfer OAM information across the A bis interface.[1]

The base station subsystem management part (BSSMAP) and the direct transfer application part (DTAP) are simple protocols that provide message distribution services: BSSMAP, between BSC and MSC, and DTAP, between MS and MSC.

---

[1]This term is used by Mouly and Pautet, and not by GSM. See the *GSM System for Mobile Communications*, by Michel Mouly and Marie-Bernadette Pautet.

GSM ADDRESSES AND IDENTIFIERS

The GSM systems use several addresses and identifiers at the air and network interfaces. Figure 4–9 shows the structure of several of the values that deal with addresses. The information in the figure will be helpful to use as a reference guide during this discussion.

Each mobile subscriber is identified uniquely with a set of values, illustrated in Figure 4–10. These values are used to identify the country in which the mobile system resides, the mobile network, and the mobile subscriber. These sets of values are known as the international mobile subscriber number (IMSI) and are used as a fixed identifier within a network (Figure 4–10a). The IMSI is also called the IMSN, for the international mobile subscriber number. The first three digits are the mobile country code (MCC), which is administered by the ITU-T. The next two digits comprise the mobile network code (MNC), which is a unique identifier of a network provider, also called the public land mobile network (PLMN). As examples, an MCC of 505 identifies Australia; an MCC of 234 identifies the UK. An MNC of 01 identifies Telecom Australia, and an MNC of 15 identifies UK Vodafone. The MNC does not have any geographical significance.

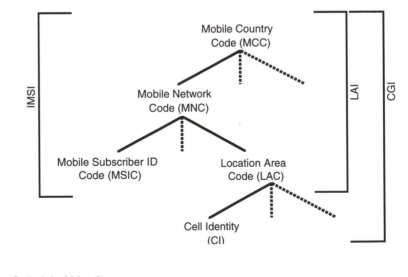

where:
    CGI   Cell global identity
    IMSI   International mobile subscriber number
    LAI   Location area identity

Figure 4–9   GSM identifiers.

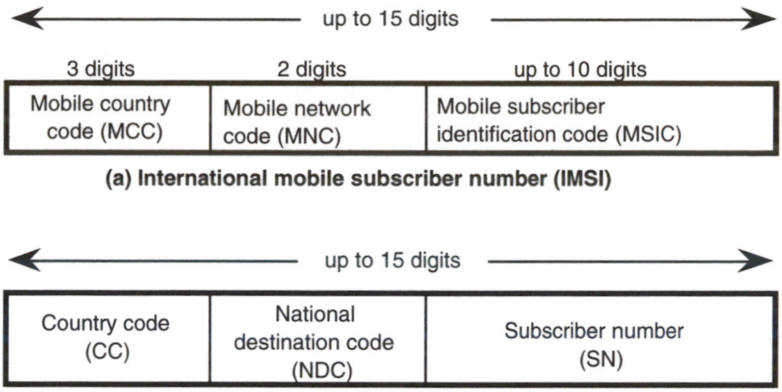

up to 15 digits

3 digits	2 digits	up to 10 digits
Mobile country code (MCC)	Mobile network code (MNC)	Mobile subscriber identification code (MSIC)

(a) International mobile subscriber number (IMSI)

up to 15 digits

Country code (CC)	National destination code (NDC)	Subscriber number (SN)

(b) The mobile station ISDN number (MSISDN)

Note: CC of MSISDN is different from MCC of IMSI (CC is variable length)

Figure 4–10   Mobile station identifiers.

The remainder of the IMSI is made up of the mobile subscriber identification code (MSIC), which is the customer identification number. The IMSI also is used for an MSC/VLR to find out the subscriber's home PLMN.

The IMSI is a unique non-dialable number that is used for signaling. It is stored in the subscriber identity module (SIM), HLR, AUC, and VLR when a mobile subscriber registers with the network.

The SIM is located in the subscriber's mobile unit. In addition to containing the IMSI, the SIM contains subscriber-specific information such as phone numbers, a personal identification number (PIN), and security/authentication parameters.

The SIM can be a small plug-in module that is placed (somewhat permanently) in the mobile unit, or it can be a card (like a credit card) that is also inserted into the unit. In the latter option, its use is like a smart card. The mobile unit is not usable (except for emergency calls) if the SIM is not inserted into the mobile unit terminal.

A modular, portable SIM allows a user to use different terminal sets. For example, a traveler need not carry a mobile unit, but can rent one from a car-rental agency and customize the unit to the subscriber's needs by inserting the smart card into the unit. Instead of the mobile station roaming, the smart card allows "SIM-roaming."

A temporary mobile subscriber identity (TMSI) is used to provide subscriber identity confidentiality. Under normal operations, GSM does not permit IMSI values to be sent in the clear over the air interface where they might be intercepted. Instead, the TMSI is used. The VLR controls the allocation of TMSIs and simply picks a number from a pool of numbers whenever a new mobile station registers in a cell. The number remains valid as long as the mobile station is resident in the cell. In effect, the MSC/VLR directs the mobile station to use this particular TMSI value in place of the IMSI value. TMSI is of local significance only and the method of being chosen is left up to the cellular operator. The TMSI contents are not defined; thus it is an unstructured number and can range up to four octets in length.

For additional addressing, another address is required, called the mobile station ISDN number (MSISDN), as shown in Figure 4–10b. It is so named because it uses the same format as the ISDN address (based on ITU-T Recommendation E.164). This number is used to reach a called party in a GSM network.

Unlike a conventional telephone call, a GSM call to a mobile station does not identify the called party, but an HLR. The HLR uses this number to provide routing instructions to other components in order to reach the subscriber. The best way to think of the MSISDN is that it is a directory number.

The country code (CC) of the MSISDN is different from the mobile country code of the IMSI. The CC is variable length and the MCC is fixed length. Also, the value of the codes differ. For example, the CC for the United States is 1, and the MCC ranges between 310–316.

The national destination code (NDC) use varies. One use is to identify a destination network, and another use is to identify a geographical area. In the United States, the NDC is used to identify a numbering plan area (NPA) or area code. The NDC and the SN are administered by each country.

How the Identifiers Are Used

Figure 4–11 shows an example of how several of the GSM identifiers are used. In event 1, the dialed number (MSISDN) is relayed to a gateway MSC. This number is used to access a database to correlate the number with the subscriber's HLR. In event 2, the gateway MSC sends a query to the HLR that contains the called MSISDN. Next, the HLR examines its records to find out where the called subscriber is located. It sends a query to the visited MSC/VLR but uses the IMSI in this query (event 3). The MSC/VLR receives the query and sends back routing instructions that are contained in the MRSN. This operation is depicted as event 4 in the figure. Next and in event 5, the HLR forwards the MSRN

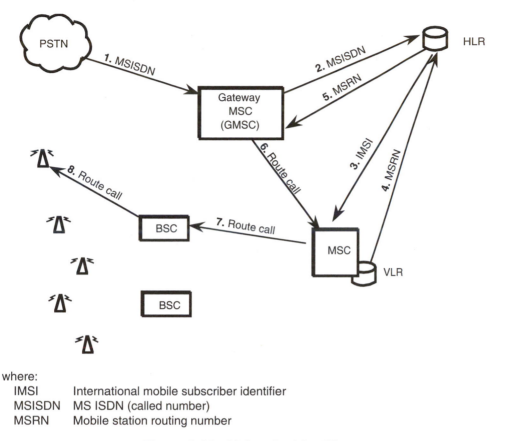

where:
  IMSI   International mobile subscriber identifier
  MSISDN MS ISDN (called number)
  MSRN   Mobile station routing number

Figure 4–11   Using the identifiers.

to the gateway MSC, which uses this routing information to route the call to the MSC that is servicing the subscriber (event 6). In event 7, the MSC routes the call to the proper BSC and, finally, in event 8 the call is sent to the called subscriber. Since the called subscriber has already registered with the network it is operating across the air interface with the TMSI.

The Location Area Identifier (LAI)

Another identifier used in GSM is called the location area identifier (LAI). It is similar in content to the IMSI, except it identifies a cell, or more commonly, a group of cells. The top part of Figure 4–12 shows the format for the LAI. The mobile country code (MCC) and mobile network code were explained earlier. The location area code (LAC) identifies a cell

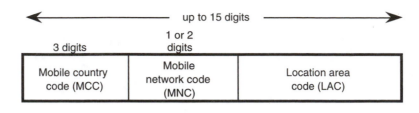

Mobile country code (MCC)	Mobile network code (MNC)	Location area code (LAC)

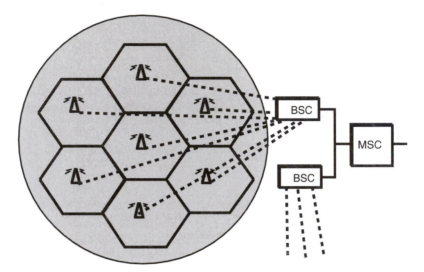

Figure 4–12   Location area identifier (LAI).

or a group of cells. This latter field plays a role in handoff operations. When a mobile station roams into another cell, if it is in the same LAI, no information is exchanged with any external network, which of course reduces the amount of signaling that occurs in the system. If the LAI is different, the mobile station sends a location update message to the network in order to update the location of the mobile station.

The International Mobile Station Equipment Identity (IMEI)

The international mobile station equipment identity (IMEI) is assigned to the GSM unit at the factory (Figure 4–13). In concept, when a GSM component passes conformance and interoperability tests, it is given a type approval code (TAC). Additionally, a final assembly code (FAC) is added to identify the place of final manufacture and/or assembly. The serial number (SNR) is assigned to each piece of equipment within each TAC/FAC. This number is assigned by the manufacturer. A spare digit is available for further assignment.

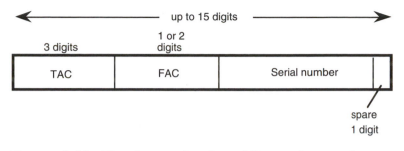

Figure 4–13 The international mobile station equipment identity (IMEI).

THE GSM CHANNEL ORGANIZATION

The second generation TDMA mobile, wireless systems use similar techniques to establish the physical and logical channels on the air interface. The principal differences are the frequencies used for the physical channels, which are shown in the bottom part of Figure 4–14. The logical channels (time slots) are quite similar and will be examined in more detail later in this chapter. For this discussion, the logical channels are categorized as traffic channels (TCH) or control channels (CCH). The physical channels are designated by n, where n is ARFCN (the absolute radio frequency channel number).

The GSM 900 system uses two 25 MHz bands for the uplink and downlink. Within that spectrum, 200 kHz channels are allocated. The uplink and downlink are separated by a 45 MHz spacing. The ARFCN ranges from 1 to 124. The allocation of the 200 kHz channels varies, and is dependent upon the traffic patterns and cell size of the system.

The GSM 1800 system uses two 75 MHz bands for the uplink and downlink. Like GSM 900, 200 kHz channels are allocated within those bands. The uplink and downlink are separated by a 95 MHz spacing. The ARFCN ranges from 512 to 885.

For PCS 1900, the system uses two 60 MHz bands for the uplink and downlink. Like the other systems, PCS 1900 also uses 200 kHz channels with the uplink and downlink separated by an 80 MHz spacing. In the United States, this bandwidth is divided for use among multiple wireless operators in a given geographical region (see Figure 1–17).

As shown in the bottom part of Figure 4–13, the logical channels are numbered from 1–124, 512–885, and 512–810 for GSM 900, GSM 1800, and PCS 1900 respectively. The ARFCN values are based on the frequency bands derived from the simple formula shown in Figure 4–14.

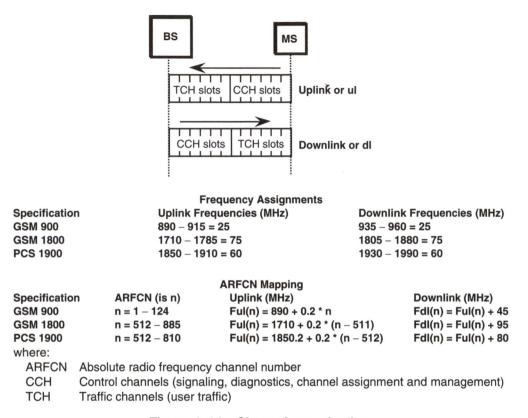

Frequency Assignments

Specification	Uplink Frequencies (MHz)	Downlink Frequencies (MHz)
GSM 900	890 – 915 = 25	935 – 960 = 25
GSM 1800	1710 – 1785 = 75	1805 – 1880 = 75
PCS 1900	1850 – 1910 = 60	1930 – 1990 = 60

ARFCN Mapping

Specification	ARFCN (is n)	Uplink (MHz)	Downlink (MHz)
GSM 900	n = 1 – 124	Ful(n) = 890 + 0.2 * n	Fdl(n) = Ful(n) + 45
GSM 1800	n = 512 – 885	Ful(n) = 1710 + 0.2 * (n – 511)	Fdl(n) = Ful(n) + 95
PCS 1900	n = 512 – 810	Ful(n) = 1850.2 + 0.2 * (n – 512)	Fdl(n) = Ful(n) + 80

where:

ARFCN   Absolute radio frequency channel number
CCH   Control channels (signaling, diagnostics, channel assignment and management)
TCH   Traffic channels (user traffic)

Figure 4–14   Channel organization.

GSM physical channels are managed through various time division multiplexing techniques. The resulting schemes create logical channels on the physical link. Logical channels are a well known concept used in many systems such as X.25, Frame Relay, and ATM. A logical channel is not a dedicated physical channel but one that is shared by multiple users. GSM uses this approach not only to allow the multiplexing of a physical channel but to provide different formats for the traffic and also different types of channels as well. GSM uses the conveyor belt concept described in Chapter 1.

Figure 4–15 shows the general organization of GSM channels. Traffic channels carrying user payload are noted with the initials of TCH. GSM defines a full rate TCH and half-rate TCH and these are shown in this figure as TCH/f and TCH/s, respectively. The TCH/s is a new addi-

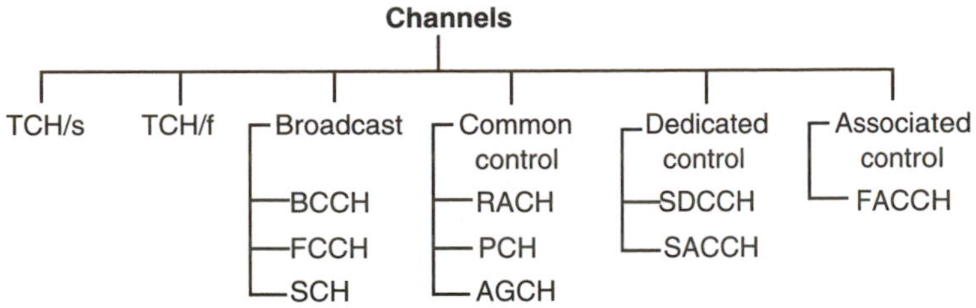

```
                              Channels
        ┌─────┬─────┬──────────┬──────────┬──────────┬──────────┐
      TCH/s  TCH/f  ┌Broadcast  ┌Common    ┌Dedicated  ┌Associated
                    │           │ control   │ control   │ control
                    ├BCCH       ├RACH       ├SDCCH      └ FACCH
                    ├FCCH       ├PCH        └SACCH
                    └SCH        └AGCH
```

Summary of Channels' Functions and Directions of Transfer:

TCH/s	**Half rate**		**Both directions**
TCH/f	**Full rate (13 kbit/s speech)**		**Both directions**
Broadcast (BCH)			
	BCCH	**Initialization, exchange LAC, MNC, etc.**	**BS-to-MS**
	FCCH	**Frequency reference**	**BS-to-MS**
	SCH	**Timing reference**	**BS-to-MS**
Common Control (CCCH)			
	RACH	**Request a dedicated channel**	**MS-to-BS**
	PCH	**Page**	**BS-to-MS**
	AGCH	**Response to RACH**	**BS-to-MS**
Dedicated Control (DCCH)			
	SDCCH	**Signaling information**	**Both directions**
	SACCH	**Channel maintenance**	**Both directions**
	Fast Associated Control (FAACH)		
		Slot stealing	**Both directions**
Data	**2.4–9.6 kbit/s**		
	FDX	**TCH/F9.6/F4.8/F2.4**	**Both directions**
	HDX	**TCH/H4.8/.4**	**Both directions**

where:
  AGCH   Access grant channel
  BCCH   Broadcast control channel
  FACCH   Fast associated control channel (steals slots from TCH or SDCCH)
  FCCH   Frequency correction channel
  PCH   Paging channel
  RACH   Random access channel
  SACCH   Slow associated control channel
  SCH   Synchronization channel
  SDCCH   Stand-alone dedicated control channel
  TCH   Traffic channels (user payload)

Figure 4–15   The GSM channels.

tion that doubles the capacity of the TCH/f channel. The latter channel runs at 13 kbit/s to carry digitized speech transmissions. Both TCH/f and TCH/s can accommodate data traffic as well. The full rate operates at 13, 12, 6, and 3.6 kbit/s, which is adequate to support modem speeds of 9.6, 4.8, and 2.4 kbit/s. The half-rate supports only 4.8 and 2.4 kbit/s data transmissions. Once TCH channels are allocated to the user, the user has dedicated bandwidth on that channel.

Each traffic channel is associated with another channel used for signaling. It also is a dedicated channel and is called the slow associated control channel (SACCH). It uses the term associated because it is always associated with the user channel (as one option). It may also be associated with a stand-alone dedicated control channel (SDCCH), which also is used for the transfer of signaling information between the base station and the mobile station. These two dedicated control channels are used in a variety of ways that are explained further in this section.

The associated control channel, called the fast associated control channel (FACCH), is not a dedicated channel although it might carry the same information as the SDCCH. As we noted earlier, the SDCCH is a dedicated channel unto itself. In contrast, the FACCH is part of a traffic channel. Indeed, it can borrow some bandwidth from the traffic channel under certain conditions. As we shall see in the next section, there is a flag in the message that announces that FACCH is stealing some bursts from the traffic channel. Some literature substitutes the term FACCH with the term fast associated signaling (FAS).

Three broadcast channels are available in the GSM system. The broadcast control channel (BCCH) is used to send various system parameters to all mobile stations. These parameters include the operator identifiers, the location of the cell, the name of the cell, frequency information, and so on. The frequency correction channel (FCCH), as its name implies, is used by the base station to give the mobile station information about frequency references and is used for a frequency correction burst. The synchronization channel (SCH) is used by the base station to provide the mobile station synchronization training sequences. And, as we shall see in the next section, the SCH channel is actually mapped into a synchronization burst format.

Three channels are grouped under common control channels. These channels are used for the establishment of links between the mobile station and the base station as well as for ongoing call management, such as call setup and call disconnect. The random access channel (RACH) is used by the mobile station and not the base station. RACH is mapped into a random burst format and it contains information used by the mobile station to request a dedicated channel from GSM. It is the first message sent from the mobile unit to the base station.

The base station uses the paging channel (PCH) to communicate with individual mobile stations within its cell. And, finally, the mobile station receives information about the dedicated channel it is supposed to use on the access grant channel (AGCH). This information also contains data about timing and synchronization.

In effect, all these channels are considered logical or physical channels in GSM. In practice, many of them are simply a different way of formatting messages and/or putting the messages in various time slots on the physical channel.

A CLOSER LOOK AT THE TDMA FRAMES AND SLOTS

Earlier we learned that the GSM burst was a duration of .577 milliseconds (ms). Figure 4–16 shows the slot in relation to an 8-slot frame that yields a time period of 4.615 ms (rounded off). The figure also shows one option for sending traffic on the channel—to multiplex 26 frames together for a 120 ms time period. This structure is called a 26-frame multiframe. We shall see shortly that other multiplexing schemes are available for combining traffic.

The Normal Burst

This figure also shows the format and bit configuration for one of the bursts on the channel. This example is for a normal burst, which contains ongoing user traffic. As discussed earlier, each burst contains 114 bits of user data, which includes considerable overhead to add resiliency to the signal. For a normal burst, the data are divided into two subslots each consisting of 57 bits. The tail (T) bits are at the beginning and ending of a burst and are used for ramping up and ramping down the signal during periods when the signal is in transition. The tail bits are always set to 0. In addition, 2 bits in this figure are labeled the S bits, which mean signaling flags, and are used to indicate if the traffic contained in the burst is signaling traffic or user traffic.

In addition, this figure shows some guard period (GP) that is at the end of the burst. No data are sent during the guard period. The guard period is approximately 8.25 bits, and since each bit is 1.69 μs in duration, the guard period is 30.4 μs.

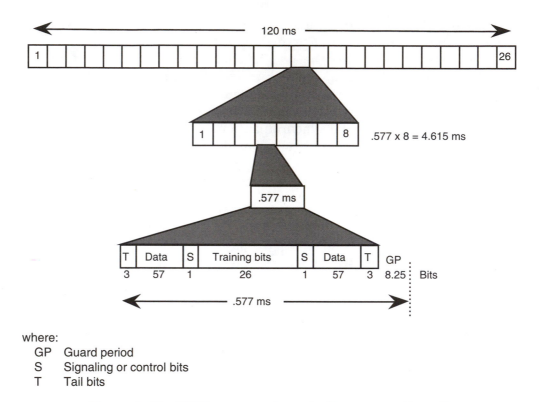

Figure 4–16   GSM message formats (for a normal burst).

where:
  GP   Guard period
  S   Signaling or control bits
  T   Tail bits

Finally, the training bits are placed in the middle of the burst to allow the receivers to synchronize themselves to the burst. These bits are especially useful in this technology because they help compensate for multipath fading and the resulting delay spread. GSM uses eight different training sequences because signals might be arriving at the receiver at approximately the same time. If the training sequences are the same, there is no easy way for the receiver to distinguish these signals. Thus, the training sequences in GSM are noted for their distinct bit structure in that they are not correlated to each other. The training sequences are used by an equalizer to detect the location of the training sequence bits in the signal.

In addition to the normal burst and the 26-frame multiframe, a 51-frame multiframe makes up another channel set (another set of bursts), as shown in Figure 4–17. The purposes of this channel set are varied, but it is used primarily for frequency alignment, timing alignment, and initial channel access. The 51-frame structure consists of four burst types: (a) the frequency correction burst, (b) the synchronization burst, (c) the access (or random access) burst, and (d) the dummy burst.

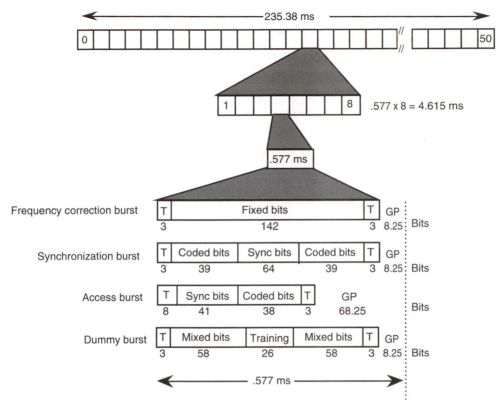

Figure 4–17　Other burst formats.

The access burst is an initial boot strapping operation; it is used by the base station to find out about the mobile station and to measure the initial time delay of a mobile station's burst. It is used by the mobile station to gain access to the system. The access burst resides in the RACH. The frequency-correction burst is used by the MS to synchronize or re-synchronize on a carrier frequency. The synchronization is used to synchronize in the time domain to ensure the MSs do not send overlapping frames on the same frequency. The dummy burst is used to fill slots when they would otherwise be empty.

Some of these bursts are associated with channels. The relationship is as follows:

RACH = Random burst
FCCH = Frequency correction burst
SCH　 = Synchronization burst

The Frequency Correction Burst

The frequency correction burst contains Os in the slot (142 bits). It is sent on the air interface to enable the mobile station to synchronize itself with the system master frequency.

The Synchronization Burst

The synchronization burst is used by the mobile station to align itself in time with the base station. The sync bits in the slot are one of the eight training sequences described earlier. The coded bits contain information to enable the mobile station to know the position and identity of all the channels (slots) in the TDMA transmissions and receptions. The coded bits also contain identifiers, such as the base station information code (BSIC), national code, and so on.

The Access Burst

The access burst is used by the mobile station to gain initial access to the network. The sync bits in the slot are used by the receiver to train on the slot, and the coded data contains information to ascertain if the mobile station's random access attempt is successful. The long guard period of 68.25 bits (3.69 µs bit × 68.25 bits = 252 µs) is used to ensure the burst "survives" for a long period. Assuming the signal propagates at the speed of light, the duration of the period is 75.5 km (252 µs × 3 × 10^8 µs).

The Complete Framing Structure

Figure 4–18 is another and more complete view of the framing structure. The longest recurring time period is the hyperframe. It has a duration of 3 hours, 28 minutes, 53 seconds, 760 milliseconds (or 12533.76 seconds). Within the hyperframe, the TDMA frame number (FN) is numbered from 0 to 2715647.

The next recurrent time period consists of superframes. The hyperframe is divided into 2048 superframes. The superframe has a duration of 6.12 seconds. As Figure 4–18 shows, the superframe is made up of the 26-frame multiframe and the 51-frame multiframe, which were explained earlier. It has a length of 26 × 51 = 1326 frames.

Why does GSM have such a complex TDMA structure? The reason for the superframe organization is that it is the least common multiple of both the 26 and 51 multiframes (26 × 51 = 1326), which represents the least number of frames that can be used without there being no spare slots. Stated another way, it is the smallest multiple of all cycles.

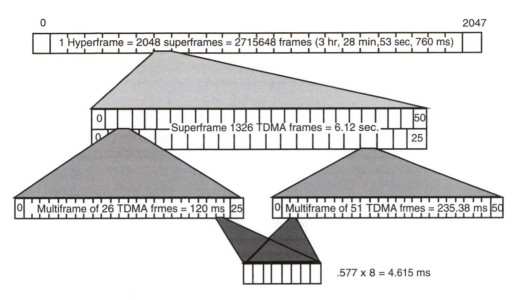

Figure 4–18   The complete framing structure.

How the Slots and Frames Are Identified

Since the GSM frame is cyclic, counters are used to keep track of which frames are being sent and received. Three counters are employed:

- T1: Superframe counter
- T2: Speech frame counter
- T3: Signaling frame counter

The T1 counter ranges between 0–2047; T2 ranges between 0–25, and T3 ranges between 0–50. When the counters reach their limit, they are reset from 0, and the counting continues. With this approach, if the receiver knows the T1, T2, T3 values, it knows the exact position of each slot on the air interface.

Some other details should be emphasized at this point in our discussion. First, the SACCH is assigned to each TCH; it occurs on the interface about two messages per second and is used for signaling. The FACCH uses some of the slots on the TCH for carrying additional signaling traffic (slot stealing). The SDCCH exists as separate slots, and FACCH uses part of the traffic channel.

Second, the SDCCH is another control channel that is associated with the TCH and is used for signaling. It is a low rate and is referred to in some literature as TCH/8, meaning that it is 1/8 the bandwidth of the TCH.

Options for Channel Organization

Figure 4–19 shows the frame layout for traffic channels. It consists of 26 frames with a duration of 120 ms. The SACCH is always associated and allocated with a TCH (some books refer to this channel combination of TCH and SACCH as TACH). It is not necessary to have a one-to-one bandwidth relationship between a signaling channel and a traffic channel because signaling messages are asynchronous, occurring only on occasion. Consequently, the SACCH slot is used to support multiple TCHs.

GSM provides for a very powerful feature for managing the air interface channels: The control channels can be configured in a variety of ways to accommodate the different types and amounts of traffic, the size of the cell, and so on. Therefore, the control channels can take several forms; that is, the slots can carry different combinations of the control channels. Figure 4–20 shows one of the more common formats, which is called combination IV. The downlink is multiplexed with the FCCH, SCH, BCCH, and CCCH (PCH or AGCH) slots plus one idle slot. The uplink contains only RACH slots.

The downlink provides for 36 slots for the CCCH, which is used to page an MS (on the PCH) or assign a channel to an MS (on the AGCH). Five slots each are provided for the FCCH (frequency-correction channel) and SCH (synchronization channel). Four slots are provided for the BCCH (broadcast control channel). As just stated, on the downlink, all slots are reserved for the RACH (random access channel).

Figure 4–21 shows the combination V organization of the channels for a smaller system that employs smaller cells and has fewer carriers and less traffic. The structure is quite similar to combination IV, it exists only once in a cell, and it is always found in time slot 0. It is used in place of combination IV for a smaller system. The term SDCCH/4 is used to connote the fact that four SDCCHs can be used on this configuration along with their associated channels. Thus, SDCCH 0 means SDCCH

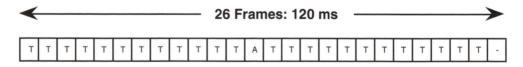

where:
  A = SACCH (slow associated control channel)
  T = traffic channels (TCH)
  - = idle slot

Figure 4–19   Frame layout for traffic channels.

Downlink:

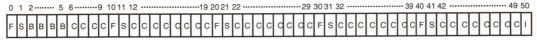

Uplink:

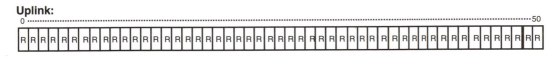

where:
    B   BCCH
    C   CCCH (PCH, AGCH)
    F   FCCH
    R   RACH
    S   SCH

Figure 4–20   Channel organization for a 51-frame multi-frame (combination IV).

BCCH + CCCH + 4 SDCCH/4 (Downlink):

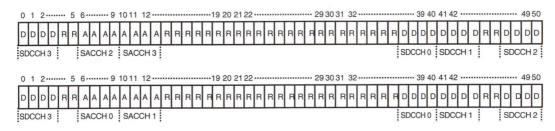

BCCH + CCCH + 4 SDCCH/4 (Uplink):

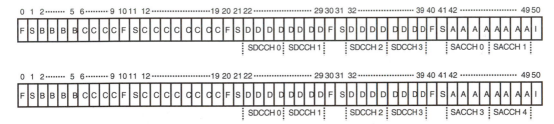

Figure 4–21   The channel organization for combination V.

subchannel 0, and so forth. The figure shows two multiframes for the up-link and two multiframes for the downlink. This illustration is drawn to make the point that an FACCH is transmitted in every other multiframe. In other words, the information is contained across four frames. These frames are associated with each other. Thus, for this combination, there is exactly one-half as much FACCH bandwidth as there for the associated SDCCH bandwidth.

One of the ideas behind this organization is for the SDCCH and its corresponding subchannels to be spaced from each other in time. For example, if either the network or the mobile station sends information to the other, the spacing of the time slots give the receiving station time for the response.

GSM AUTHENTICATION AND ENCRYPTION

This part of our analysis shows an example of how GSM uses private keys for authentication and the ciphering (encryption/decryption) of user traffic. Refer to Figure 4–22 during this discussion.

One of the most important operations in the handshake of any mobile system is the proper authentication of the user. GSM provides authentication by checking the validity of a subscriber's SIM card. This authentication is based on the A3 algorithm that is stored in both the SIM card and AUC, and a private key Ki, which is also stored on the SIM and in the network AUC.

The AUC is responsible for the creation of the signed response (SRES) (see Figure 4–22a). A Ki value is associated with each IMSI. The A3 algorithm uses Ki and a 128-bit random number (RAND) to produce the SRES. As shown in Figure 4–22b, the AUC downline loads several sets of the RAND, SRES pairs to the HLR (which are also called challenge, response pairs). In turn, the HLR makes these values available to a VLR as needed. When the VLR exhausts the set (by using one set each time the MS registers in a cell for which the VLR is responsible), it can request more sets from the HLR.

To authenticate (Figure 4–22c) the network sends to the subscriber a RAND in a message. The message is a "challenge" to the user. The mobile station uses RAND as input to the A3 calculation along with the authentication key, Ki. Remember, this value is stored only on the SIM card and by the network. The input of Ki and RAND into the A3 algorithm produces the signed response (SRES). This value is returned to the VLR and checked to determine if it has been coded properly. In this man-

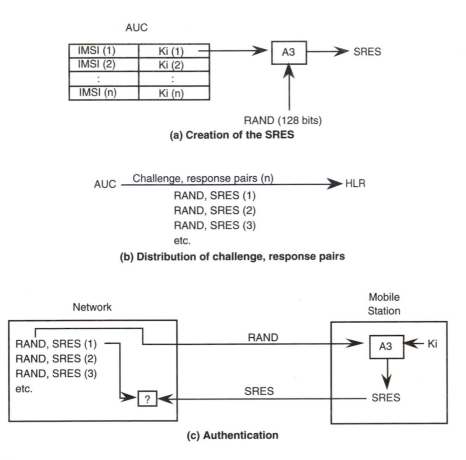

(a) Creation of the SRES

(b) Distribution of challenge, response pairs

(c) Authentication

where:
  RAND   Random number
  SRES   Signed response

Figure 4–22   Example of GSM authentication.

ner, the network is able to verify the proper identify of the user. Obviously, if SRES does not equal the precomputed value stored at the VLR, then the user is not authenticated.

Typically, a set of RAND and SRES values are stored by the network (at the HLR and VLR), and managed by the AUC. This approach allows different values to be used with each authentication. If the HLR exhausts the list of numbers, additional values can be requested from the AUC. A3 and Ki are not sent across any of the communications channels.

Ciphering is accomplished by applying an exclusive OR operation to the GSM 114-bit burst. This operation is performed at the transmitter with a complementary operation performed at the receiver. By doing this at the transmitter and receiver, the 114 bits will retain their original value. GSM uses an algorithm called A5 to perform this operation. The A5 algorithm is implemented in both the mobile station and network (see Figure 4–23).

The A5 algorithm uses a key designated as Kc. This key is calculated from RAND and Ki through an algorithm designated as A8, as shown in Figure 4–23a. The result of this operation is a ciphering key Kc, which is calculated by AUC and sent to the HLR (remember, the AUC and HLR may be indistinguishable), as shown in Figure 4–23b. The A8 algorithm is stored at the mobile station on the SIM card. The Kc key is then used with the ciphering algorithm A5. The network instructs the mobile station to begin a ciphering sequence and upon this instruction, the mobile station transmits ciphered data, as shown in Figure 4–23c.

The idea of these operations is to make the production of SRES an easy affair if Ki and RAND are known. In contrast, deriving Ki from RAND and SRES is quite complex, which is the essence of this approach.

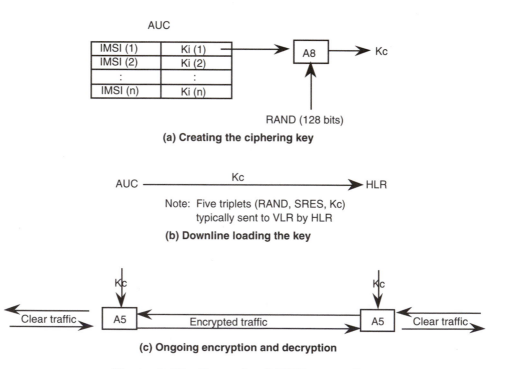

(a) Creating the ciphering key

(b) Downline loading the key

(c) Ongoing encryption and decryption

Figure 4–23   Example of GSM encryption.

Security of the IMSI

There are a variety of procedures defined for managing the temporary mobile subscriber identity (TMSI). Recall that the TMSI is a local number having meaning in a given location area (and it is always accompanied by the location area identification [LAI] to avoid ambiguities). It is the job of the network VLR to maintain mapping relationships between TMSIs and IMSIs. If a TMSI is received by the VLR that does not correspond to its LAI, then this VLR must request from the VLR in charge of the indicated location area the IMSI of the MS. Attempts are made to not send the IMSI across the air interface. However, if a VLR receives the LAI and TMSI and still cannot identify the "old VLR" this means that any relationship between the old TMSI and the IMSI is lost. Consequently, in this situation, the MS is requested to send the IMSI in the clear but hereafter a TMSI is assigned for the duration of the connection.

With this background information in mind, Figure 4–24 shows one of several scenarios for TMSI exchange. This particular procedure is one in which the mobile station has moved to a new location area in which the VLR is different from the original location area. Upon receiving the LAI and old TMSI from the mobile station, the new VLR queries the old VLR (event 2) and receives back from the VLR the IMSI security related information that it had previously stored. Upon receiving this information the new VLR allocates a new TMSI and assigns this value to the mobile station as depicted in event 3. Thereafter, operations proceed as usual with the HLR undergoing location updating operations with the new serving area (event 4) and canceling the records of this mobile station in the old VLR (event 5), which also entails the deallocation of the old TMSI at the old VLR.

THE GSM MESSAGES

The layer 3 messages are coded as shown in Figure 4–25. The header for this message consists of protocol discriminator, the transaction indicator, the message type, and the information elements.

The protocol discriminator is coded as follows:

Bits 4321	Call control
0011	Call control and call related SS messages
0101	Mobility management messages
0110	Radio resource management messages

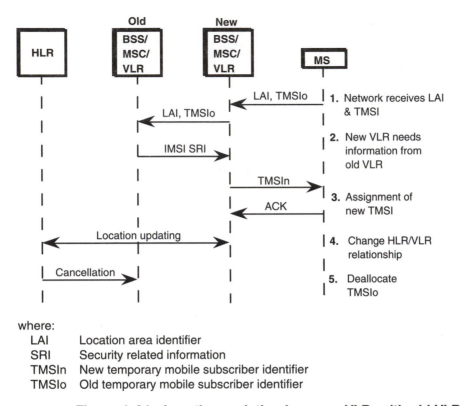

where:
   LAI   Location area identifier
   SRI   Security related information
   TMSIn   New temporary mobile subscriber identifier
   TMSIo   Old temporary mobile subscriber identifier

Figure 4–24   Location updating in a new VLR, with old VLR reachable.

The message type field, as its name implies, identifies the type of message, such as ciphering mode command, channel release, paging request, and so on. The bits in this field are coded to identify each of the individual messages discussed in the previous section. GSM provides for a wide variety of messages to support the mobile user services. The next section provides several examples of how these messages are employed.

PUTTING IT ALL TOGETHER

Let us now tie together many of the concepts that have been explained thus far in this chapter by showing several examples of GSM operations. The first set of operations that take place between the MS and the network is the establishment of control channels and configuration and system parameters. These operations entail three tasks, shown in Figure 4–26 as events 1, 2, and 3.

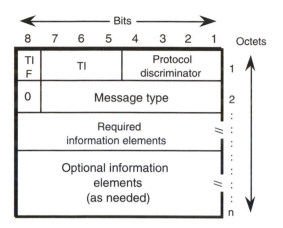

where:
  TI   Transaction identifier
  TIF Transaction identifier flag

Figure 4–25   The Q.931+ message.

The first task is to find and lock onto a strong frequency in one of the RF channels and then to find the FCCH. The FCCH exhibits a power burst performance that can be detected by the MS. This operation allows the MS to find the proper frequency domain.

The next task (event 2) involves the time domain; that is, locating the SCH slot. The MS locates this channel because it knows where the SCH is located in the next frame. Using the SCH, the MS obtains synchronization and training information.

After locating the SCH, the BCCH is easily found, because the MS knows the relative position of the BCCH in the frame. It reads this channel to obtain system parameters, such as cell and system values (LAC, etc.), as shown in event 3. During all this activity, the MS has been in a receive mode only.

In event 4, the MS uses the RACH to request a stand-alone dedicated channel, the SDCCH. The BSC grants this request through the AGCH. This response from the BSC also contains *timing advance* information. This information is based on the BSC's analysis of the MS's signal on the RACH, which enables it to measure the delay of the MS signals. The purpose is to ensure that the MS bursts do not interfere with bursts from other MSs on the same physical channel.

After the SDCCH channel has been established, the MS in event 5 asks for a location update. It knows to perform this request, because it has stored in memory the previous area in which is was located, and it received in event 3 information that indicated that it had moved to a new

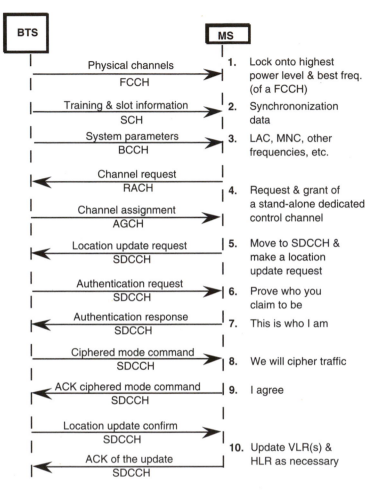

Figure 4–26   Initial channel usage.

area. Although not shown here, the network can initiate a location update itself, by an indication in the BCCH signal.

Before the MS can exchange any more information with the network the identity of the user must be authenticated. These operations are depicted as events 6 and 7. After successful authentication, the network informs the MS that all traffic will be ciphered (in events 8 and 9).

The location update request operations are complete with the exchange of messages shown as event 10. The MS is now ready to originate and accept calls.

In the example in Figure 4–27, we show how the channels are used to establish a call to the MS. In event 1, upon receiving an incoming call indi-

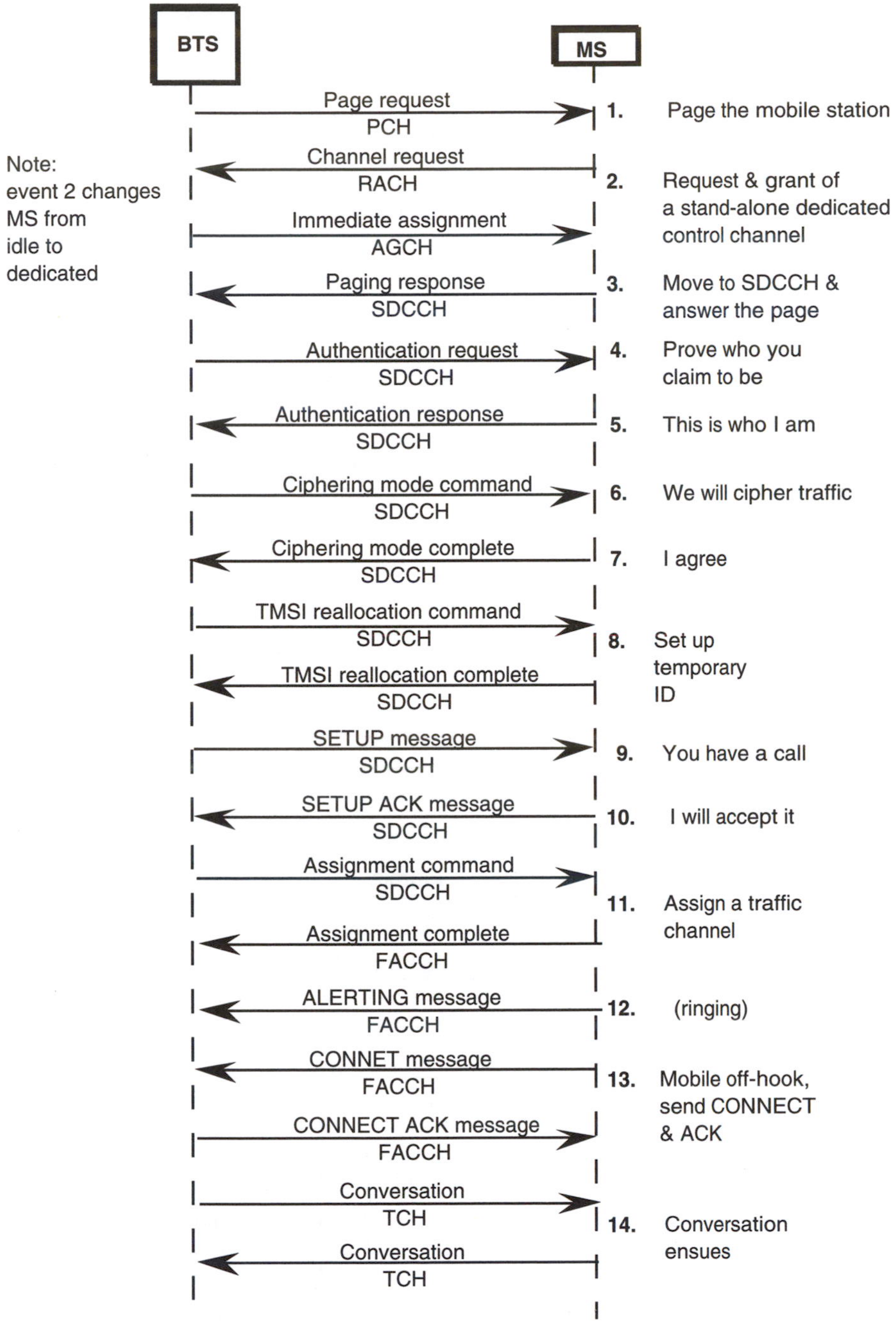

Figure 4–27 Call establishment to MS.

cation, the BSC uses the PCH to send a page to the MS. Event 2 is the same as the last example. In event 3, the MS answers the page on the assigned SDCCH. Events 4 through 7 are the same as the last example. Event 8 is concerned with establishing a TMSI for the duration of the session.

Events 9 through 13 are interlaced with Q.931+ messages and the assignment of a TCH for the call. In event 11, the TCH is assigned. Notice the use of the FACCH for some of these exchanges. During the exchange of a lot of signaling messages, the FACCH can use (take the place of) the TCH. In effect, the FACCH is allowed to steal bandwidth from the traffic channel, and so indicates by a code in the message.

After the Q.931+ ACK CONNECT message is sent from the MS to the BSC/MSC (in event 13), conversation can take place on the TCHs.

Figure 4–28 shows the MAP messages that are used between the GMSC, HLR, and VLR to locate the MS and set up a call. The numbered events should be self-descriptive at this point in the discussions. Events 1 through 4 correspond to the events shown in Figure 4–11. Event 5 is the connection establishment message that is sent to the MSC in charge of the mobile station's call. It is an SS7 ISDN user part (ISUP) message called the IAM (for initial address message).

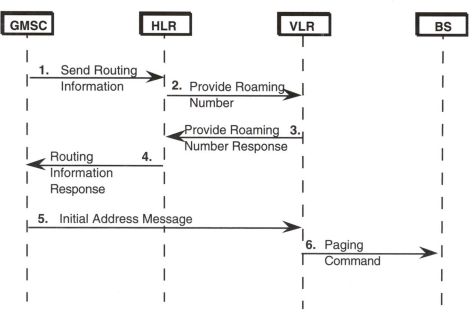

Figure 4–28   Call establishment to MS, prior to air interface message exchanges.

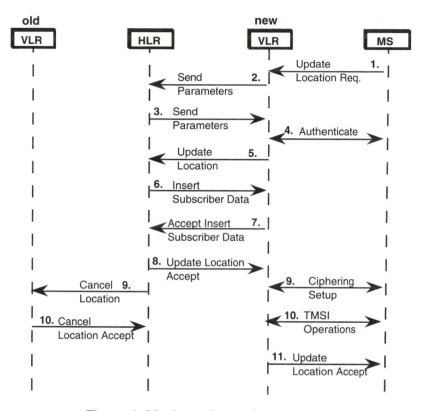

Figure 4–29   Location update operation.

Figure 4–29 shows the MAP messages that are used to perform a location update operation. The numbered events should be self-descriptive at this point in the chapter.

Other Examples of GSM Operations

The remainder of this chapter provides three more examples of GSM operations.

Figure 4–30 pieces together the previous material and shows the full MAP message flow when the MS originates a call. All these operations have been explained in earlier event lists, but not as a complete figure, and several of these events group together individual events of previous examples.

In conclusion, Figure 4–31 shows a full MAP message flow when an MS receives a call. I have added in this figure the ISUP address complete

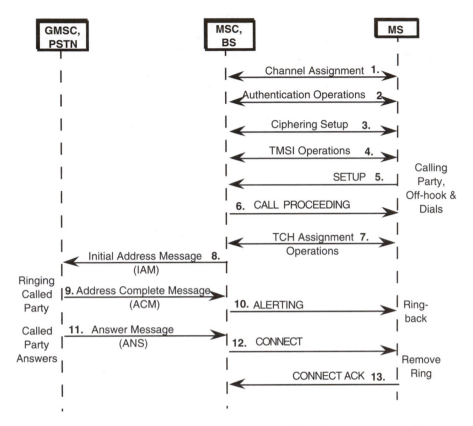

Figure 4–30   The full message flow: MS originates the call.

message (ACM) and the answer message (ANS). Also, notice the effect all these messages have on the called and calling parties:[2]

- The ALERTING message is sent when ringing operations are performed to the called MS.
- The ACM is used to provide ringback to the calling party.
- The CONNECT message is sent upon the called user answering the call.
- The ANS message is used to remove ringback at the calling party.

---

[2]The ISUP messages (events 1, 11, and 14) do not originate and terminate with the calling party. For example, the calling party's dialed numbers of DTMF digits are mapped into the IAM at the originating control office (CO) and sent through the telephone network to the GMSC.

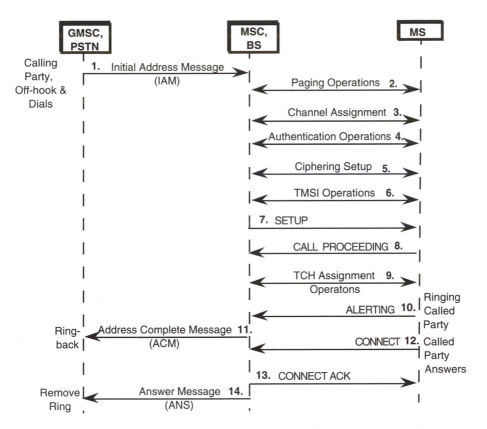

Figure 4–31   The full message flow: MS receives the call.

SUMMARY

The GSM is a European-based technology and is the foundation for the Digital Cellular System 1800 (GSM 1800, now called GSM 1800) and the Personal Communications System 1900 (PCS 1900). GSM is the most widely used second generation system in the world. It defines both the air interface with a TDMA 8-slot operation as well as the network side with MAPs and variations of SS7 and ISDN operations.

APPENDIX 4A   EUROPEAN AND NORTH AMERICAN LAYER 1 GSM STANDARDS

The North American and European GSM specifications are similar with regard to radio frequency power levels, but they do differ. For the

North American specifications, the mobile station is classified in regard to its rated output power into three classes: power class 1, power class 2, and power class 3. These classes are summarized in Table 4A–1 and provide the maximum output power permitted by a mobile station with a limit on the maximum output power tolerance, also shown in this table. In no cases will the mobile station be allowed to exceed a maximum of 2 Watts (+33 dBm). In addition, the mobile station power class 3 is restricted to transportable or vehicular mounted mobile units.

Additional power level requirements for the mobile station are summarized in Table 4A–2. The table defines the power levels that are needed for adaptive power control, which starts from the lowest power control level to a maximum power control level. Note also that the power control level tolerance is decided both for a normal and extreme operation. The interval between the power steps must be 2 dB ± 1.5 dB with exception of the step between power control levels 30 and 31.

The BTS transmitter output power requirements are summarized in Tables 4A–3 and 4A–4. The power class is organized into four categories, each places a limit on the maximum output power in Watts and dBms. In no case shall the BTS exceed a maximum of 1640 Watts EIRP in accordance with FCC rules.

The radio frequency power levels for GSM 900 and DCS 1800 are provided in these tables. Table 4A–5 provides the power levels for GSM, Table 4A–6 for DCS 1800, and Table 4A–7 for upcoming micro cells, which is part of Phase II, of GSM 900 and DCS 1800.

Table 4A–1   MS Dynamic Power Classes (North American)

Mobile Station Power Class	Maximum Output Power	Maximum Output Power	Maximum Output Power Tolerance
1	1 Watt (+30 dBm)	±2 dB	±2.5 dB
2	0.25 Watt (+24 dBm)	±2 dB	±2.5 dB
3	2 Watts (+33 dBm)	±2 dB	±2.5 dB

Note: The lowest power control level for MS power classes 1-3 is 15, with a nominal power level of 0 dBm.

Table 4A–2   MS Dynamic Power Control Range (North American)

Power Control Level	Output Power (dBm)	Tolerance for Conditions	
		Normal	Extreme
22–29	Reserved	Reserved	Reserved
30	33	±2 dB	±2.5 dB
31	32	±2 dB	±2.5 dB
0	30	±3 dB[1]	±4 dB[1]
1	28	±3 dB	±4 dB
2	26	±3 dB	±4 dB
3	24	±3 dB[1]	±4 dB[1]
4	22	±3 dB	±4 dB
5	20	±3 dB	±4 dB
6	18	±3 dB	±4 dB
7	16	±3 dB	±4 dB
8	14	±3 dB	±4 dB
9	12	±4 dB	±5 dB
10	10	±4 dB	±5 dB
11	8	±4 dB	±5 dB
12	6	±4 dB	±5 dB
13	4	±4 dB	±5 dB
14	2	±5 dB	±6 dB
15	0	±5 dB	±6 dB
16-21	Reserved	Reserved	Reserved

Note 1: Tolerance for MS Power Classes 1 and 2 is ±2 dB normal and ±2.5 dB extreme at Power Control Levels 0 and 3 respectively.

Table 4A–3   Standard BTS TRX Power Classes (North American)

TRX Power Class	Maximum Output Power (Watts)	Maximum Output Power (dBm)
1	20≤Po<40	43.0≤Po<46.0
2	10≤Po<20	40.0≤Po<43.0
3	5≤Po<10	37.0≤Po<40.0
4	2≤Po<5	34.0≤Po<37.0

Table 4A–4   Micro BTS TRX Power Classes (North American)

Micro BTS Power Class	Maximum Output Power (Watts)	Maximum Output Power (dBm)
M1	0.5≤Po<1.6	27≤Po<32 dBm
M2	0.16≤Po<0.5	22≤Po<27 dBm
M3	0.05≤Po<0.16	17≤Po<22 dBm

Table 4A–5   Dynamic Power Control Range (GSM 900)

Power Class	Output Power of MS W(dBm)	Output Power of BS W(dBm)
1	20(43)	320(55)
2	8(39)	160(52)
3	5(37)	80(49)
4	2(33)	40(46)
5	0.8(29)	20(43)
6		10(40)
7		5(37)
8		2.5(34)

Table 4A–6   Dynamic Power Control Range (DCS 1800)

Power Class	Output Power of MS W(dBm)	Output Power of BS W(dBm)
1	1(30)	20(43)
2	0.25(24)	10(40)
3		5(37)
4		2.5(34)

Table 4A–7   Dynamic Power Control Range, Micro Cells (GSM and DCS) at the Base Station

Power Class	Output Power of GSM W(dBm)	Output Power of DCS W(dBm)
M1	0.25(24)	1.6(32)
M2	0.08(19)	0.5(27)
M3	0.03(14)	0.16(22)

APPENDIX B   NORTH AMERICAN GSM SUPPLEMENTARY SERVICES

The GSM network includes a variety of supplementary services. Table 4B–1 provides a view of the supplementary services that are under consideration for the North American GSM version.

Most of the services pertain to common telephone-type supplementary services such as call waiting and call forwarding.

Table 4B–1   The PCS 1900 Supplementary Services

Category or Abbreviation	Name and Function
Line ID	
CLIP	Calling line ID presentation
CLIR	Calling line ID restriction
CLOP	Connected line ID presentation
COLR	Connected line ID restriction
Call Offering	
CFU	Call forwarding unconditional
CFB	Call forwarding on mobile subscriber busy
DFNRy	Call forwarding on no reply
CFNRc	Call forwarding on subscriber not reachable
Call Completion	
CW	Call waiting
CH	Call hold
MPTY	Multiparty service
CUG	Closed user group (community of interest)
Charging	
AoCI	Advice of charge
AoCC	Advice of change
Call Restriction	
BAOC	Barring of outgoing calls
BOIC/exHC	Barring of outgoing international calls except those directed to home PCN country
BOIC	Barring of international calls
BAIC	Barring of all incoming calls
BIC-Roam	Barring of incoming calls when roaming outside the home PCN country
USSD	Unstructured supplementary service operations

These services operate at layer 3 of the radio interface and assume the use of the ongoing physical and data link layers. The Q.931+ messages are data-filled with information elements for supplementary services. The REGISTER, FACILITY, and REGISTER COMPLETE messages are the primary messages used for this service.

The services are controlled through requesting them during the establishment of a call, during the call, and even during the clearing of a call. Some of the services can be obtained independently from a call.

This table lists and describes the supplementary services currently in the draft standards.

The North American version of GSM defines five other supplementary services, which are listed and briefly described in Table 4B–2. Most of these services are part of the terminal adaptation services that were described earlier in this course.

The point-to-point and broadcast short message services are applications that sit on top of the GSM bearer services. They include separate protocols that can run on a TCH, if one is allocated. Otherwise, the messages can be exchanged on the SDCCH or SACCH.

For data transmissions over the air interface, the Radio Link Protocol (RLP) is used. It has many of the features that were described in LAPDm.

Table 4B–2   Other Supplementary Services

Name	Function
Short message service (SMS), Point-to-point	• Transfers messages between PCN and MS. • Options to use TCH or SDCCH/SACCH if TCH not allocated • User traffic is mapped into TCAP/MAP • LAPDm SAPI 3 is used
Short message service cell broadcast (SMSC)	• Transfers broadcast messages from a PCN to multiple MSs • Reception by MS is only possible in the idle mode
Performance requirements	• Establishes parameters (timing) for handover, IMSI detach, TMSI allocations, channel assignments, paging responses, and many other operations
Rate adaptation	• Amplifies the terminal adaptation requirements with more information on V.110
Radio link protocol (RLP) for data and telematic services	• Specifies the RLP for data transmissions • Based on HDLC, LAPD, and X.25's LAPB • Similar to LAPDm, and has an FCS check

5

IS-136

T his chapter introduces a second generation TDMA system developed in North America and published by the TIA as IS-136. The IS-136 is an air interface but includes some references to the network side. Since these references are related to IS-41, which is discussed in Chapter 7, this chapter concentrates on the air interface operations.

During this analysis, you will surely notice the similarities of the IS-136 TDMA operations to the GSM TDMA operations described in Chapter 4. They are variations on the same theme.

Because IS-136 and GSM have much in common (interleaving, convolutional coding, and so on) the approach in this chapter is to analyze the IS-136 TDMA system from another perspective: its layered architecture. The emphasis in this chapter is also on the specific content of the messages. In addition, the TDMA frame structure of IS-136 and GSM are compared.

The PCS 1900 IS-136 specification uses the initials BMI for "base station, MSC and interworking function," which is a catch-all phrase to describe the network components and operations in the system. In keeping with the overall structure of this book, the term base station (BS) is used in place of BMI. If the focus of the analysis is on the air interface, the BMI idea is a useful concept since many of the operations at the air interface are created from components other than the base station. The base station acts as a conduit for these processes. But this distinction is not important enough to warrant diverging from the practice of using the term base station to signify signals/messages coming from or going to the "network side" of the mobile wireless system.

EVOLUTION TO IS-136

Chapter 3 explains that Digital AMPS (D-AMPS) was introduced in North America in the early 1990s to overcome some of the limitations of the original AMPS technology. IS-136 is a relatively new specification that builds on the D-AMPS operations. Recall that D-AMPS provides an option to use the traffic channels for conventional FDMA operations or TDMA, but the control channels remain as AMPS analog. IS-136 replaces the analog control channels with TDMA control channels. The name of this control channel is the digital control channel (DCCH).

Figure 5–1 shows the relation of AMPS to IS-136, with the arrows depicting the steps in the evolution from AMPS to IS-136. The notation "maybe" in the figure means that it is not required that D-AMPS evolve to IS-136. While it is a natural progression, the D-AMPS technology can remain in the market and co-exist with IS-136. My view is that the analog aspects of AMPS will become obsolete in the near future.

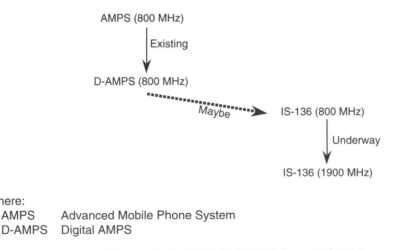

where:
   AMPS   Advanced Mobile Phone System
   D-AMPS Digital AMPS

Figure 5–1   AMPS, D-AMPS, and IS-136.

As of this writing, the IS-136 deployments have been on the 800 MHz band. Work is underway to up-band IS-136 onto the PCS spectrum of 1900 MHz.

IS-136 DEPLOYMENT

Since IS-136 was developed as a North American standard, it has achieved most of its success in North America. It is not present in Europe and has limited success in the Far East. It is enjoying great success in South America.

Market forecasts state that the second generation TDMA market in the United States will be dominated by IS-136 with GSM trailing as a distant second. However, this position is reversed in the worldwide market with GSM dominating the marketplace. It is likely that both technologies will gradually diminish in use over the next several years as the CDMA technology matures and improves. In fact, third generation systems plan on using CDMA and TDMA at the air interface.

THE IS-136 AIR INTERFACE

Figure 5–2 shows the air interface for IS-136. The basic concepts of this interface are quite similar to those of GSM, discussed in Chapter 4, except that the differences make the two interfaces incompatible. The frame structure consists of 6 slots per frame. Each frame duration is 40 ms, with a transfer rate of 25 frames per second. IS-136 uses another term to describe the frame structure; it is called the TDMA block, and is one-half of a TDMA frame.

The number of data bits (coded information bits) in a slot varies. In the forward direction from the network to the mobile station, the length of the data field is 260 bits in length. In the reverse direction, the field is either 244 bits or 200 bits in length, depending on the format of the slot.

IS-136 IDENTIFICATION NUMBERS

AMPS-Based Identifiers

Three identification numbers are used in AMPS and IS-136. They are (a) the mobile station's electronic serial number (ESN), (b) the sys-

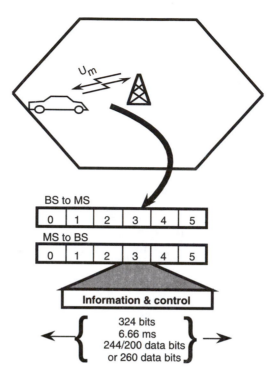

BS to MS

| 0 | 1 | 2 | 3 | 4 | 5 |

MS to BS

| 0 | 1 | 2 | 3 | 4 | 5 |

Information & control

324 bits
6.66 ms
244/200 data bits
or 260 data bits

where: 6 burst periods of 6.66 ms = 40 ms

Figure 5–2   The IS-136 U$_m$ interface.

tem identification (SID) number, and (c) the mobile station's mobile identification number (MIN).

To review briefly from Chapter 2, the FCC requires the ESN to be used for each mobile station. The ESN is a 32-bit binary number that uniquely identifies a cellular unit. The ESN is burned into ROM so that circuitry providing the number is secure and any attempt to change the serial number is supposed to make the mobile station unusable.

System identification numbers (SIDs) are 15-bit binary numbers that are assigned to cellular systems. Each cellular system is identified by a unique SID number. The mobile station in the cell must transmit the SID to a base station so the cellular receiver can determine the system through which they are communicating. The FCC assigns one SID to each cellular system and these systems may transmit only their assigned SIDs (or another SID, if this other group so permits).

The mobile identification number (MIN) is a 34-bit number that is derived from the mobile station's 10-digit telephone number. The specification refers to MIN1 (24 bits that correspond to the 7-digit directory number) and MIN2 (10 bits that correspond to the 3-digit area code).

GSM-Based Identifiers

IS-136 identifiers are also based on the GSM identifiers. All mobile stations can be identified by one or more of the following mobile identification formats (MSID) (see Figure 5–3):

- IMSI (encoded as a 50-bit MSID)
- TMSI (a 20- or 24-bit MSID)
- MIN (a 34-bit MSID)

The IMSI is the conventional specification defined in ITU-T E.212, which provides a maximum length of 15 decimal digits (see Figure 5–3a). The convention for coding IMSI over the air interface is with the 50-bit MSID (which consists of 15 decimal digits). In case the entire IMSI address space is not needed, the extra decimal digits are padded out with leading zeros, beginning with d15. Each 3-digit group is coded into a 10-bit binary equivalent (for example, 271 = 0100001111), as shown in Figure 5–3b.

The TMSI is coded as either a 20- or 24-bit MSID and is sent over the air interface to be assigned by the network to the mobile stations. The TMSI can also be used by the network to page or deliver a message to the mobile station on a channel reserved for short messages. The

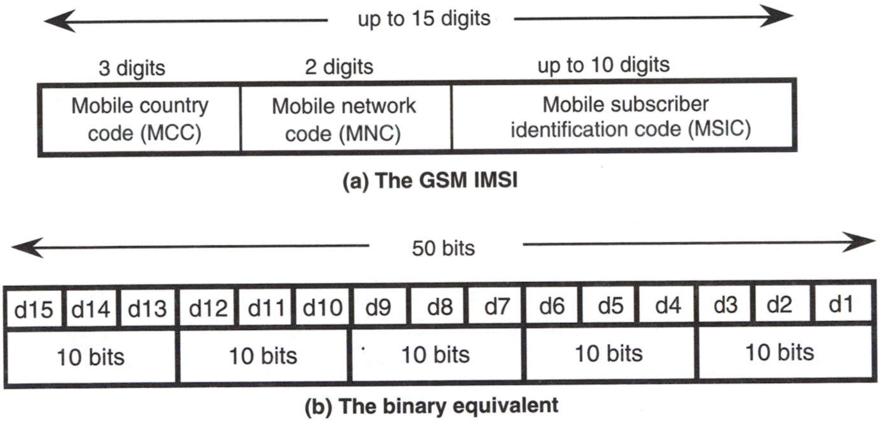

(a) The GSM IMSI

	up to 15 digits	
3 digits	2 digits	up to 10 digits
Mobile country code (MCC)	Mobile network code (MNC)	Mobile subscriber identification code (MSIC)

50 bits

d15	d14	d13	d12	d11	d10	d9	d8	d7	d6	d5	d4	d3	d2	d1
10 bits			10 bits			10 bits			10 bits			10 bits		

(b) The binary equivalent

Figure 5–3 IS-136's use of the international mobile subscriber number (IMSI).

TMSI can also be used by the MS to make accesses on a random access channel.

The mobile station identification number (MIN) is a 32-bit MSID and is derived from the 10-digit network address and defined in ITU-T E.164. Like the TMSI, the MIN can also be used by MS to make accesses on the RACH.

IS-136 establishes rules on how to determine which MSID to use (see document PN3388-1, section 8.1.4 for more information).

IS-136 IN THE 800 AND 1900 MHz BANDS

The frequency allocations for channels in the 800 MHz band are in accordance with the original AMPS frequency spectrum, shown in Table 2–1 of Chapter 2. For IS-136 that operates in the 1900 MHz bandwidth, the channel numbers and frequency assignments are allocated as shown in Table 5–1. Channel spacing is 30 kHz for the mobile station and base station, and the transmitter center frequency in MHz corresponds to the integer N as follows:

Mobile: 0.030N + 1850.010
Base: 0.030N + 1929.990

INITIAL ACCESS TO THE SYSTEM

In order for the mobile station to discover how it is to operate within a system, it must obtain information carried on the DCCH. It is important for the mobile station to be able to search and lock onto a DCCH as quickly as possible.

In the United States, the radio spectrum is divided into several frequency bands that reflect the number of operators located in a particular area. It could take considerable time for a mobile station to search for its appropriate DCCH within these frequency bands. Consequently, to narrow the search and the time to perform the search, IS-136 sets up procedures to search for bands that are more likely to exist for the mobile station's appropriate DCCH. These frequency bands are organized into probability blocks. The probability blocks are assigned a relative order of probability with regard to the potential for DCCH support.

To further aid the process, an identifier is used to assist the mobile station in searching for (a) DCCHs within the 1900 MHz band,

Table 5–1   Channel Numbers and Frequencies for 1900 MHz Operations

Band	Bandwidth (MHz)	Number of Channels	Boundary Channel Number	Frequency (MHz) Mobile	Frequency (MHz) Base
A	15	499	1	1850.040	1930.020
			499	1864.980	1944.960
Not used		1	500	1865.010	1944.990
D	5	165	501	1865.040	1945.020
			665	1869.960	1949.940
Not used		1	666	1869.990	1949.970
Not used		1	667	1870.020	1950.000
B	15	498	668	1870.050	1950.030
			1165	1884.960	1964.940
Not used		1	1166	1884.990	1964.970
Not used		1	1167	1885.020	1965.000
E	5	165	1168	1885.050	1965.030
			1332	1889.970	1969.950
Not used		1	1333	1890.000	1969.980
Not used		1	1334	1890.030	1970.010
F	5	165	1335	1890.060	1970.040
			1499	1894.980	1974.960
Not used		1	1500	1895.010	1974.990
C	15	499	1501	1895.040	1975.020
			1999	1909.980	1989.960

(b) DCCHs within the 800 MHz band, and (c) service providers (designated as band A, B, C, D, E, and F) operating on the 1900 MHz band. These service providers are those that won licenses from the PCS auctions and are designated with A through F to represent that portion of the frequency band to which they have allocated by the FCC (see Chapter 1, Figure 1–19).

IS-136 CHANNEL ORGANIZATION

IS-136 uses TDMA slots to define different types of operations. These slots are called channels and are depicted in Figure 5–4. The DCCH is organized into the uplink channel (the reverse DCCH, or

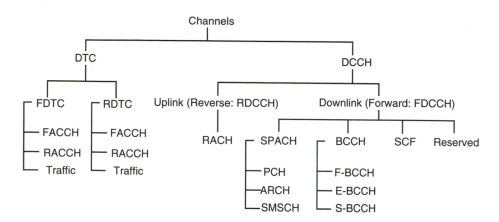

where:
ARCH	Access response channel
BCCH	Broadcast control channel
DCCH	Digital control channel
E-BCCH	Extended broadcast control channel
F-BCCH	Fast broadcast control channel
FACCH	Fast associated control channel
FDCCH	Forward DCCH
FDTC	Forward digital traffic channel
PCH	Paging channel
RACH	Random access channel
RDCCH	Reverse DCCH
RDTC	Reverse digital traffic channel
S-BCCH	SMS broadcast control channel
SACCH	Slow associated control channel
SCF	Shared channel feedback
SMSCH	SMS channel
SPACH	SMS (short message service) point-to-point, shared, ACKed channel

Figure 5–4   IS-136 channel organization.

RDCCH), which only contains the random access channel (RACH) and several downlink channels: (a) the SMS point-to-point, paging and access response channel (SPACH), (b) the broadcast control channel (BCCH), (c) the shared channel feedback (SCH), (d) and some reserved channels. The SPACH and BCCH are further organized into other channels.

The RACH is an uplink channel used to gain access to the system. In addition, this channel is used to respond to pages and send registration messages and a variety of other information. The RDCCH is a special slot used to send traffic to the BS.

The SPACH is organized into the PCH, ARCH, and SMSCH. The PCH is used to send various control messages to the MS, such as pages, alerting, and message-waiting messages. The ARCH is used by the MS to receive various kinds of control information, such as responses to an MS access operation, channel assignment, cell hand-off, and so on. The SMSCH is used to send short messages to the MS.

The BCCH is organized into the F-BCCH, E-BCCH, and S-BCCH. The F-BCCH contains general information such as the types and number of slots that are configured, information on authentication, and power levels. The E-BCCH also carries general information, such as information on neighbor cells and services supported by neighbor cells. The S-BCCH is used to deliver short messages.

The SCF is used to coordinate random access operations. It informs the MS about the outcome of access attempts and which slots can be used for these access attempts.

Table 5-2 provides a summary of the IS-136 channel organization scheme.

Table 5-2 Summary of Channels' Functions and Directions of Transfer

Digital Traffic Channel (DTC)		
FDTC	User information and signaling	BS-to-MS
RDTC	User information and signaling	MS-to-BS
FACCH	Bust signaling	Both directions
SACCH	Continuous signaling	Both directions
Digital Control Channel (DCCH)		
Reverse Digital Control Channel (RDCCH)		
RACH	Used to gain access to system	MS-to-BS
Forward Digital Control Channel (FDCCH)		
SMS, Point-to-Point, Paging, ACKed Channel (SPACH)		
PCH	Page	BS-to-MS
ARCH	MS moves to ARCH after RACH operation	BS-to-MS
SMSCH	Short message channel	BS-to-MS
Broadcast Control Channel (BCCH)		
F-BCCH	Initialization, exchange Ids, etc.	BS-to-MS
E-BCCH	Less time critical information	BS-to-MS
S-BCCH	SMS broadcasts	BS-to-MS
Shared Channel Feedback (SCF)		
	Controls RACH access	BS-to-MS

SELECTING A DCCH

It is possible that there may be a number of DCCHs in a cell, and IS-136 permits a number of slots to be allocated to the DCCHs. The mobile station is assigned to a DCCH through a hashing function that hashes the mobile station to a DCCH based on a specific identifier, the number of DCCHs in a cell, and the number of slots allocated to the DCCHs. This identifier is called the PCH allocation ID (PAID).

The hashing process consists of the obtaining a list of the DCCHs available in a cell and using the PAID to select the appropriate DCCH channel and slot from this list of DCCHs.

The mobile station uses the following criteria to determine if a candidate DCCH is suitable for use.[1] As the criteria show, the principal criteria are based on the power received on a candidate DCCH channel.

1. $C\_SEL_{cand} > 0$ dBm
   AND
2. $(MS\_ACC\_PWR_{cand} \leq 4$ dBm
   AND
   $Mobile\_Station\_Power\_Class = 4)$
   OR
   $MS\_ACC\_PWR_{cand} \geq 8$ dBm

where:

C_SEL_{cand} is: $RSS_{dBm} - RSS\_ACC\_MIN_{dBm} - MAX(MS\_ACC\_PWR_{dBm} - P_{dBm}, 0_{dBm})$ for the candidate control channel. C_SEL is set to a negative value if requirement 2 above is not met.

RSS is the received signal strength, averaged over the last 5 measurements. The minimum time between 2 consecutive measurements shall be 20 milliseconds.

RSS_ACC_MIN is a parameter broadcasted on the F-BCCH Control Channel Selection Parameters message. It is the minimum received signal level required to access the cell

MS_ACC_PWR is a parameter broadcasted on the F0BCCH Access Parameters message. It is the maximum nominal output power that the mobile station may use when initially accessing the network.

P is the maximum nominal output power of the mobile station as defined by its power class.

If the candidate DCCH does not meet the requirements established in these criteria, it is marked as ineligible. The mobile station then remains in a scanning state and looks for the next candidate DCCH.

---

[1]*Source:* TIA PN 3388-1, Section 6.3.2.1.

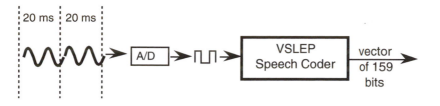

Figure 5–5 Functional view of vector-sum excited linear predictive coding (VSLEP).

THE IS-136 CODEC

IS-136 uses three operations to combat transmission impairments. First, it employs convolutional coding to protect certain bits of the codec bitstream. Second, it interleaves each speech frame over to time slots (to mitigate the effects of Rayleigh fading). Third, it uses a cyclic redundancy check (CRC) over the more significant bits of the code output.

Voice coding for IS-136 is shown in Figure 3–5.[2] The pattern of a speech signal is defined in 20 durations called speech segments. The segments are processed in the speech coder (vocoder). This operation uses two excitation codebooks and a long term filter to create a 159-bit output.[3]

The vocoder compresses each 20 ms speech segment into 159 bits, which are placed into a slot in the frame. Since 25 frames are transmitted each second and 2 slots are used in each frame, the compressed speech is 7950 bit/s.

Both D-AMPS and IS-136 stipulate the analog-to-digital translation process to be performed with conventional standards (ITU-T G.711), which produces a PCM format of 13 bits per sample. This data is used as input to the vocoder, as shown in Figure 5–5.

The 159 bits have other bits added to them, as shown in Figure 5–6. The original 159 bits are divided into 77 class 1 bits and 82 class 2 bits. The idea is to offer more protection to the more significant bits in the bit-

---

[2] This example is based on the first commercial implementations of IS-136. As of this writing, this technique is in most of the IS-136 systems. It will eventually be replaced by an enhanced vocoder. But this statement is true of all the second generation systems. The vocoders will continue to improve, and the resulting data rates (in bit/s) will continue to go down.

[3] The reader is directed to TIA PN3388-2, Section 2 for the details of these operations, which specify weighting algorithms, codebook code vectors, and vector quantization procedures.

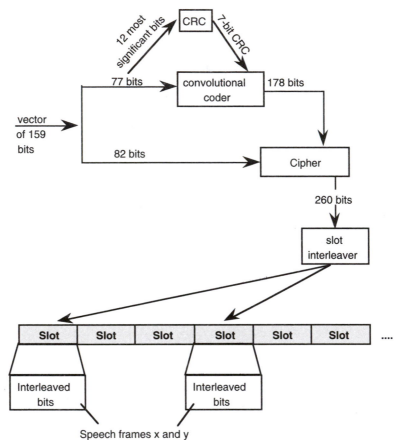

Figure 5–6   Coding and slot interleaving on IS-136.

stream. These bits are the class 1 bits, and they receive two forms of protection: the 12 most significant bits are taken through a 7-bit CRC operation, and all 77 bits are processed through a convolutional encoder that recodes each bit with 2 bits. The result is a 178-bit output from the convolutional coder. These bits and the class 2 bits are subjected to a ciphering function, then placed into the two slots in the frame through the slot interleaver.

The interleaver places the encoded speech data over the two time slots with speech data from adjacent speech frames. In other words, each time slot contains traffic from two speech frames. The interleaved speech frames are called x and y frames, where x is the previous speech frame and y is the present speech frame.

THE IS-136 LAYERS AND MESSAGE MAPPING

The organization of the IS-136 channels is similar in concept to GSM, with the use of frames and superframes, but the two schemes do have significant differences in how these similar concepts are implemented. Figure 5–7 shows the IS-136 channel scheme.

Let us start this analysis by examining layers 3 and 2 first. The layer 3 information has a header placed around it. This header is based on the ISDN L_3 protocol, Q.931, and is almost identical to GSM's L_3 message format (see Chapter 4, Figure 4-25). The PD (protocol discriminator) is set to indicate that IS-136 conformant messages are used (PD = 01). The MT (message type) indicates the type of message is in the message field (CONNECT, etc.). The information elements are fields whose values and presence depend upon the message type.

This information is passed to layer 2, and this layer adds its headers and trailers, consisting of a variety of L_2 headers (depending upon the type of L_2 protocol data unit that is to be sent, a cyclic redundancy check (CRC) field, and the tail bits. The specific functions of these fields are described later. This information is passed to layer 1, which is explained in Figure 5–8.

Continuing with the precious example, as shown in Figure 5–8, the L_2 protocol data unit is passed to L_1. The physical layer performs coding and interleaving operations on the traffic, topics that are discussed later. This layer maps the coded traffic into slots, then blocks, then frames, and

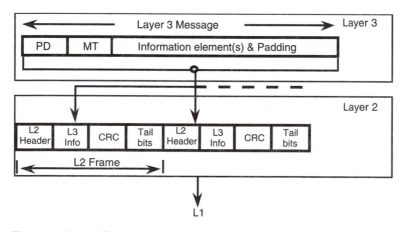

Figure 5–7 IS-136 channel organization and message mapping.

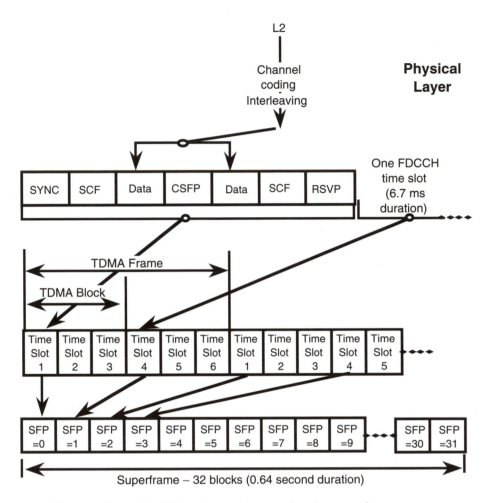

Figure 5–8 IS-136 channel organization and message mapping.

then superframes. The superframe consists of 32 blocks and is .64 seconds in duration (5.7 ms slot × 3 slots to block × 32 blocks = .64 sec).

The SYNC field is used for slot synchronization, equalizer training, as well as time slot identification. The shared channel feedback (SCF) field is used to indicate if a certain RDCCH RACH slot is busy, reserved, or idle. It is used to aid the mobile station in gaining access to the RACH.

The coded superframe phase (CSFP) field is used to provide information on the superframe phase. It allows the mobile station to find the start of the superframe. It is also used to discriminate between DCCH and DTC because the CSFP of a DCCH and the DCVCC of a DTC have

Hyperframe 0										Hyperframe 1
Superframe 0					Superframe 1					Superframe 2
Primary					Secondary					Primary
F	E0	S0	R	SPACHi	F	E1	S1	R	SPACHj	•••••

where:

F	F-BCCH
E	E-BCCH
S	S-BCCH
R	Reserved
SACH	Short message service point-to-point, shared ACKed channel

Figure 5–9   The hyperframe structure.

no common values. The term superframe phase (SFP) refers to the 32 blocks of the superframe.

The next level of slot aggregation is called the hyperframe, as shown in Figure 5–9. It consists of two superframes and forms the complete TDMA conveyor belt. One superframe is called the primary superframe and the other is called the secondary superframe. Each PCH running in the primary superframe is repeated in the secondary superframe. The SPACH slots can vary in their information content from frame to frame. The E-BCCH information can vary from superframe to superframe. Fields in the slots indicate changes that occur in the next hyperframe.

Each superframe on the FDCCH is organized into a specific sequence of logical channels. The number of these channels that can be supported within the superframe can vary, thus giving the network manager options in how to configure these channels. Figure 5–10 shows the composition of the superframe.

With any TDMA air interface, the mobile station must have some means to identify each slotted channel on the TDMA conveyor belt. The superframe phase field (SFP), shown in Figure 5–10, is used for this purpose. It is used by the mobile station to find the start of the superframe.

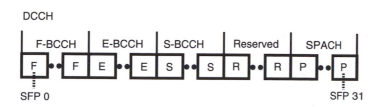

Figure 5–10   Another look at the superframe.

RELATIONSHIPS OF THE LAYERS AND THE CHANNELS

An effective way to analyze the major operations of IS-136 is to focus on its operations in the three IS-136 layers. With this in mind, Figure 5–11 illustrates the organization of the DCCH at the mobile station, and Figure 5–12 shows the DCCH at the base station. This part of our analysis will focus on these figures in a general way, and subsequent discussions will explain them in more detail.

Service Access Point (SAP) Concepts

Layer 3 operates on top of layer 2 through a service access point (SAP). Services are provided from the lower layer to the upper layer through the SAP. The SAP is an identifier. It identifies the entity in an upper layer that is receiving the service(s) from a lower layer.

For example, an entity in the mobile station can invoke services in the base station through the use of SAPs. It is the responsibility of the receiving lower layer (in concert with the operating system in the receiving machine) to pass the traffic through the proper destination SAP to the upper layer. Some people view the SAP as a software "port." It is akin to the socket concept found in the UNIX operating system environment.

Notice that two SAPs are used to define the RDCCH and FDCCH operations between these layers. Layer 3 and layer 2 communicate with each other by the exchange of transactions between the layers (through the SAPs). The figure pertaining to the base station model is similar to that of the mobile station except that more than two SAPs are used to provide the interface between layer 3 and layer 2. As noted in the Figure 5–12, five SAPs are associated respectively for S-BCCH, E-BCCH, F-BCCH, SPACH, and RDCCH. For both Figures 5–11 and 5–12, notice that the notations L3 MSG, L3 LI, MSID, and so on are noted in relation to the SAPs. This notation simply means that the layer 3 message and its length indicator as well as associated parameters (such as mobile station id (MSID)) are sent back and forth between the two layers.

The SAPs and their supporting operations between the layers are completely transparent to the end user and the operations of the SAPs do not manifest themselves on the air interface. However, they are a very important means to the end in the transferal of these messages across the air interface between the mobile station and the base station.

Let us focus our attention now on layer 2 and its boundaries between layer 3 and layer 1. For the mobile station reference, the layer 2 deals with RDCCH transmit process and an abbreviated RDCCH trans-

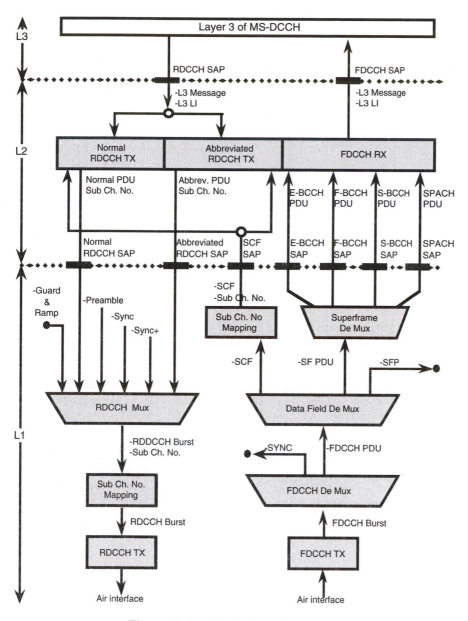

Figure 5–11   DCCH at the mobile station.

mit process. It also supports the FDCCH receive process. Subchannel numbers are handled here, although the subchannel mapping is performed at layer 1 (discussed later). For the layer 2 operations at the base station, the system still deals with the FDCCH transmit, the normal

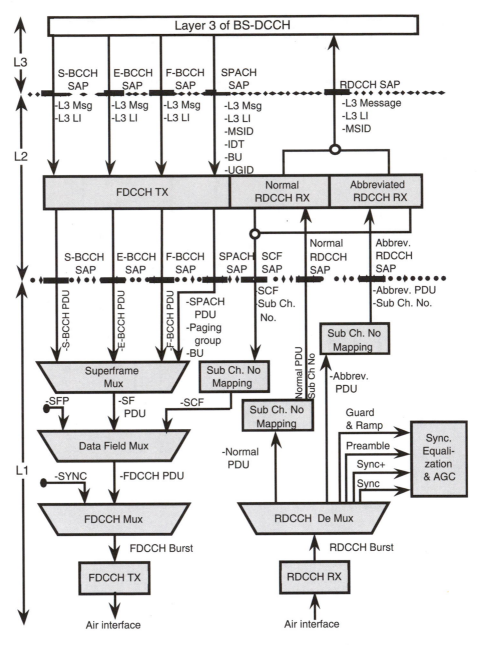

Figure 5–12   DCCH at the base station.

RDCCH receive, and the abbreviated RDCCH receive. For both figures, notice that SAPs define the boundary and operations between layer 2 and layer 1.

The layer 1 operations are responsible for transmitting and receiving the traffic across the RDCCH and FDCCH. Synchronization features are added at this layer as well as functions such as processing preambles, sync bits, handling guard and ramp operations, as well as channel number mapping and error correction procedures. As with the other layers, the operations of the base station's layer 1 is a mirror image of the operations of the mobile station's layer 1.

LAYER 1 OPERATIONS

The previous discussions have focused on the overall architecture of IS-136, with some general explanations of Layer 1. The next part of the chapter delves into more detail on three layers of IS-136. We start at layer 1, and to begin the analysis, let us take a look at the TDMA slots on the air interface.

The Slot Organization

The slot organization for traffic channels and control channels differ. This section examines the channels and their respective slot organizations.

The Digital Traffic Channel Structure.   The two time slot formats for the digital traffic channel are shown in Figure 5–13 and are also called "signals" in some literature. The digital traffic channel (DTC) employs two channels that are used to supervise call setup and tear down and manage the ongoing call. These channels are called the fast associated control channel (FACCH) and the slow associated control channel (SACCH).

The shortened burst slot (not shown in figure) is used for calculating the distance of the mobile station to the base station. It aligns the MS and BS in the time domain, a concept explained in Chapter 3.

Figure 5–13 shows the formats for the slots. The contents of the slots are:

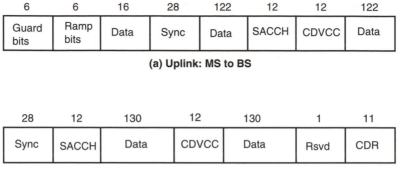

(a) Uplink: MS to BS

(b) Downlink: BS to MS

Figure 5–13   Uplink and downlink data slots for IS-136.

- Guard time: Used on uplink to compensate for different distances and timing variations between the MS and BS.
- Ramp bits: Allows some time for the build-up and decay of the RF signal.
- Data: The traffic (voice) that was explained earlier. Signaling traffic may be placed in the data field in the event of heavy signaling traffic. This traffic is called the fast associated control channel (FACCH).
- Sync: Used by equalizers for discerning the correct time alignment on the slot.
- SACCH: The slow associated control channel, used as a signaling and control channel.
- CDVVC: The coded digital voice color code, used like the AMPS color code for co-channel identification.
- CDL: Used for other control functions.

The DCCH Channel Structure.   Figure 5–14 shows the slot structure of the DCCH. Several of the fields in these slots perform the same functions as those described with the digital traffic channel slots (guard time, ramp time, sync). The other fields have been described in material in this chapter or will be described in the following sections.

The earlier parts of this chapter have explained many features of layer 1, such as the frame structure and the burst sizes. Some additional comments are made in this section to round out the earlier discussions.

All traffic sent on the forward and reverse channels is interleaved before being placed in the data field of the L2 frame. For the forward

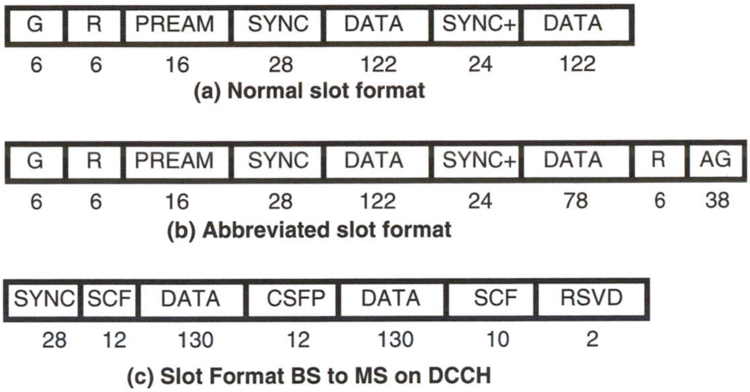

G	R	PREAM	SYNC	DATA	SYNC+	DATA
6	6	16	28	122	24	122

(a) Normal slot format

G	R	PREAM	SYNC	DATA	SYNC+	DATA	R	AG
6	6	16	28	122	24	78	6	38

(b) Abbreviated slot format

SYNC	SCF	DATA	CSFP	DATA	SCF	RSVD
28	12	130	12	130	10	2

(c) Slot Format BS to MS on DCCH

where:

AG	Guard time for abbreviated RACH burst
CSFP	Coded super frame phase
G	Guard time
PREAM	Preamble
R	Ramp time
RSVD	Reserved
SCF	Shared channel feedback
SYNC	Synchronization
SYNC+	Additional synchronization

Figure 5–14   The DCCH channel structure.

DCCH, the 216 bits are interleaved in a 13 rows by 20 columns matrix. For the reverse DCCH with a normal length burst, the 244 bits are interleaved in a 12 rows by 21 columns matrix. For the reverse DCCH with an abbreviated length burst, the 200 bits are interleaved in a 12 rows by 17 columns matrix. The three matrices for the forward DCCH and reverse DCCH are shown in Tables 5–3, 5–4, and 5–5. The bits transmitted for

Table 5–3   CDVCC Table

0	12	24	. . .	180	192
1	13	25	. . .	181	193
. . .	. . .	. . .	. . .	. . .	. . .
7	19	31	. . .	187	199
8	20	32	. . .	188	N/A
9	21	33	. . .	189	N/A
10	22	34	. . .	190	N/A
11	23	35	. . .	191	N/A

Table 5–4   Reverse DCCH Table

0	12	24	. . .	228	240
1	13	25	. . .	229	241
2	14	26	. . .	230	242
3	15	27	. . .	231	243
. . .	. . .	. . .	. . .	. . .	N/A
11	23	35	. . .	191	N/A

N/A = Non-applicable

both channels are transmitted in row, then column order For example, for the forward DCCH, the bits are transmitted: 0, 13, . . . 247 (row 0).

The preamble field (PREAM) shown Figure 5–14 allows the receiver to perform automatic gain control (AGC) and to enhance symbol synchronization before the data and synchronization portions of the burst are reached in the transmission. The preamble field is specified by the following changes in radians shown in Figure 5–15.

The ramp time field (R) denotes a ramp-up or ramp-down power interval and is three symbols (six bits) in duration. As mentioned earlier, the SYNC field is used for slot synchronization, equalizer training, as well as time slot identification. The SYNC word is coded to identify full-rate or half-rate users as well. However, for the actual synchronization sequences (beyond the bits that provide full- or half-rate channel identification), the SYNC words are specified by the following phase changes in radians, and depicted in Table 5–6.

Subchanneling of the RACH

Since the RACH is used by multiple mobile stations to send data to the network, there must be some means to convey to the mobile station

Table 5–5   Forward DCCH

0	13	26	. . .	234	247
1	14	27	. . .	235	248
2	15	28	. . .	236	249
. . .	. . .	. . .	. . .	. . .	. . .
11	24	37	. . .	245	258
12	25	38	. . .	246	259

N/A = Non-applicable

$$\left|-\frac{\pi}{4}\right|-\frac{\pi}{4}\left|-\frac{\pi}{4}\right|-\frac{\pi}{4}\left|-\frac{\pi}{4}\right|-\frac{\pi}{4}\left|-\frac{\pi}{4}\right|-\frac{\pi}{4}$$

Figure 5–15 The PREAM.

when to use the slots on the RACH so as to eliminate/diminish the possibility of multiple mobile stations sending at the same time. The operation to manage this aspect of the air interfaces is called RACH subchanneling. The idea is to allow the network to inform the mobile station about slots that are free on the RACH and to allow enough time at both the base station and the mobile station to overlap these events.

These operations allow us to examine the shared channel feedback (SCF) concept in more detail. The SCF flags are used to indicate the availability of the RDCH (busy, reserved, idle). Consequently, the mobile station can examine the arriving SCF flags to determine when to begin transmitting in the RACH.

Figure 5–16 shows the concept of RACH subchanneling, as specified in TIA/EIA PN3388-1, section 4.11.2. The FDCCH information indicates that the next burst T1 in the RDCCH is available (that is, it is idle). The mobile station receives this information and can begin sending its first burst at that time (which is actually 64.8 ms after receiving the full P1 slot in the FDCCH). In addition, the mobile station begins reading the SCF flags in the next P1 FDCCH slot (and 41.8 ms after completing transmission of its access burst) to determine the base station reception status of its initial access burst attempt.

Table 5–6 Synchronization Sequences

Sync														
1	$-\frac{\pi}{4}$	$-\frac{\pi}{4}$	$-\frac{\pi}{4}$	$3\frac{\pi}{4}$	$\frac{\pi}{4}$	$3\frac{\pi}{4}$	$-3\frac{\pi}{4}$	$3\frac{\pi}{4}$	$-3\frac{\pi}{4}$	$-\frac{\pi}{4}$	$3\frac{\pi}{4}$	$\frac{\pi}{4}$	$-\frac{\pi}{4}$	$-\frac{\pi}{4}$
2	$-\frac{\pi}{4}$	$-\frac{\pi}{4}$	$-\frac{\pi}{4}$	$3\frac{\pi}{4}$	$-3\frac{\pi}{4}$	$3\frac{\pi}{4}$	$\frac{\pi}{4}$	$3\frac{\pi}{4}$	$\frac{\pi}{4}$	$-\frac{\pi}{4}$	$3\frac{\pi}{4}$	$-3\frac{\pi}{4}$	$-\frac{\pi}{4}$	$-\frac{\pi}{4}$
3	$-3\frac{\pi}{4}$	$\frac{\pi}{4}$	$3\frac{\pi}{4}$	$-3\frac{\pi}{4}$	$-3\frac{\pi}{4}$	$-\frac{\pi}{4}$	$\frac{\pi}{4}$	$-3\frac{\pi}{4}$	$-3\frac{\pi}{4}$	$\frac{\pi}{4}$	$\frac{\pi}{4}$	$\frac{\pi}{4}$	$-3\frac{\pi}{4}$	$\frac{\pi}{4}$
4	$\frac{\pi}{4}$	$-3\frac{\pi}{4}$	$3\frac{\pi}{4}$	$\frac{\pi}{4}$	$\frac{\pi}{4}$	$-\frac{\pi}{4}$	$-3\frac{\pi}{4}$	$\frac{\pi}{4}$	$\frac{\pi}{4}$	$-3\frac{\pi}{4}$	$-3\frac{\pi}{4}$	$-3\frac{\pi}{4}$	$\frac{\pi}{4}$	$-3\frac{\pi}{4}$
4	$\frac{\pi}{4}$	$3\frac{\pi}{4}$	$\frac{\pi}{4}$	$-3\frac{\pi}{4}$	$-3\frac{\pi}{4}$	$-\frac{\pi}{4}$	$\frac{\pi}{4}$	$-\frac{\pi}{4}$	$\frac{\pi}{4}$	$-3\frac{\pi}{4}$	$-3\frac{\pi}{4}$	$3\frac{\pi}{4}$	$\frac{\pi}{4}$	$3\frac{\pi}{4}$
6	$-3\frac{\pi}{4}$	$3\frac{\pi}{4}$	$-3\frac{\pi}{4}$	$\frac{\pi}{4}$	$\frac{\pi}{4}$	$-\frac{\pi}{4}$	$-3\frac{\pi}{4}$	$-\frac{\pi}{4}$	$-3\frac{\pi}{4}$	$\frac{\pi}{4}$	$\frac{\pi}{4}$	$3\frac{\pi}{4}$	$-3\frac{\pi}{4}$	$3\frac{\pi}{4}$

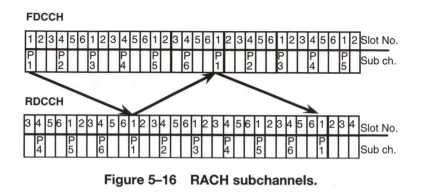

Figure 5–16   RACH subchannels.

In this manner, the RACH can be usually be accessed with the assurance that there is no contention. In case of problems, the feedback provided in the next 41.8 ms indicates if the access attempt was correct or incorrect, which allows the mobile station to decide if it needs to attempt the access once again.

LAYER 2 OPERATIONS

The principal purpose of layer 2 operations is the transport of layer 3 messages between the mobile station and base station. As Figure 5–17 shows, the operations at the L_3/L_2 SAPs are mapped to/from the SAPs at the L_2/L_1 boundary. The operations occur through the exchange of primitives, which are identified in Figure 5–17 as "request" and "indication." An explanation of these primitives will help in understanding several key operations of IS-136, and the following material provides a description of each primitive. You will also find it helpful to refer to Figures 5–11 and 5–12 during this discussion.

Primitives and Service Definitions

The primitive is used by the layer to invoke the services and create any headers that will be used by the peer layer in the remote station. This point is quite important. The primitives are received by adjacent layers in the local site (for example, the base station) and are used to create the headers used by peer layers at the remote site (for example, the mobile station).

At the receiving site, the primitive is used to convey the data to the next and adjacent upper layer and to inform this layer about the actions of the lower layer.

Mobile Station Side

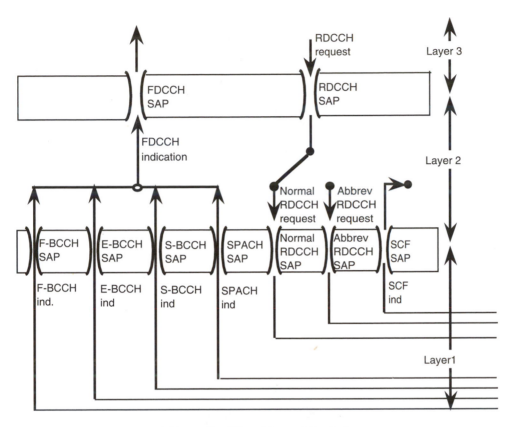

(a) Layer 2 entities at the mobile station

Figure 5–17   Layer 2 entities.

The OSI Model uses four types of primitives to perform the actions between the layers: (a) request, (b) indication, (c) response, and (d) confirm. The manner in which they are invoked varies. Not all four primitives must be invoked with each operation, and IS-136 uses only the request and indication primitives. For example, if the remote machine has no need to respond to the local machine, it need not return a response primitive. In this situation, a request primitive would be invoked at the local site to get the operation started. At the remote site, the indication primitive would be invoked to complete the process.

Of course, if the remote station were to send traffic back, it would invoke the operation with a response primitive, which would be mapped to the confirm primitive at the local machine.

Base Station Side

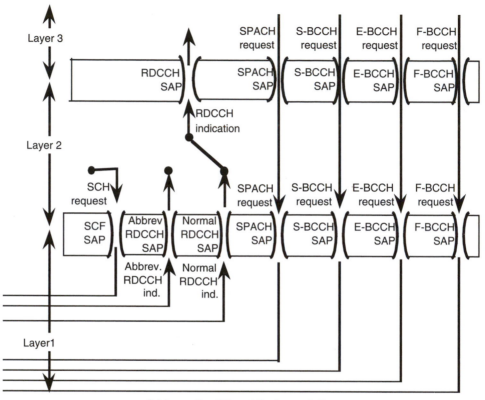

(b) Layer 2 entities at the base station.

Figure 5–17   Continued

One method of assuring that the primitives are related to the same operation is through the use of SAPs, and IS-136 borrows this OSI concept in its layer management operations.

Primitives at the Mobile Station

The RDCCH request primitive is sent from layer 3 to layer 2 to initiate the mobile station's attempt to gain access on the RACH. The parameters in this primitive include one or more layer 3 messages as well as a length indicator (LI) indicating how long the messages are. The third parameter is a message encryption indicator that is used to identify the form of encryption (if any) that will be applied to layer 3 messages subject to encryption. While this parameter is carried in the RDCCH request primitive, it does not affect the RACH channel because messages cited here are not subject to encryption.

The FDCCH indication primitive is sent from layer 2 to layer 3 when the mobile station correctly receives a layer 3 message. As indicated in Figure 5–17a, this primitive contains information emanating from these FDCCH channels: (a) F-BCCH, (b) E-BCCH, (c) S-BCCH, and (d) SPACH. Consequently, the indication primitives representing these four channels are mapped into the FDCCH indication primitive.

We have learned that the PCH channel is part of the overall SPACH channel. The mobile station listens to its assigned PCH subchannel through the SPACH and the FDCCH SAP while in the DCCH camping state. The DCCH camping state means the mobile station is locked onto a specific DCCH and is receiving information on this DCCH. The SPACH channel uses an address at layer 2 to check against the addresses coming in across the air interface. If these addresses match, the mobile station recognizes that it has received a page.

The ARCH is also part of the SPACH. The mobile station listens to the ARCH to determine if its access attempt was successful. The ARCH also contains a layer 2 address that is recognized by the mobile station, which allows the mobile station to determine if the ARCH message is destined for it.

The SMSCH is also part of the SPACH and the mobile station listens to the SMSCH to receive terminating point-to-point short message service messages. Once again, layer 2 provides an address that allows the mobile station to check for these messages to make sure it receives those messages intended for this mobile station.

Primitives at the Base Station

Figure 5–17b shows the layered operations at the base station with the associated SAPs and primitives. The RDCCH indication primitive is sent from layer 2 to layer 3 and carries information from the mobile station on the RDCCH/RACH. The primitive contains one or more layer 3 messages, a length indicator for these messages, a mobile station ID (MSID), the mobile station ID type (IDT), and the message encryption indicator.

The F-BCCH request primitive is sent from layer 3 to layer 2 and carries the layer 3 messages pertinent to the F-BCCH. Likewise, the E-BCCH request primitive follows the same procedure. The S-BCCH request primitive has not been defined as of this writing and is left for further study. This also holds true for the S-BCCH primitive at the mobile station shown in Figure 5–17a.

The SPACH primitive is sent from layer 3 to layer 2 and is used to page the mobile station on the PCH. The primitive contains layer 3 messages as well as their associated length indicators and: (a) up to 5 MSIDs, (b) information defining the format MSID (for example, the MSID can take the form of 20-bit TMSI, a 24-bit TMSI, a 32-bit MIN, or a 50-bit IMSI), (c) a polling indicator that indicates if the base station is soliciting a response from the mobile station (which is carried in an automatic request for repeat (ARQ) status frame and is discussed later in this section), (d) the burst usage (to discriminate if the SPACH request is on the PCH, ARCH, or SMSCH), and (e) a message encryption indicator.

Formats and Operations of the Layer 2 Frames

The L_2 frames are formatted into a header, L_3 length indicator (LI), L_3 Data, and CRC, shown in Figure 5–18. The headers are many and diverse; 36 different formats are defined for the channels and primitives shown in Figure 5–18. Obviously, the reader must study IS-136 for this level of detail. I will show one example of L_2 frames—those used for the RACH protocol. A summary picture of the 14 RACH frames is provided in Figure 5–18, and the next part of the chapter explains the functions of the fields in the header.

The contents of the header depicted in Figure 5–18 consists of the burst type that defines if the frame is the beginning, continuation, or ending of a segmented piece of information. The change indicator field starts at zero and is toggled with each new frame transmitted. If the frame is resent, the change indicator value remains the same. For certain types of traffic, an extension header is employed to contain supple-

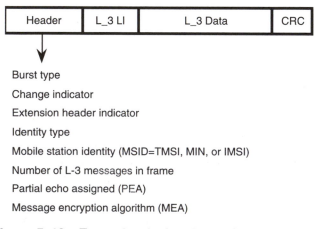

Figure 5–18   Example of a L_2 frame (on the RACH).

mentary header information. For this operation, the extension header indicator is used to define if the header extension is present or not present. The identity type defines the type of MISD carried in the next field is the frame (a connection setup message, data message, etc.). The message station identity (MSID) may be a TMSI, MIN, or an IMSI. The next field indicates how many layer 3 messages reside in the frame.

The partial echo assign field (PEA) is used for automatic retransmission request (ARQ) operations. The PEA is stored to identify ARQ transactions and identify a specific mobile station ARQ frame. The PEA actually defines the unique instance of each ARQ transmission. The mobile station sends out this frame with the ARQ value sent to a specific value and waits to receive a response from the base station. If the mobile station does not receive a matching PEA value within a specific period, it can issue another ARQ frame.

The last field in the header is the message encryption algorithm (MEA) field which is used to indicate specific types of signaling on the channel.

LAYER 3 OPERATIONS

As discussed several times in this book, the layer 3 operations of all the second generation mobile wireless systems are similar. They are concerned with connection management, mobility management, and to some extent, radio resource management. As we have learned, many of the functions of radio resource management are delegated to the base station or base station controller and the mobile station.

Tables 5–7, 5–10, and 5–11 list the IS-136 layer 3 messages and their associated channels. The S-136 layer 3 messages operate over (a) the BCCH, (b) the SPACH, and (c) the RACH. The BCCH messages in Table 5–7 are organized to operate over the subchannels: (a) F-BCCH, (b) E-BCCH, and (c) S-BCCH. The SPACH messages in Table 5–10 are organized to operate over (a) SMSCH, (b) PCH, and (c) ARCH. The RACH messages in Table 5–11 do not operate over any subchannels. The RACH channel is considered its own subchannel and is called RACH. We examine the BCCH messages first (see Table 5–7).

F-BCCH Operations

The F-BCCH carries the information that is needed by the mobile station to find the structure of the DCCH and operations parameters pertaining to the cell in which the mobile station is located. The complete F-BCCH must begin and end in the same superframe.

Table 5–7 IS-136 BCCH Messages

Messages	F-BCCH	E-BCCH	S-BCCH
DCCH Structure	M		
Access Parameters	M		
Control Channel Selection Parameter	M		
Registration Parameters	M		
System Identity	M		
Overload Class (OLC)	O		
Mobile Assisted Channel Allocation	O	O	
Neighbor Cell		M	
Regulatory Configuration		M	
BSMC Message Delivery	O	O	
Emergency Information Broadcast		O	
Neighbor Service Information		O	
Service Menu	O	O	
SOC/BSMC Identification Code	O	O	
SOC Message Delivery	O	O	
Time and Date		O	

Note: M indicates mandatory and O indicates optional use

Before any layer 3 messages are exchanged, the mobile station must be powered on and perform control channel scanning operations in order to lock onto an appropriate DCCH. The ability to find a DCCH depends on the mobile station finding a strong channel, which entails searching for DCCH and reading a full cycle of F-BCCH and E-BCCH. These operations are performed by the layer 3 entity in the mobile station. The mobile station is considered to be in a DCCH camping state as long as it is connected to the "best DCCH" according to several rules in the selection criteria. The mobile station will remain in the DCCH camping state unless it wishes to access the base station, originate a message, receive a page, perform a registration, perform an shared secret data (SSD) update (described in Chapter 7), or execute a point-to-point short message service transfer (SMS).

The mobile station is in an idle state in this camping state. It stays in the camping state even while reading F-BCCH information from its assigned DCCH or from a neighbor DCCH.

In order for the mobile station to discover how it is to operate within a system, it must obtain information carried on the DCCH, and it is important for the mobile station to be able to search and lock onto a DCCH as quickly as possible.

As explained in Chapter 1, the U.S. radio spectrum is divided into several frequency bands that reflect the number of operators located in a particular area. It could take considerable time for a mobile station to search for its appropriate DCCH within frequency bands. Consequently, to narrow the search and the time to perform the search, IS-136 sets up procedures to search for bands that are more likely to occur the mobile station's appropriate DCCH. These frequency bands are organized into probability blocks. The probability blocks are assigned a relative order of probability with regard to the potential for DCCH support.

To further aid the process, an identifier is used to assist the mobile station in searching for (a) DCCHs within the 1900 MHz band, (b) DCCHs within the 800 MHz band, and (c) service providers (designated as band A, B, C, D, E, and F) operating on the 1900 MHz band. These service providers are those that won licenses from the PCS auctions and are designated with A through F to represent that portion of the frequency band to which they have allocated by the FCC.

The DCCH Structure Message

All L_3 messages begin with the protocol discriminator and message type information elements. The other information elements in the message depend on the message type. Several of the information elements in the IS-136 DCCH message provide information to the mobile station about the channels/slots on the air interface conveyor belt. For the DCCH structure message, the following information elements are required (optional information elements are not covered here).

Number of F-BCCH, E-BCCH, S-BCCH, and Reserved Slots

The number of slot allocations for these channels can vary. This approach gives the network manager some flexibility in configuring the channels to support different kinds of cell traffic, from large cells in rural areas with sparse signaling needs, to small cells in metropolitan areas where many mobile stations create heavy signaling demands. In addition, the DCCH can be configured as full-rate or half-rate. The total number of slots per superframe is 32 for a full-rate DCCH, and 16 for a half-rate DCCH. Table 5–8 shows the slot allocations for the half-rate and full-rate DCCH.

Hyperframe counter (HFC): The HFC is used at the mobile station to determine the time position of the TDMA slot rotation.

Table 5–8   Slot Allocations

	Full-Rate DCCH		Half-Rate DCCH	
	Min	Max	Min	Max
F-BCCH (F)	3	10	3	10
E-BCCH (E)	1	8	1	8
S-BCCH (S)	0	15	0	11
RESERVED (R)	0	7	0	7
SPACH [1]	1	28	1	12

[1]Some SPACH slots may be restricted from allocation as PCH subchannels (see Sections 4.10.2 and 6.4.1.1.1.1 of PN3388-1).

Primary superframe indicator: This information element is used to inform the mobile station about the position of the DCCH on the logical channels. The primary superframe indicator delineates the positioning of the channel with regard to the TDMA blocks.

Slot configuration: Each mobile station is allocated a specific PCH subchannel within the paging frame of a specific DCCH. The slot configuration parameter provides information to guide the mobile station in selecting a DCCH and a PCH within the DCCH. The mobile station uses an algorithm that yields exactly one DCCH channel and one slot assignment for a given mobile station's PCH allocation identifiers. In other words, the use of this field allows a mobile station to select the appropriate DCCH channel and a slot from an ordered list.

Digital verification color code (DVCC): The DVCC and the user information bits are used to calculate a CRC (cyclic redundancy check). IS-136 supports the CRC's algorithm's inputs to be variable based on the DVCC information element in this message.

MAX_SUPPORTED_PFC: Paging frames are assigned to paging frame classes (PFC). A paging frame is defined as the number of hyperframes over which the mobile station has a single instance of a PCH allocation. As examples, a PFC of 1 indicates that a paging frame is in each hyperframe, and a PFC of 2 indicates a paging frame is in alternating hyperframes. The PFCs and the periodicity in the hyperframe are shown in Table 5–9.

A mobile station is assigned a PFC class during its initial registration procedures. The PFC value defines the highest PFC supported by the base station. If the value of this field is less than its assigned PFC, the mobile station simply sets its assigned PFC to this value.

PCH_DISPLACEMENT: This information element is sent by the base station to direct the mobile station to continue the reading of a con-

Table 5–9   Paging Frame Classes and Periodicity

PFC	Periodicity in Hyperframe
1	1
2	2
3	3
4	6
5	12
6	24
7	48
8	96

tiguous number of SPACH slots after it first reads its assigned PCH. The idea of this operation is to allow the mobile station to power down (sleep) until the next occurrence of its assigned PCH subchannel occurs. The parameter in the PCH_DISPLACEMENT information element gives the mobile station the information it needs to know when to sleep or not to sleep and when to look for its PCH.

PFM_DIRECTION: This information element is used with the PCH_DISPLACEMENT value to modify the mobile station's assigned displacement.

Once the mobile station has received the operating parameters in the DCCH structure message just described, the normal sequence of events is for registration operations to take place. This entails the exchange of layer 3 registration or test registration messages between the mobile station and the network. The registration procedures entail the mobile station exchanging its information with the network as well as performing authentication procedures for purposes of privacy and security. These operations are described in the chapter dealing with IS-41 operations (Chapter 7).

It is possible that the mobile station will be asked to perform a registration update procedure. This is based on parameters stored at the base station that have expired. The idea of the registration update is to periodically verify the authenticity of the mobile station as well as to validate certain operating parameters.

During the registration procedures or registration update procedures, the mobile station may be asked to reauthenticate (as just discussed) and also to resend a system identity message that consists of the mobiles station's SID and other identifying information.

In addition, after registration procedures have occurred successfully, the IS-136 mobile station is capable of mobile assisted handoff that was introduced in the D-AMPS chapter. This procedure uses the mobile assisted channel allocation (MACO) message that enables the mobile station to report radio measurements on designated channels. These measurements are sent to the network, which allows the network to determine if the mobile station is camped on to appropriate channels and an appropriate cell.

Since second generation mobile wireless systems typically offer an array of optional services and these services are defined by the actual implementation, it is important for the network to be able to inform the mobile station about these capabilities. For IS-136, these services are "advertised" to the mobile station through the layer 3 service menu message. This message informs the mobile station that the network does or does not support the following operations: (a) voice privacy, (b) data privacy, (c) VSELP digital coded speech on a full rate DTC, (d) message encryption, (e) ARQ support on the FACCH/SACCH, and (f) point-to-point SMS.

Since a mobile station is roaming through a geographical area, it will often need to change cells and corresponding channels. To aid in this process, the network sends the neighbor cell message to the mobile station to provide information about the neighboring cells' characteristics. This message might invoke the IS-136 operation known as the control channel reselection, which is executed to allow a mobile station to determine if a given neighbor control channel is better than the one on which it is currently camped. The mobile station is aided in this process by receiving a list of neighbor cells in the neighbor cell message. This information allows the mobile station to measure the signal strength of these neighbor channels to determine if it should change the channels and cells on which it is currently camped. Other procedures for control channel reselection are quite detailed and beyond the scope of our general description. The interested reader should refer to section 6.3.3 of PN3388-1.

SPACH Messages

The next discussion will focus on the major aspects of SPACH messages (see Table 5–10). For purposes of efficiency and brevity, I will list these messages and provide a brief description of their functions. Before these messages are described, we spend a few moments on the mobile station PCH allocation operations.

On a specific DCCH, each mobile station is allocated a specific PCH subchannel. The mobile station calculates the PCH subchannel to which it is assigned by one of two methods. The first method is by using an assigned user group ID (UGID). The second alternative is to use the permanent mobile station identity (PMSID). The PMSID can be identified with

Table 5–10   IS-136 SPACH Messages

Messages	SMSCH	PCH	ARCH
Audit Order		X	
Base Station Challenge Order Confirm			X
BSMC Message Delivery	X	X	X
Capability Request		X	
Digital Traffic Channel Description			X
Directed Retry			X
Message Waiting		X	
Page		X	X
Parameter Update		X	
R-DATA	X		
R-DATA ACCEPT	X		
R-DATA REJECT	X		
Registration Accept			X
Registration Reject			X
Release			X
Reorder/Intercept			X
SOC Message Delivery	X	X	X
SPACH Notification		X	
SSD Update Order		X	X
Test Registration Response			X
Unique Challenge Order		X	
User Alert		X	

Note: X indicates mandatory or optional use

either a MIN or an IMSI. Whatever the method chosen, the network and mobile station are configured to provide one of these values to enable the mobile station to find its PCH subchannel on a specific DCCH. Consequently, a mobile station monitors only a single PCH subchannel as determined by the UGID or the PMSID.

- **Audit order:** This message is sent by the base station to order the mobile station to return a subaddress to the network and perhaps implement a forced reregistration.
- **Base station challenge order confirmation:** This message is sent in response to the base station challenge order, this message contains the authentication algorithm output.

- **BSMC message delivery:** This message is not defined in the specification and is implementation-specific.
- **Capability request:** This is a general message sent by the mobile station to find out about the capabilities of a mobile station. The mobile station may also be configured with optional capabilities and this message will find out about those capabilities.
- **Digital traffic channel designation:** This message is sent by the network to assign the mobile station a digital traffic channel (DTC). This message contains the digital verification color code (DVCC), the digital mobile attenuation code (DMAC), the channel number, and other information such as time, information, protocol version, and so on. The DVCC is a digital 8-bit code that is used for the generation of information to determine that the correct traffic from the base station other than co-channel traffic (from another base station) is being decoded. The DMAC is a field that commands the mobile station to adjust to a particular power level for its transmissions.
- **Directed retry:** With this message, the network can force a mobile station to reject a particular DCCH and reattempt to access on an alternate channel from its neighbor list.
- **Message waiting:** As this name implies, this message is used to inform the mobile station that it has a message waiting for it.
- **Page:** This message informs the mobile station that an attempt is underway to set up a mobile station terminated call. The interesting contents of this message are the calling party number and additional information about the profile of the calling party (if supported).
- **Parameter update:** This message is used on the PCH to update any parameters that were downline loaded to the mobile station
- **R-data:** This message is used to support short message services. The R-data accept and reject messages are used in conjunction with this message.
- **Registration accept and reject:** As described in Chapter 7, registration operations are a part of the IS-136 roaming and authentication procedures, and registration operations are described in Chapter 7.
- **Release:** This message is used when the network clears a mobile station from a mobile station terminated call.
- **Order/interrupt:** This message is sent when the network rejects

an origination from the mobile station and/or a R-data message from the mobile station.

- **SOC message delivery:** This message, as its name implies, is used to carry SOC information, but the specification does not define the contents of this message. It is left up to the particular operator to use this message if necessary.

- **SPACH notification:** This message is used by the network to inform the mobile station that the base station intends to deliver a message on the RACH or SMSCH.

- **SSD update order:** This message is used in the authentication procedure, which is described in Chapter 7.

- **Test registration response:** This message is used to support ongoing registration and informs the mobile station if it is likely to receive service upon registration.

- **Unique challenge order:** This message is used in authentication and is described in Chapter 7.

- **User alert:** This message is used to activate a user at a mobile station. Its most common operation is to alert the user of incoming traffic.

RACH Messages

The last set of layer 3 messages are the RACH messages, see Table 5–11. Since the messages are carried on RACH, they convey information carried from the mobile station to the network. Many of these messages are invoked in response to the layer 3 messages sent from the network (described in the previous sections). Therefore, our approach here will be to review some of these messages and point out unique and interesting features that were not covered earlier in this discussion.

- **Capability report:** The capability report message is sent by the mobile station to inform the network about the capability of the mobile station. Examples of the information contained in this message are: (a) the software version residing in the mobile station, (b) the firmware version, (c) the model number of mobile station, (d) the manufacturer code, (e) support or nonsupport of asynchronous data transmission, (f) support or nonsupport of G3 fax operations, (g) support of ANSI/IA5 character operations, (h) support of short message services broadcast, as well as other information.

Table 5–11   IS-136 RACH Messages

Messages	RACH
Audit Confirmation	X
Authentication	X
Base Station Challenge Order	X
BSMC Message Deliver	X
Capability Report	X
MACA Report	X
Origination (Setup)	X
Page Response	X
R-DATA	X
R-DATA ACCEPT	X
R-DATA REJECT	X
Registration	X
Serial Number	X
SOC Message Delivery	X
SPACH Confirmation	X
SSD Update Order Confirmation	X
Test Registration	X
Unique Challenge Order Confirmation	X

- **Origination (setup):** This message is used to begin the setup of a call from the mobile station to the network. As such, it must contain the called party number and an optional calling party number. The reason the calling party number is optional is that the network may be able to infer the calling party number from its ongoing connection to the mobile station and other operating parameters. Other information pertains to the protocol version being used at the mobile station and an indication if the call is an emergency call (in which case it must be handled by special procedures).
- **Page response:** This message is sent by the mobile station in response to a page from the network. Pages are discussed earlier in this chapter.
- **Rdata:** This message relays SMS traffic to the network from the mobile station.
- **Registration:** This message is used for registration procedures and contains: (a) registration type, (b) the station class mark

(SCM), (c) version of IS-136, (d) C-number (a preferred network to use), (e) paging frame class (PFC) request, (e) DCCH member, and others. The only mandatory information elements in the registration message are registration type, SCM and protocol version. The registration type indicates the type of registration the mobile station is making, as shown in Table 5–12.

- **Serial Number:** This message contains the ESN.
- **SOC message delivery:** This message contains a system operator code (SOC), and is not defined in the IS-136 specification.
- **SPACH confirmation:** This message obviously is an SPACH confirmation. It can contain an authentication message if the mobile station was directed to authenticate.
- **SSD update order confirmation:** This message is described in Chapter 7.
- **Test registration:** This message is sent to the base station to inquire if the mobile station will receive service if it uses two specific IS-136 identifiers to register. These identifiers are the private system identification (PSID) and the residential system identification (RSID). No further details are provided in IS-136.
- **Unique challenge order confirmation:** This message is described in Chapter 7.

Table 5–12   Registration Types

Value	Function
0000	Power down
0001	Power up
0010	Location Area
0011	Forced
0100	Periodic
0101	Deregistration
0110	New System
0111	Reserved
1000	TMSI timeout
1001	User Group

All other values are reserved

SUMMARY

IS-136 is a TDMA-based air interface using a 3-slot-per-frame structure. IS-136 has many features that are quite similar to its European cousin, GSM. In spite of these conceptual similarities, the air interfaces are completely incompatible and requires a dual-mode and dual-band handset for a user to be able to use both systems.

APPENDIX 5A   PROCEDURE FOR DIGITAL CONTROL CHANNEL ASSIGNMENTS

This appendix provides a summary of the PCS and AMPS spectrum allocations and the guidance used by IS-136 to search for the DCCH within these frequency bands. These tables are extracted from TIA PN 3388-1, which are derived from the FCC PCS rulings. As discussed in the main body of this chapter, the approach is quite important because it provides a mechanism for the mobile to reduce the time of the searches to camp on an appropriate DCCH. Table 5A–1 shows the scheme for searching on the system A 800 MHz spectrum space, and Table 5A–2 shows the spectrum space for system B and the search guidance based on the relative probability indicator in the far right columns.

The next six tables (Tables 5A–3 through 5A–8) show the channel allocation and block numbers for PCS bands A, B, C, D, E, and F, the number of channels associated with these frequency bands and (once again) the relative priority listing for finding these channels as well as the appropriate DCCH on the channels.

Table 5A-1 Recommended A Band DCCH Allocation

Block Number	Channel Number	Band	Number of Channels	Relative Probability
1	1–26	A	26	4
2	27–52	A	26	5
3	53–78	A	26	6
4	79–104	A	26	7
5	105–130	A	26	8
6	131–156	A	26	9
7	157–182	A	26	10
8	138–208	A	26	11
9	209–234	A	26	12
10	235–260	A	26	13
11	261–286	A	26	14
12	287–312	A	26	15
13	313–333	A	21	16 (Lowest)
14	667–691	A'	25	3
15	692–716	A'	25	2
16	991–1023	A''	33	1 (Highest)

Table 5A-2 Recommended B Band DCCH Allocation

Block Number	Channel Number	Band	Number of Channels	Relative Probability
1	334–354	B	21	16 (Lowest)
2	355–380	B	26	15
3	381–406	B	26	14
4	407–432	B	26	13
5	433–458	B	26	12
6	459–484	B	26	11
7	485–510	B	26	10
8	511–536	B	26	9
9	537–562	B	26	8
10	563–588	B	26	7
11	589–614	B	26	6
12	615–640	B	26	5
13	641–666	B	26	4
14	717–741	B'	25	3
15	742–766	B'	25	2
16	767–799	B'	33	1 (Highest)

Table 5A–3   Recommended 1900 MHz A Band DCCH Allocation

Block Number	Channel Number	Band	Number of Channels	Relative Probability
1	1–31	A	31	16 (Lowest)
2	32–62	A	31	15
3	63–93	A	31	14
4	94–124	A	31	13
5	125–155	A	31	12
6	156–186	A	31	11
7	187–217	A	31	10
8	218–248	A	31	9
9	249–279	A	31	8
10	280–310	A	31	7
11	311–341	A	31	6
12	342–372	A	31	5
13	373–403	A	31	4
14	404–434	A	31	3
15	435–465	A	31	2
16	466–499	A	34	1 (Highest)

Table 5A–4   Recommended 1900 MHz B Band DCCH Allocation

Block Number	Channel Number	Band	Number of Channels	Relative Probability
1	668–698	B	31	16 (Lowest)
2	699–729	B	31	15
3	730–760	B	31	14
4	761–791	B	31	13
5	792–822	B	31	12
6	823–853	B	31	11
7	854–884	B	31	10
8	885–915	B	31	9
9	916–946	B	31	8
10	947–977	B	31	7
11	978–1008	B	31	6
12	1009–1039	B	31	5
13	1040–1070	B	31	4
14	1071–1101	B	31	3
15	1102–1132	B	31	2
16	1133–1165	B	33	1 (Highest)

Table 5A–5 Recommended 1900 MHz C Band DCCH Allocation

Block Number	Channel Number	Band	Number of Channels	Relative Probability
1	1501–1531	C	31	16 (Lowest)
2	1532–1562	C	31	15
3	1563–1593	C	31	14
4	1594–1624	C	31	13
5	1625–1655	C	31	12
6	1656–1686	C	31	11
7	1687–1717	C	31	10
8	1718–1748	C	31	9
9	1749–1779	C	31	8
10	1780–1810	C	31	7
11	1811–1841	C	31	6
12	1842–1872	C	31	5
13	1873–1903	C	31	4
14	1904–1934	C	31	3
15	1935–1965	C	31	2
16	1966–1999	C	34	1 (Highest)

Table 5A–6 Recommended 1900 MHz D Band DCCH Allocation

Block Number	Channel Number	Band	Number of Channels	Relative Probability
1	501–510	D	10	16 (Lowest)
2	511–520	D	10	15
3	521–530	D	10	14
4	531–540	D	10	13
5	541–550	D	10	12
6	551–560	D	10	11
7	561–570	D	10	10
8	571–580	D	10	9
9	581–590	D	10	8
10	591–600	D	10	7
11	601–610	D	10	6
12	611–620	D	10	5
13	621–630	D	10	4
14	631–640	D	10	3
15	641–650	D	10	2
16	651–660	D	15	1 (Highest)

Table 5A–7   Recommended 1900 MHz E Band DCCH Allocation

Block Number	Channel Number	Band	Number of Channels	Relative Probability
1	1168–1177	E	10	16 (Lowest)
2	1178–1187	E	10	15
3	1188–1197	E	10	14
4	1198–1207	E	10	13
5	1208–1217	E	10	12
6	1218–1227	E	10	11
7	1228–1237	E	10	10
8	1238–1247	E	10	9
9	1248–1257	E	10	8
10	1258–1267	E	10	7
11	1268–1277	E	10	6
12	1278–1287	E	10	5
13	1288–1297	E	10	4
14	1298–1307	E	10	3
15	1308–1317	E	10	2
16	1318–1332	E	15	1 (Highest)

Table 5A–8   Recommended 1900 MHz F Band DCCH Allocation

Block Number	Channel Number	Band	Number of Channels	Relative Probability
1	1335–1344	F	10	16 (Lowest)
2	1345–1354	F	10	15
3	1355–1364	F	10	14
4	1365–1374	F	10	13
5	1375–1384	F	10	12
6	1385–1394	F	10	11
7	1395–1404	F	10	10
8	1405–1414	F	10	9
9	1415–1424	F	10	8
10	1425–1434	F	10	7
11	1435–1444	F	10	6
12	1445–1454	F	10	5
13	1455–1464	F	10	4
14	1465–1474	F	10	3
15	1475–1484	F	10	2
16	1485–1499	F	15	1 (Highest)

6
IS-95

This chapter describes the major operations of IS-95 (and version A of IS-95, IS-95-A). The term IS-95 is used in the chapter to describe version A. The first part of the chapter reviews the status of the deployment of CDMA systems in the United States, where it is more widely used. Following this brief survey, the CDMA technology is explained, and the remainder of the chapter explains the major features of IS-95.

CDMA DEPLOYMENT IN THE UNITED STATES

In the mobile cellular industry, CDMA is a relatively new technology, and it did not see commercial deployment in the United States until late 1996. The first commercial deployments were in South Korea and Hong Kong in 1995. The deployment in the United States came about largely due to the need to expand and improve on the first generation cellular AMPS systems and the maturation of the CDMA technology.

As Figures 6–1 and 6–2 show, the growth of CDMA and its air interface protocol IS-95 is occurring at an accelerating pace in the United States. The maps in the figures will eventually be almost all black as CDMA continues its penetration into the second generation marketplace.

Figure 6–1 Deployment of IS-95 CDMA, March 1997.
(*Source: PCS Week* and *Phillips PCS Source Book*.)

One reason for this growth is the fact the service providers are required to have systems in place based on deadlines imposed by the Federal Communications Commission (FCC). In addition, once service providers were awarded licenses, it was important to get the systems deployed as soon as possible in order to obtain revenue. Another reason is that many of the service providers that were granted licenses chose IS-95 as the technology for the air interface.

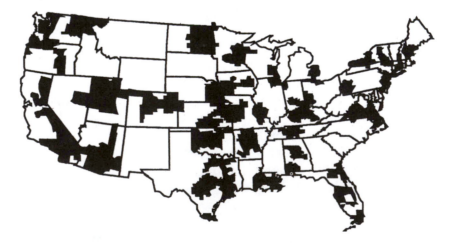

Figure 6–2 Deployment of IS-95 CDMA, March 1998.
(*Source: PCS Week* and *Phillips PCS Source Book*.)

Several should be made about these maps. First, in most situations, the CDMA service is not available in all the areas with the blacked-out regions. In fact, in some of these areas, the coverage is spotty, with the coverage in the more densely populated areas. Second, deployment has also occurred in parts of Hawaii and Puerto Rico.

This material is sourced from *PCS Week* and *Philips PCS Source Book*, both references from Phillips Business Information, Inc., 1201 Seven Locks Rd., Potomac MD 20859-0043. The *Phillips PCS Source Book* is a useful guide that also contains information on each service provider (carrier), the specific market area, and population coverage.

REVIEW OF SPECTRUM SHARING CONCEPTS

Before we begin the analysis of CDMA and IS-95, we should review some basic concepts pertaining to spectrum sharing. Recall that there are three major techniques used for radio frequency (RF) spectrum utilization: (a) frequency division multiple access (FDMA), (b) time division multiple access (TDMA), and (c) code division multiple access (CDMA). These concepts are illustrated in Figure 6–3.

CDMA does not divide the time spectrum nor the frequency spectrum into pieces. As this picture illustrates, CDMA places users in a cell onto the same frequency spectrum at the same time. More than one CDMA RF channel can be used in a cell. Each user is identified on the channel with a unique code. This code is used at the transmitting site to encode the traffic and also to spread it across the frequency spectrum. At the receiver, the code is used to extract a user's information.

THE IS-95 SPECIFICATION

The IS-95 specification is published by the Telecommunications Industries Association/Electronic Industries Association (TIA/EIA). IS-95 is designed as a dual-mode operation that permits the mobile station to operate in the conventional AMPS environment or the CDMA environment. For both operations, the ongoing AMPS frequency spectrum is used (a spectrum allocated initially in 1983 for the AMPS operators). Therefore, for the CDMA operation, multiple AMPS channels are grouped together for a CDMA operation of 1.228 MHz.

One might question why the AMPS spectrum space is utilized for IS-95. The reason is simple. By using the current AMPS infrastructure,

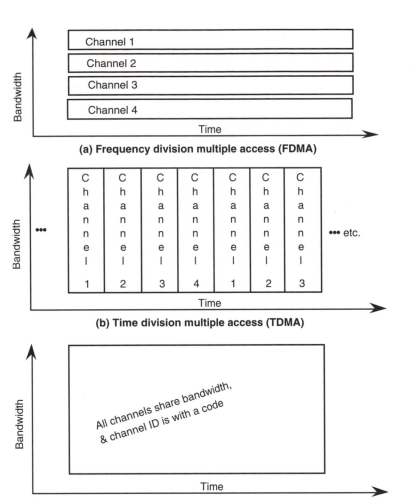

(a) Frequency division multiple access (FDMA)

(b) Time division multiple access (TDMA)

(c) Code division multiple access (CDMA)

Figure 6–3   Review on sharing the spectrum.

it is less expensive to overlay the CDMA over the current cells than to build a completely new system. This approach allows the deployment of the CDMA spread-spectrum technology in a more timely fashion.

IS-95 defines a variety of operations for the air interface. As just stated, it describes the operations for a CDMA-AMPS, dual-mode mobile station. This station is expected to operate in accordance with the AMPS specification published as EIA/TIA-553 as well as the D-AMPS specification published as EIA/TIA IS-54-B. Additionally, the mobile station analog operation should be able to support the TIA/EIA IS-91 specification. The rules hold true also for the base station operations.

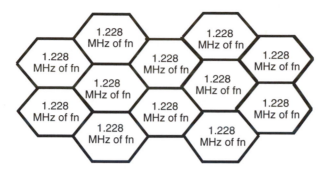

Figure 6–4   Cell architecture of IS-95.

IS-95 uses the same 1.228 Mhz bandwidth in each cell of the system, which translates into a frequency reuse factor of 1. Figure 6–4 shows this concept. This chapter concentrates on the use of the AMPS spectrum, wherein the two CDMA channels (forward and reverse) are separated by 45 MHz. Most of the IS-95 architecture will be upbanded to the PCS spectrum, and the forward and reverse channels are separated by 80 MHz. Figure 6–5 shows this concept.

IS-95 also stipulates operations for authentication and encryption. These operations are in consonance with the overall North American standards published in IS-54-B and IS-136 and supported by the network as defined in IS-41.

OPERATIONS ON THE FORWARD AND REVERSE CHANNELS

IS-95 defines a variety of characteristics and operations for the forward and reverse traffic channels (see Figure 6–6). Even though some of the operations on these two channels are identified by the same name, in

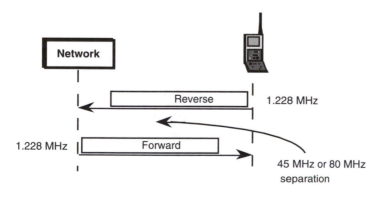

Figure 6–5   AMPS or PCS spectrum can be used.

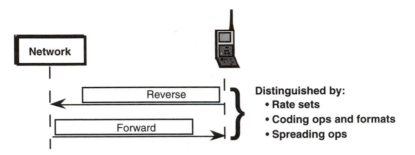

Figure 6–6   Channels and rate sets.

many situations the operations differ. For example, an operation called "bit interleaving" is used on both forward and reverse channels to reposition bits within the transmission stream, but the specific manner in which the operation is performed differs on the forward and reverse channels.

As a general guideline, these characteristics and operations may be different in regard to: (a) the transmission rates (in bit/s), (b) the coding operations, and (c) the manner in which the bits are spread with a spreading code.

Regarding rates, IS-95 defines two rate sets: (a) rate set 1 (operating at a high rate of 8 kbit/s) and (b) rate set 2 (operating at a high rate of 13 kbit/s). The sets have different coding and syntax characteristics. These rates are negotiated between the mobile station and the network during the connection setup and handshake.

CDMA TIMING OPERATIONS

CDMA operations on the air interface require precise timing between the base station and the mobile station. The base station is responsible for providing this timing across the air interface. This timing is sourced from the Global Positioning System (GPS), as shown in Figure 6–7. The GPS is traceable and synchronous with Universal Coordinated Time (UTC). However, GPS and UTC vary by an integer number of seconds that encompasses the number of leap second corrections added to UTC since January 6, 1980. The start of CDMA-system time is January 6, 1980 00:00:00:UTC, which coincides with the start of the GPS time.

CDMA system time is the absolute time referenced at the base station, offset by the one-way or round-trip delay of the transmission. Also, CDMA system time in frames is an integer value t: $t = s/0.02$, where s represents system time in seconds.

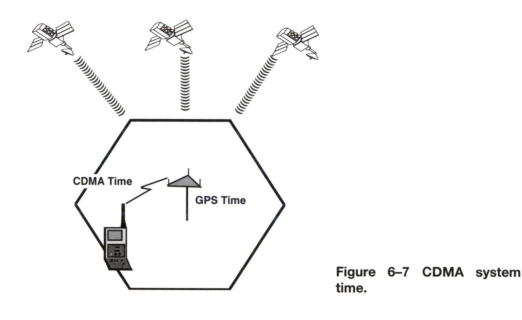

Figure 6–7 CDMA system time.

The intent of these operations is to ensure that the base station and mobile station are synchronized with regard to their transmissions and receptions. If the system is performing correctly, it assures a correlation of the long code mask with the I-pilot-PN sequence and the Q-pilot-PN sequence. These relationships (masks and PN sequences) are discussed later in this chapter.

INTRODUCTION TO THE IS-95 CHANNEL STRUCTURE

Figure 6–8 shows the organization of the forward (downlink) and reverse (uplink) channels. The forward channels are divided into control and traffic channels with each channel identified by a specific Walsh code.[1] Three types of control channels are used on the forward interface: (a) one pilot channel, (b) one sync channel, and (c) one to seven paging channels.

On the reverse interface, the channels consist of either access channels or traffic channels. All these channels are identified with a long pseudonoise (PN) sequence (a periodic binary sequence), with each access

---

[1]The theory of CDMA is beyond the scope of this book. For the reader who wishes more details, I recommend *Applications of CDMA in Wireless/Personal Communications,* by Vijay K. Garag, Kenneth Smolik, and Joseph E. Wilkes, published by Prentice Hall.

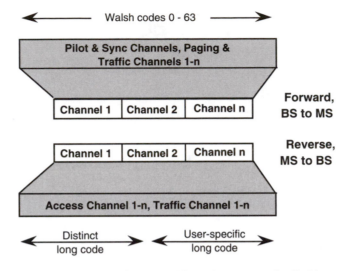

Figure 6–8   Forward (downlink) and reverse (uplink) organization.

channel identified by distinct access channel long code sequence. Each traffic channel by a distinct user long code sequence. The codes differ in order to uniquely identify each access channel and each traffic channel.

A More Detailed View of the Channel Structure

Figure 6–9 provides a more detailed view of the IS-95 channel structure. As just stated, in the IS-95 CDMA system, the reverse traffic channel (MS-to-BS) is set up for each MS to use a user-specific long code. This allows the BS to decode the information from each MS. The reverse channel also has access channels for control operations. These channels are identified by a distinct channel long code sequence. Up to 32 access channels are supported. The traffic on the uplink channel is grouped into 20 ms frames.

The forward channel (BS-to-MS) consists of control and user information. All information is coded with a Walsh function and then modulated by a pair of PN sequences at a fixed chip rate of 1.2288 megachips per second (Mcps).

The base stations in the system may be using the same frequency spectrum, and some means must be available to identify each base station. This identifier is provided by a common code that is offset in bit-times to distinguish the base stations.

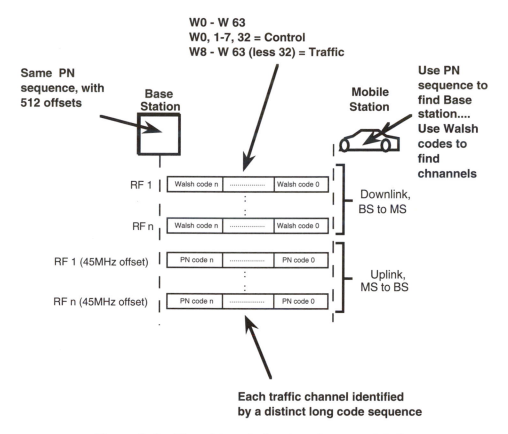

W0 - W 63
W0, 1-7, 32 = Control
W8 - W 63 (less 32) = Traffic

Same PN sequence, with 512 offsets

Base Station

Mobile Station

Use PN sequence to find Base station....
Use Walsh codes to find chnannels

RF 1 | Walsh code n .... Walsh code 0

RF n | Walsh code n .... Walsh code 0

Downlink, BS to MS

RF 1 (45MHz offset) | PN code n .... PN code 0

RF n (45MHz offset) | PN code n .... PN code 0

Uplink, MS to BS

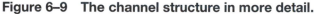

Each traffic channel identified by a distinct long code sequence

Figure 6–9   The channel structure in more detail.

THE PSEUDONOISE (PN) CODE

IS-95 employs a pseudonoise (PN) code for the coding and spreading of the traffic. The term *pseudonoise* is so named because the code pattern has the properties of noise in that the code appears to be randomized noise when received by a receiver that does not have the proper PN decoding sequence. In actuality, the sequences are not purely random, thus the term pseudonoise sequence. The pattern is indeed deterministic but it appears to be a random signal to a receiver that does not have the correct decoding capability.

The PN sequences must conform to the following properties. The number of 1s and 0s within the code sequence can differ by no more than one digit (a 1 or 0). This attribute is called a balance property. In addition, the PN sequence must exhibit the run property, which is defined of the PN sequences in which 50% of the sequence must have a run length of 1 and

25% must have a run length of 2. Stated another way, the PN code exhibits a Bernoulli sequence. That is: (a) the relative frequencies of 0 and 1 are 1/2, and (b) run lengths of 0s and 1s follow the coin-flipping experiment:

1. 1/2 of 1 or 0 run lengths are unity
2. 1/4 of the run lengths are of length two
3. 1/8 of the run lengths are of length 3
4. A fraction 1/2 of all runs are of length N for all finite

The PN sequences must exhibit a correlation property, which means that if the PN sequence is compared with a non-zero offset of itself, then the number of agreements differs from the number of disagreements by no more than one. The PN sequence is orthogonal to a copy of itself, which is offset by non-zero number of bits. For example, assume:

PN sequence (without offset)   110001001101011
PN sequence (with 4-bit offset)   101111000100110
Agreements and disagements   100001110110010
Resulting in 7 disagreements and 8 agreements.

Figure 6–10 shows an example of how the information bits are spread with the spreading code.

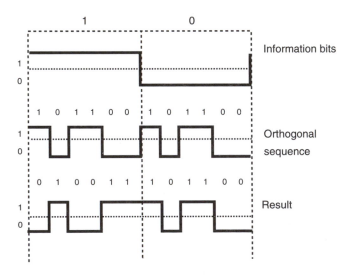

Figure 6–10   Example of the spreading operation.

Generating the PN Sequences

The PN sequences are generated with a linear feedback shift register as shown in Figure 6–11. The sequences are generated by combining the outputs of the feedback shifts. The binary values are shifted through the shift register in accordance with a clocking function. The contents of

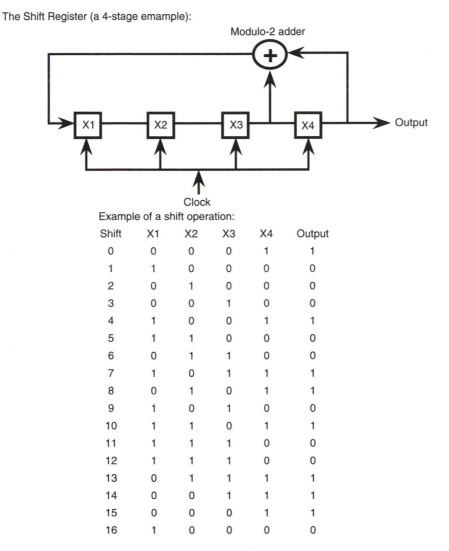

The Shift Register (a 4-stage emample):

Example of a shift operation:

Shift	X1	X2	X3	X4	Output
0	0	0	0	1	1
1	1	0	0	0	0
2	0	1	0	0	0
3	0	0	1	0	0
4	1	0	0	1	1
5	1	1	0	0	0
6	0	1	1	0	0
7	1	0	1	1	1
8	0	1	0	1	1
9	1	0	1	0	0
10	1	1	0	1	1
11	1	1	1	0	0
12	1	1	1	0	0
13	0	1	1	1	1
14	0	0	1	1	1
15	0	0	0	1	1
16	1	0	0	0	0

Figure 6–11 Using a shift register to generate PN sequence. (*Source:* Garag, Smolik, Wilkes, *Applications of CDMA in Wireless/Personal Communications,* Prentice Hall.)

the stages are combined to produce the input to the first stage. There-after, the stages determine the successive contents of the other stages. The register is called linear because the feedback logic is based on modulo-2 adders. For IS-95, the shift register varies in length to produce either a short PN code or a long PN code. The shift register with length N will produce a PN sequence of $2^N - 1$. This example is sourced from *Applications of CDMA in Wireless/Personal Communications*, a Prentice Hall book, by Vijay K. Garag, Kenneth Smolik, and Joseph E. Wilkes.

Several observations are germane to this discussion. First, the register cannot be seeded with all 0s. The reason is that a linear feedback shift register, if it reaches the zero state or is set to a zero state, remains in the zero state. Additionally, the register of linear n-stages cannot exceed $2^N - 1$.

SHORT CODES AND LONG CODES

We learned earlier that IS-95 uses two different PN codes. One is called the short code and the other is called the long code. The short code is produced with a register length of 15 and the long code is produced with a register length of 42. The short code is $2^{15} - 1$, which produces 32,767 bits. Since these codes are generated at a 1.2288 MHz rate, the codes repeat themselves every 26.67 ms. Later in this chapter we will see that the short codes are used for spreading the signal on both the reverse and forward channels. The purpose of the short code at the base station is to uniquely identify that base station by generating the same short code among all base stations but with different offsets in time.

As just mentioned, the PN long codes are $2^{42} - 1$ bits in length. Consequently, these codes do not repeat themselves for 41 days. The long codes are used for two purposes. For the reverse channel, they are used to identify each channel, and for the forward channel they are used for scrambling.

OFFSETTING THE PN SEQUENCE

The specific base station is identified by a PN sequence that is offset in time. There are 512 offsets available, and a pilot channel is identified by an offset index value, ranging from 0–511 inclusive. The specification stipulates that "... the zero offset PN sequence shall be such that the start of the sequence shall be output at the beginning of every even sec-

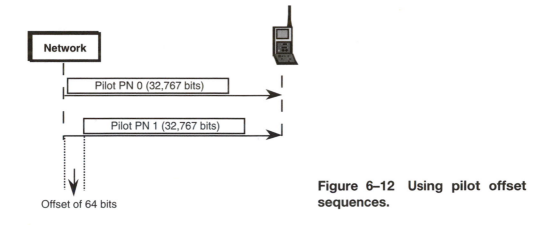

Figure 6–12 Using pilot offset sequences.

ond in time, referenced to base station transmission time . . . The start of the zero offset pilot PN sequence for either the I or Q sequence shall be defined as the state of the sequence for which the previous 15 outputs were '0'" (see IS-95-A, section 7.1.3.2.1). The PN sequence offset idea is shown in Figure 6–12.

KEY TERMS AND CONCEPTS

Before we proceed further, several terms and concepts should be clarified. These terms and concepts will be used in this chapter.

First, the term *soft handoff* refers to the handoff of the mobile station from one base station to another base station. CDMA handoffs are characterized by beginning communications with a new base station on the same CDMA frequency band before terminating with the old base station.

The term *aging* refers to a mechanism where the mobile station maintains a list of other base stations that have been sent to it recently from the currently acting base station.

The mobile station groups pilots into four sets, which are intialized by the base station at the call setup. Once the sets are set up, they can be changed by the pilots moving among the sets, an operation known as set transitioning or set maintenance.

The term *active set* refers to a list of base stations the mobile station is communicating with (our salutations to Winston Churchill for this sentence structure).

The term *neighbor set* refers to a set of pilot channels associated with CDMA channels that are neighbors and may be used by the mobile station.

As a general practice, the neighbor set contains the pilots associated with CDMA channels that are in geographical regions near the mobile station.

The term *candidate set* refers to pilots that have been received with sufficient strength to indicate that they can be moved to the active set. They are so moved when the mobile station informs the base station, and the base station accepts.

The *remaining set* includes all pilots in the system that are not in the other three sets.

SOFT HANDOFFS

So, the term soft handoff refers to an operation in which the mobile station is in communication with more than one base station and is making decisions about which base station to use, based on the signal strength (SS) of the pilots of the base stations. With hard handoff, the mobile station abandons one base station and picks up another.

The mobile station keeps an active set of base stations in which a pilot channel is associated with forward traffic channels. As Figure 6–13 shows, the mobile station initially has BS 1 in the active set (Figure 6–13a). As the mobile station moves closer to BS 2, this base station is added to the active set. This decision is made when the signal strength (SS) from BS 2 exceeds an add threshold value (Figure 6–13b).

Depending on the movement of the mobile station and factors such as terrain, BS 1 may be removed from the active list if its signal strength (SS) goes below a drop threshold value (Figure 6–13c).

Although not shown in Figure 6–13, the entries in the active set may fluctuate (BS 1 in the set, BS 1 out of the set, and so on), due to the base station's ongoing signal to the mobile station.

HARD HANDOFFS

In addition to the soft handoff, IS-95 also supports a hard handoff in which the mobile station communicates with one BS at a time. This handoff is called a "break before make" operation, in contrast to the soft handoff, which is a "make before break" procedure. The mobile station relinquishes resources in the "old" BS and then tunes to a new BS.

Hard handoff is typically done when (a) moving between BSs served by different switches, (b) encountering BSs of different vendors, and (c) encountering BSs that support different air interfaces. IS-95 defines hard handoffs for: (a) CDMA-to/from-CDMA, and (b) CDMA-to-AMPS.

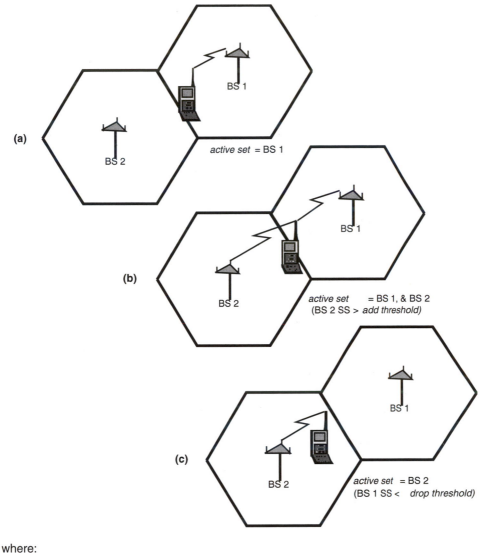

(a)

active set = BS 1

(b)

active set = BS 1, & BS 2
(BS 2 SS > *add threshold*)

(c)

active set = BS 2
(BS 1 SS < *drop threshold*)

where:
  SS   Signal strength

Figure 6–13   Joining and leaving the active set.

In some situations, hard handoffs cannot be avoided, but they can create problems. For example, the mobile station may not be able to set up a connection with another base station. Also, soft handoff requires less power than hard handoff. Finally, a hard handoff may be discernible to the users of the system.

THE IS-95 LAYERS

Like most mobile, wireless systems, IS-95 is organized into logical layers, as shown in Figure 6–14. The three layers are known in the Open Systems Interconnection (OSI) Model as the bearer layers and are named: (a) layer 1, the physical layer; (b) layer 2, the data link layer; and (c) layer 3, the network layer. The term bearer comes from the fact that these lower layers are tasked with bearing (carrying) the traffic of the upper layers (for example, an upper layer for user traffic).

Layer 1 is the CDMA layer and is responsible for most of the functions we have discussed thus far in this chapter, such as the digital bit transformations. Layer 2 is divided into two sublayers. The multiplex sublayer is used to share the physical channel between signaling and data traffic. The other sublayer (labeled "layer 2" in this figure) operates as a support layer for layer 3. Its functions vary, depending upon the type of layer 3 (or an upper layer) that is positioned above it. The layer 2 (labeled "Signaling" in Figure 6–14) is responsible for the reliable delivery of layer 3 signaling traffic across the air interface. The signaling layer 3 (labeled "Signaling, Call Processing, and Control" in the figure) is responsible for the management of calls, handoffs, power control operations, and a variety of other functions described later.

Primary traffic, as the name implies, is the principal traffic sent across the air interface. Secondary traffic is other (additional) traffic sent across the air interface.

Upper Layers (Primary Traffic)	Upper Layers (Secondary Traffic)	Layer 3 (Signaling, Call Processing, and Control)	
Layer 2 (Primary Traffic)	Layer 2 (Secondary Traffic)	Layer 2 (Signaling)	Layer 2 (Paging & Access Channels)
Multiplex Sublayer (Traffic Channel)			
Layer 1 (Physical)			

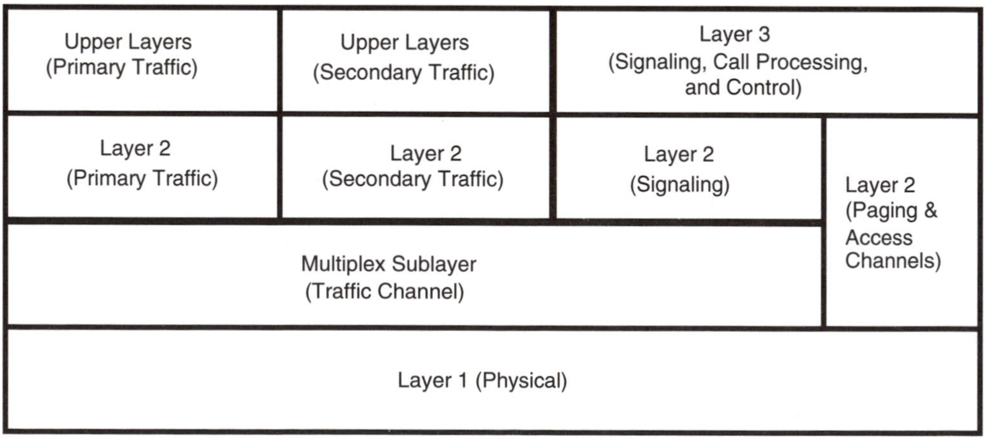

Figure 6–14   The layered protocol stack.

Several definitions are needed at this point in the discussion. First, a *blank-and-burst* operation is one in which a traffic channel frame's primary traffic is preempted by signaling or secondary traffic (preemption is performed on a frame-by-frame basis). Next, a *dim-and-burst* operation is one in which primary traffic is multiplexed with either signaling or secondary traffic. Signaling traffic may be sent either as blank-and-burst or dim-and-burst, and secondary traffic may be sent in the same manner.

Layer 2 and layer 3 messages are distinguished by the fields in the messages and not by the message syntax; this approach is different from conventional layered systems that define different formats and syntaxes for the two layers.

MAJOR OPERATIONS AT THE PHYSICAL LAYER

Newcomers to IS-95 and CDMA find the physical layer the most interesting because it is quite different from other mobile wireless interfaces such as FDMA and CDMA. So, considerable explanations are provided in this chapter on the physical layer.

Figure 6–15 provides a summary of the major functions involved on the physical channel interfaces. The next part of the chapter should prove useful as an introduction to more detailed information, following shortly.[2] We will use this general flow diagram to highlight the major functions at the BS and MS, and the order in which they are executed. The next part of this chapter describes these functions, and Table 6–1 represents a brief summary.

The Forward Channel

On the forward channel, the vocoder accepts PCM voice traffic and produces a compressed signal. The vocoder is defined to operate at one of four rates: full, 1/2, 1/4, or 1/8. Two types of vocoders are defined: (a) rate set 1, which produces an 8.0 kbit/s voice bit stream over a 9.6 kbit/s frame; and (b) rate set 2, which produces a 13.0 kbit/s voice bit stream over a 14.4 kbit/s frame. The sync, paging, and forward traffic channels are convolutional encoding before the signal is sent onto the air interface. IS-95 uses orthogonal functions for a spreading code on the forward channel and for modulation on the reverse channel.

---

[2]This example is based on *Wireless PCS,* by Rajan Kuruppillai, Mahi Dontamsetti, and Fil J. Cosentino, McGraw-Hill, 1997.

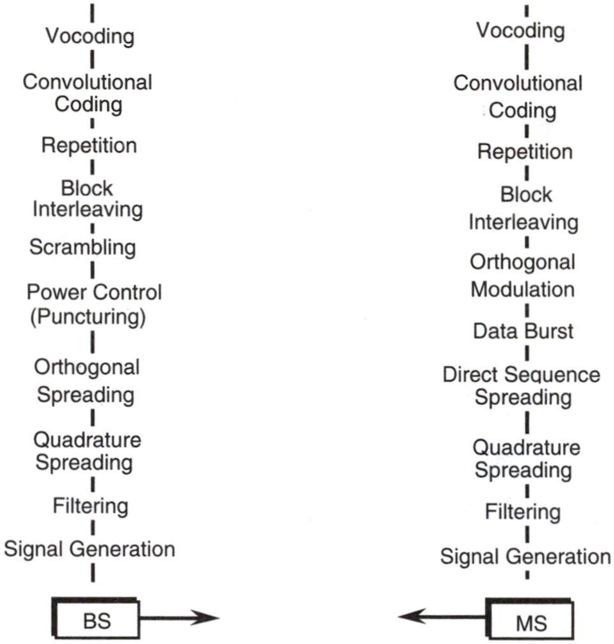

Vocoding
|
Convolutional
Coding
|
Repetition
|
Block
Interleaving
|
Scrambling
|
Power Control
(Puncturing)
|
Orthogonal
Spreading
|
Quadrature
Spreading
|
Filtering
|
Signal Generation
|

[BS] ⟶

Vocoding
|
Convolutional
Coding
|
Repetition
|
Block
Interleaving
|
Orthogonal
Modulation
|
Data Burst
|
Direct Sequence
Spreading
|
Quadrature
Spreading
|
Filtering
|
Signal Generation
|

⟵ [MS]

Figure 6–15 Major functions of the physical layer.

Table 6–1 Major Functions of the Physical Layer

Function	What?	Why?
Vocoding	Coding voice signal	Digitization & compression
Convolutional coding	Encode information bit stream	Error correction to increase reliability
Repetition	Repeat bits	Combat channel impairments & provide rate adaptation
Interleaving	Disperse redundant bits away from each other	Combat channel impairments
Scrambling	Randomize the bits	Reduce power spikes & provide some security
Power control	Provide feedback to MSs	Reduce MS co-interference
Orthogonal spreading	Spread symbols with a code	Identify channels
Quadrature spreading	Spread codes with another code	Part of phase modulation of the signal
Filtering	Restrict signal frequencies	Define passband of signal

AN ANALYSIS OF THE PHYSICAL LAYER FUNCTIONS

This part of the chapter describes the forward channel functions introduced in Figure 6–15 in more detail. As stated, the operations on the reverse channel are similar and their differences were just explained. Of purposes of brevity and efficiency, this analysis concentrates on the forward channel.

The specific type of vocoder employed in IS-95 is not defined in the specifications. Since other chapters explain vocoders, we will not revisit them here in detail. IS-96-A defines the vocoding standard for CDMA.

Convolutional Coding

If a certain amount of error can be tolerated on the channel, it is possible to reduce the amount of power required for the transmission of the signal, since a high-powered signal produces fewer errors than a low-power counterpart. Convolutional coding provides the ability to correct certain errors at the receiver, and therefore permits a lower power transmitter than what would be required if convolutional coding were not used. The technique has been employed in conventional wire-based modems for a number of years (using trellis coding techniques) and is also applied to mobile modems.

Convolutional coding is applied to the forward and reverse channels, and the algorithms for the two are similar, but different. The example in Figure 6–16 is for the forward channel. The $k = 9$ value is the constraint length, which is the length of the register and one input bit. The $R = 1/2$ value refers to the output of two symbols for every one input.

In a sense, the register has a memory: The symbol generated at each register shift is based on the new input bit and the contents of the previous registers. This approach allows the receiver to perform a complementary function and "correct" a bit if it does not fit with the expected results (the associated bits).

The Repetition Function

The next stage in the process is the repetition function. As the name implies, it repeats the input data n times to equal an output rate of 19.2 k symbols per second (ksps) for rate set 1 and 28.8 ksps for rate set 2. The number of times the data is repeated depends on the rate of the input to the repetition function. The effect of repetition is to add redundancy to the transmission, which helps combat the impairments to

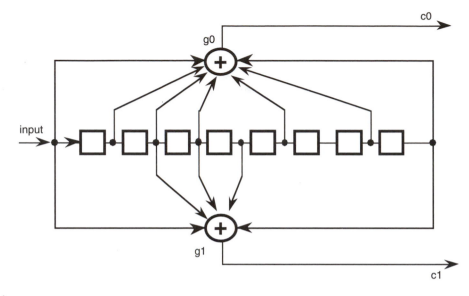

where:

K: Constraint length, and data length = K − 1
R: 1/2 = one input produces two outputs

Figure 6–16   Convolutional coding for sync, paging, and forward traffic channels (K = 9, 1/2 rate encoder example).

the bits that occur on the RF channel. Also, repetition provides "rate adaptation" in that it creates a constant input stream to the next process (19.2 or 28.8 ksps).

The sync, paging, and forward traffic channels employ symbol repetition. For the sync channel, each convolutional encoding signal is repeated one time before being placed in the block interleaving function. The paging and forward traffic channels operate slightly differently. Each convolutionally encoded symbol is repeated whenever the information rate is lower than 9600 bit/s (for 9600 bit/s, the code repetition rate is 1). If the code symbol is 4800 bit/s, the symbol is repeated one time (resulting in a code repetition rate of 2). If the data rate is 2400 bit/s, each code symbol is repeated three times (resulting in a code repetition rate of 4). For the 1200 bit/s rate, each symbol is repeated 7 times (resulting in a code repetition rate of 8). The idea is to provide a rate adaptation to have common input into the block interleaver. Consequently, these repetition operations create a standard symbol rate of 19.2 modulation symbols/second.

Block Interleaving

The next function, block interleaving, is a common operation on mobile air interfaces. Interleaving mitigates the effect of Rayleigh fading by preventing a specific transmission from occupying the physical channel for prolonged periods. The effect is to place the bits into noncontiguous slots on the channel. The IS-95 approach is to interleave 384 bits every 20 ms. After the sync, paging, and forward traffic channels have gone through the symbol repetition operation, they are placed in the block interleaving function.

Tables 6–2 and 6–3 show the input to the interleaver for the sync channel and the output from the interleaver. Remember that the sync channel operates at 1200 bit/s and each symbol is repeated one time for a total of two repetitions. The tables in this column are interpreted as: read column first and then row. For example, in Table 6–2, the input to the interleaver consists of the first input symbol positioned in column 1, rows 1 and 2; the second input symbol is positioned in column 1, rows 3 and 4; and so forth.

Table 6–3 shows the output. The table is read in the same manner as the first table, but notice that the symbols have been interleaved and spread across the array.

Table 6–2   Input to the Interleaver

1	9	17	25	33	41	49	57
1	9	17	25	33	41	49	57
2	10	18	26	34	42	50	58
2	10	18	26	34	42	50	58
3	11	19	27	35	43	51	59
3	11	19	27	35	43	51	59
4	12	20	28	36	44	52	60
4	12	20	28	36	44	52	60
5	13	21	29	37	45	53	61
5	13	21	29	37	45	53	61
6	14	22	30	38	46	54	62
6	14	22	30	38	46	54	62
7	15	23	31	39	47	55	63
7	15	23	31	39	47	55	63
8	16	24	32	40	48	56	64
8	16	24	32	40	48	56	64

Table 6–3   Output from the Interleaver

1	3	2	4	1	3	2	4
33	35	34	36	33	35	34	36
17	19	18	20	17	19	18	20
49	51	50	52	49	51	50	52
9	11	10	12	9	11	10	12
41	43	42	44	41	43	42	44
25	27	26	28	25	27	26	28
57	59	58	60	57	59	58	60
5	7	6	8	5	7	6	8
37	39	38	40	37	39	38	40
21	23	22	24	21	23	22	24
53	55	54	56	53	55	54	56
13	15	14	16	13	15	14	16
45	47	46	48	45	47	46	48
29	31	30	32	29	31	30	32
61	63	62	64	61	63	62	64

The sync channel block interleaver spans 26.666 ms, which is equivalent to 128 modulation symbols at the rate of 4800 symbols/second.

Scrambling

The interleaved slots are fed to the scrambler, shown in Figure 6–17, which alters the bitstream with a long code PN generator. The input to this function is the user's electronic serial number (ESN). In the United States, the Federal Communications Commission (FCC) requires an ESN to be used for each mobile station in the cellular system. The ESN is a 32-bit binary number that uniquely identifies a cellular unit. The ESN for a mobile station is established by the manufacturer at the factory and is not supposed to be easily altered. It is burned into ROM so that circuitry providing the number is secure and any attempt to change the serial number is supposed to make the mobile station unusable.

The data scrambling operation is performed on the output of the interleaver symbols with modulo-2 addition operations (see Figure 6–17). The operation is performed with the binary value of the long code PN chip operating at a 1.2288 MHz clock rate. However, only the first output of every 64 bits is used for the scrambling, which results in a 19.2 symbol/second rate. This operation is performed by the decimator.

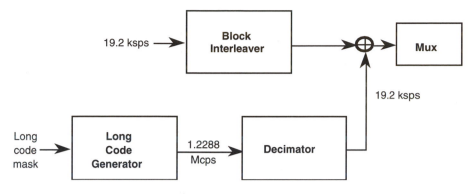

Figure 6–17 Scrambling.

By using the user's ESN, the user's traffic is uniquely identified from that of other users. This ESN is made available to the network when the MS sends its handshaking information on the uplink access channel (in an access message).

Scrambling prevents the sending of repetitive patterns on the radio link, which in turn reduces the probability of users sending at peak power at the same time, which would degrade the RF channel, due to power spikes. The randomizing is achieved by using the ESN, which itself must be different from other ESNs.

Power Control and Puncturing

The symbol bit function is used to transmit a power control subchannel on the forward traffic channel (see Figure 6–18). This subchannel transmits a 1 or 0 bit over 1.25 ms to produce an 800 bit/s transfer rate. These bits replace (on a periodic basis) two consecutive forward traffic channel modulation symbols. This "bit stealing" operation does not noticeably affect the quality of the traffic channel.

The subchannel is used to direct the mobile station to increase or decrease its output power level. The base station estimates the received power strength of the mobile station by examining its transmissions on the reverse traffic channel (over a 1.25 ms period, which is equivalent to 6 modulation symbols). It then sends the power control directions to the mobile station on the power control subchannel (with a 0 to indicate an increase in power and a 1 to indicate a decrease in power).

The power control bits are placed in the forward channel after the scrambling operation. The bits are inserted by symbol puncturing, which refers to modulation symbols being replaced by power control bits. Since

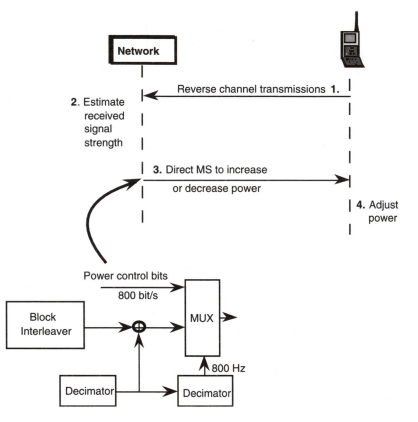

Figure 6–18 Puncturing to produce the power control sub-channel.

the bits are punctured into the stream after encoding, repetition, interleaving, and scrambling, there is very little delay in the processing (and using) these bits at the transmitter (and likewise, the same for the receiver). This approach allows the mobile station to react rapidly to the base station's commands.

Power control bits are inserted by replacing 1 bit for rate set 1 and 2 bits for rate set 2 for every 24 modulation symbols from the interleaver.

Orthogonal Spreading

The next step in the process is orthogonal spreading, which entails applying an orthogonal Walsh code to the bit stream. Walsh codes W8 through W63 are used to identify each downlink traffic channel. The full bit rate (called the chip rate) on the air interface is 1.228 Mbit/s, which is the result of spreading the 19.2 kbit/s input stream with a 64 bit Walsh code ($19.2 \times 64 = 1.228$ Mbit/s).

The results of the Walsh code operation are used as input into the quadrature spreading process, which further codes the signal with a PN sequence that is uniquely associated with a base station. In fact, all base stations in the system use the same PN sequence, but each base station uses one of 512 offsets to keep each base station uniquely identified. The signal is then filtered and modulated onto the air interface.

Figure 6–19 shows an example of the orthogonal modulation process. As just stated, each 6 symbol block is replaced with the 64-ary Walsh chip.

Quadrature Spreading

After the orthogonal spreading, each channel is then quadrature spread with a spreading sequence of length 2^{15}, for a 32,768 PN chip. The chip rate for the sequences is 1.2288 Mcps. Two PN sequences are used, the I and Q quadratures.

The pilot PN sequence period is the quadrature sequence length of 32,768 divided by the chip rate of 1,228,800 for the pilot PN sequence to equal a pilot PN sequence period of 26.666 . . . ms. Therefore, every 2 seconds, 75 PN sequence repetitions occur. The output of the quadrature spreading is then mapped into the phases as shown in Figure 6–20.

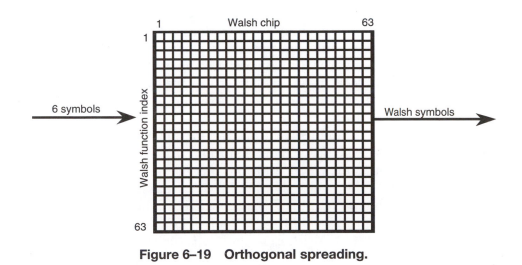

Figure 6–19 Orthogonal spreading.

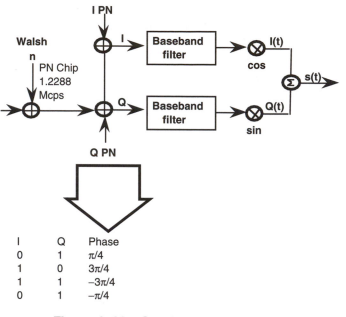

I	Q	Phase
0	1	$\pi/4$
1	0	$3\pi/4$
1	1	$-3\pi/4$
0	1	$-\pi/4$

Figure 6–20   Quadrature spreading.

The Reverse Channel

On the reverse channel, the MS vocoding, convolutional coding, symbol repetition, and block interleaving operations are similar to those operations on the forward channel, with the differences summarized in Figure 6–21. The other functions differ, as explained here.

The orthogonal modulation process replaces the traffic bits with a Walsh code. As stated earlier, the traffic stream at this point is 28.8 bit/s, and each 6-symbol block in the stream is replaced with a 64-chip Walsh code (one of 64 mutually orthogonal functions), producing a 307.2 kcps rate ($28.8 / 6 * 64 = 307.2$).

The data burst randomization process is implemented to help in reducing interference from other mobile stations. To explain why this operation is useful, remember that multiple MS users are on the same frequency spectrum. However, the actual transmission rate varies in accordance with the input rate. The transmitter divides the 20 ms frame into sixteen 1.25 ms time slots (power control groups), and uses an algorithm to distribute the MS's data into all the 1.25 slots, and thus throughout the 20 ms frame. This approach has the effect of spreading power and reducing potential interference on the channel.

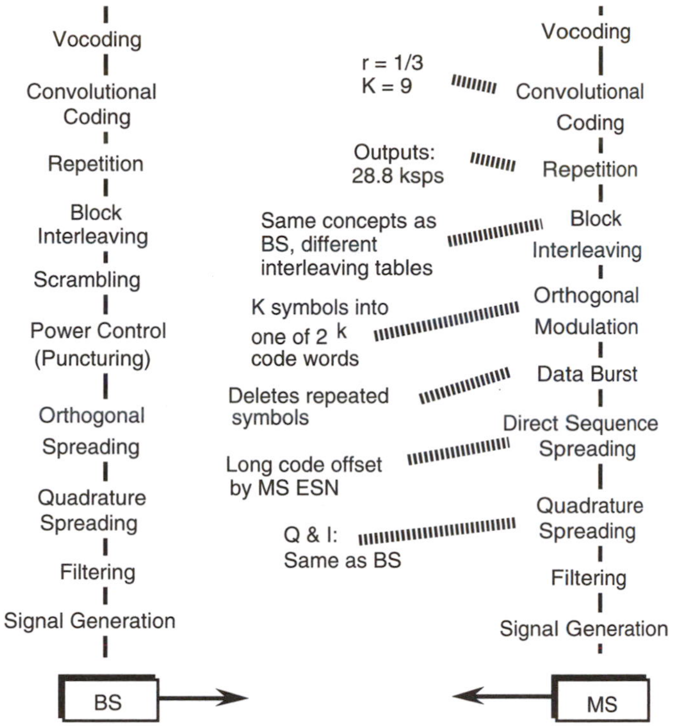

Figure 6–21   Major functions on the reverse channel.

The direct sequence spreading function uses a long code mask that is derived from the mobile station's ESN, therefore making the transmission unique to the user. This operation distinguishes mobile stations in that it is "the code" in code division multiple access.

The quadrature spreading operation uses a short PN code with a 0 offset. Therefore, the combination of the direct sequence spreading and quadrature spreading uniquely identify each user.

AN ANALYSIS OF THE CHANNELS

During our analysis of IS-95 and CDMA, I have made reference to the channels many times, but I have not described how they are created. This part of the chapter covers this subject and shows how the operations just described, such as convolutional coding and so on play a role in the creation of these channels.

The Pilot Channel

The pilot channel is transmitted continuously by the base station on each CDMA frequency. About 15 to 20% of the total power in the cell is expended on the pilot channel. The base station uses the time offset of the short PN sequence to identify the forward CDMA channel. Each specific pilot channel is identified with an offset index (of 0–511 inclusive). The identification of each pilot occurs with an offset in chips and is performed for each given pilot PN sequence reference from the 0 shift pilot PN sequence, which equals the index value multiplied by 64. As an example, if the pilot PN sequence offset index is 12, then the PN sequence offset is 12×64, which equals 768 PN chips.

The pilot channel consists of all 0s and is coded with the Walsh code function 0 (see Figure 6–22). In order to differentiate between pilot channels in adjacent cell sites, the same quadrature spreading code is applied to the traffic but with different offset values. This approach allows the mobile station to search for the synchronization information by a single pass through all code phases. The mobile station detects the strongest signal, which should yield the best cell site on which to camp. The quadrature spreading code uses the I PN and Q PN and provides for 512 possible offsets. The system must use different offsets in neighboring cells.

In summary, the pilot channel is differentiated by the use of the Walsh function 0 and each pilot channel in the system is differentiated by an offset of the same quadrature spreading code.

The Sync Channel

The sync channel is transmitted in every cell and is used by the mobile station to obtain identification information about the cellular system and a cell site-specific PN offset information. One message is sent on this

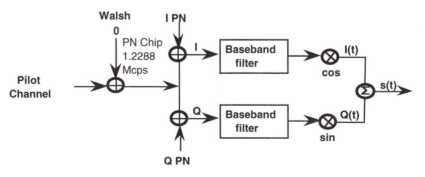

Figure 6–22   Pilot channel.

channel, called the sync channel message, and it is sent continuously. The message contains the system time, the long code state, the protocol revision, as well as information on the paging channel.

Like the pilot channel, each base station uses the same quadrature spreading code but with one of 512 offsets. The sync channel operates at 1200 bit/s with Walsh code 32 applied to the information, which is then spread with the quadrature I PN and Q PN. Figure 6–23 shows the sync channel components and functions.

The Paging Channels

Paging channels are stated as being optional within a cell and, if used, are transmitted in every cell. I know of no situation where they are not used. They are identified with Walsh codes 1–7. They are further scrambled with a long code, specific only to paging channels. The mobile stations decode the information by recognizing the code mask and Walsh function. The paging channels operate either at 4800 bit/s or 9600 bit/s (see Figure 6–24). As with the pilot and sync channels, each BS in a cell applies one of 512 offsets to the signal to differentiate between cell sites.

Paging channels contain messages for one or more mobile stations. One purpose of the page is to notify the mobile station of an incoming call, and it is usually sent from more than one cell site.

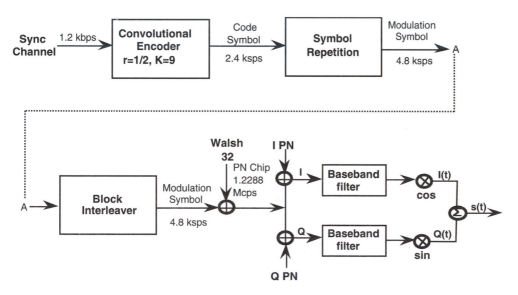

Figure 6–23   The sync channel.

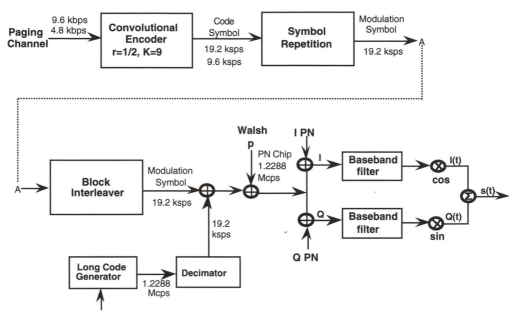

Figure 6–24   Paging channels.

In addition to conveying information about a call, the paging channel also provides a wide array of system parameters dealing with registration information and power information. The paging channels also contain information on the access channels that are used by the mobile station on the uplink interface.

Forward Traffic Channels

The forward traffic channels are identified with a Walsh function (see Figure 6–25). A vocoder can produce bit rates ranging from 1200 bit/s to 13000 bit/s. Whatever the vocoder input may be, the convolutional encoding and repetition function produces a 19.2 ksps rate. When applied to the 64-bit Walsh function, the resultant rate is 1.228 Mchip/s. The repetition rate of the chip operations is 32,768 chips every 26.66 ms.

It should prove helpful to distinguish:

Bits: raw information
Symbols: coded information
Chips: spreading information

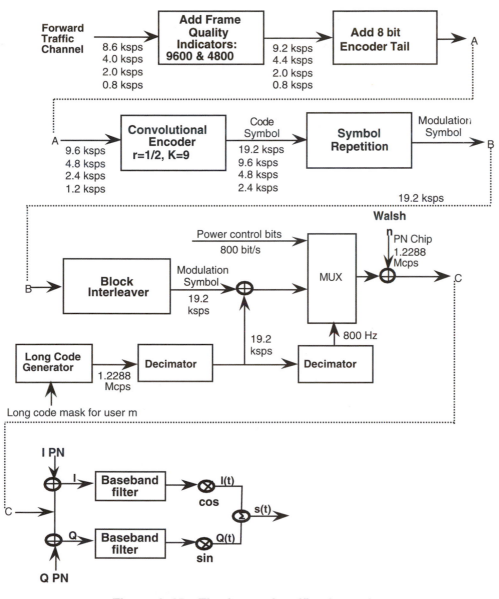

Figure 6–25 The forward traffic channels.

Reverse Traffic Channels

Figure 6–26 shows the composition of the reverse traffic channel. User traffic on the reverse channel is identified by a user-specific long code sequence based on the user's ESN. Access channels are identified by a unique long-code sequence. The uplink interface supports up to 32 ac-

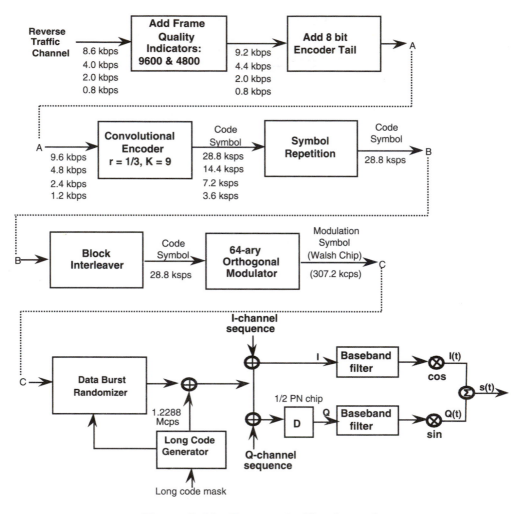

Figure 6–26   Reverse traffic channel.

cess channels and 62 traffic channels. Each access channel is associated with a downlink paging channel. In earlier discussions, I pointed out that several of the operations of the digital traffic on the reverse channel are different from those on the forward channel.

The Access Channel

The access channel is used by the mobile station to communicate with the network, so it operates on the reverse channel. Up to 32 access channels are supported. The access channel operates at 4.8 kbit/s, and can be used by more than one mobile station. The mobile stations contend for the

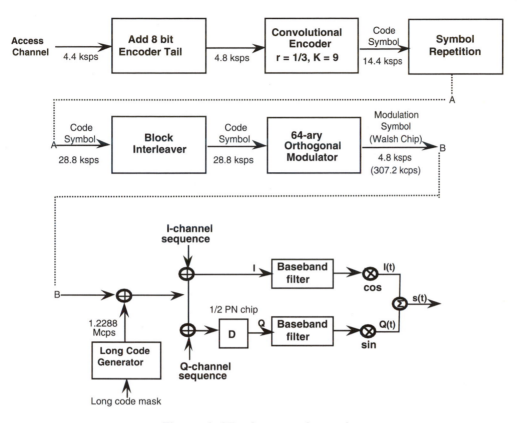

Figure 6–27   Access channel.

access channel usage, so a contention resolution procedure is employed to ensure that the mobile stations do gain access to this channel.

Figure 6–27 shows the operations that occur on the access channel. In a manner similar to the other channels, the access channel provides convolutional coding, symbol repetition, and interleaving. After these operations are performed, the bits are passed to the orthogonal modulator and are spread using a long code generated by an access channel address mask. Like the other channels, the access channel is quadrature spread with I and Q PN sequences with 0 offset.

THE DATA LINK LAYER

The IS-95 data link layer is similiar to the layer 2 operations of TDMA systems described in other chapters. One of the more important functions of this layer is message acknowledgment, and this part of the chapter explains this subject (see Figure 6–28).

The message acknowledgment procedures are used to ensure that the exchange of control and signaling messages between the mobile station and base station occurs correctly. The operation is a conventional positive acknowledgment operation and uses a field in several messages: ACK_TYPE (acknowledgment of the sent address type, ADDR_TYPE) ACK_SEQ (acknowledgment sequence number), MSG_SEQ (message sequence number), ACK_REQ (acknowledgment required), and VALID_ACK (valid acknowledgment) to support this overall operation. These fields operate at the IS-95 layer 2, which is in keeping with conventional ACKing and NAKing procedures on a communications channel.

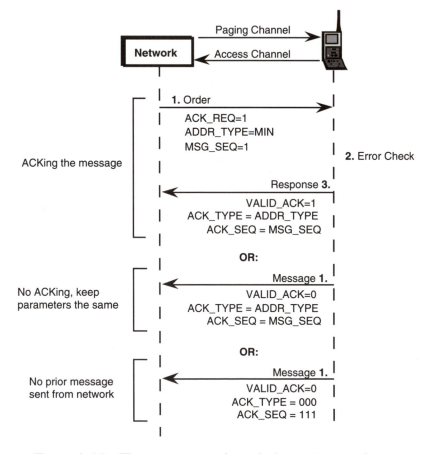

Figure 6–28   The message acknowledgment procedures.

The mobile station informs the base station that it is sending a message with an acknowledgment by setting the VALID_ACK field to 1 in the message. In addition, it sets the ACK_TYPE and ACK_SEQ fields to the values of the ADDR_TYPE and MSG_SEQ fields of the message that is being acknowledged. The ADDR_TYPE field informs the recipient of the type of address in the message (MIN, ESN, IMSI, or broadcast).

To acknowledge a page message or slotted page message, the mobile station sets the ACK_SEQ field equal to the MSG_SEQ field of the record addressed to the mobile station. For a general page message, the mobile station sends the ACK_SEQ field equal to the message MSG_SEQ field of the record addressed to the mobile station.

If the mobile station is not sending an acknowledgment in the message, it simply sets the VALID_ ACK field to 0. The mobile station is required to acknowledge any message sent to it in which this message has the ACK_REQ field set to 1.

In addition, these various sequence numbers and identifiers provide sufficient information for the mobile station to detect duplicate messages. Duplicate messages must be discarded by the mobile station.

Figure 6–28 shows examples of the acknowledgment procedures, with three scenarios or acknowledgment procedures. In the first scenario, the mobile station receives an order message from the base station. The base station has set ACK_REQ to 1, (event 1 of the first scenario), which means the mobile station must respond. The mobile station performs an error check (event 2), and responds in event 3, by coding the fields in the message in accordance with the rules discussed earlier.

In the second scenario, the mobile station is sending a message on its own, and is not responding to a message. So, it sets ACK_REQ to 0, to indicate that it is not acknowledging anything, and keeps the other fields as the same values as before.

If the network has not sent any messages to the mobile station (scenario 3) and the mobile station wishes to send a message, it sets ACK_REQ to 0, sets ACK_TYPE to 000, and ACK_SEQ to 111.

LAYER 3 OPERATIONS

The sole purpose of layers 1 and 2 of IS-95 are to support layer 3, and the purpose of layer 3 is to provide all the requisite procedures to allow a mobile user to make a call. As we shall see, the procedures are numerous and varied.

An effective way to analyze the "behavior" of layer 3 is to examine the states (operations) that a mobile station traverses (executes) during a call. Figure 6–29 shows the states (the substates and procedures are explained later with the associated states). The call processing operation at the mobile station consists of the following states:

- Mobile station initialization state: The mobile station searches, selects, and acquires a system (A or B), and decides on a primary/secondary CDMA channel number.

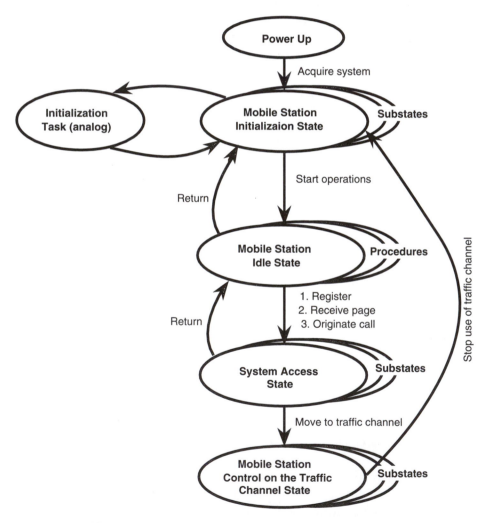

Figure 6–29   Mobile station call processing states.

- Mobile station idle state: Once having acquired the system, the mobile station monitors the paging channel.
- System access state: The mobile station uses the access channel to send messages to the base station.
- Mobile station control on the traffic channel state: The mobile station communicates with the base station on the traffic channels.

Initialization State

The mobile station initialization state consists of four substates, executed in the order shown in Figure 6–30. A description of each of these substates follows.

The system determination substate is used to determine which system to use (System A or System B) and whether analog only or CDMA operations will be employed. It will also determine the primary or secondary channel to be employed (for System A, primary channel is 283 and secondary channel is 384; for System B, primary channel is 691 and secondary channel is 777). The channel number is stored at the mobile station in a variable called CDMACH, for CDMA channel.

The ability to use System A or System B only, or select for one or the other is determined by the A and B operators. Generally, the mobile station is programmed to interwork with one provider. However, arrangements may exist in an area (a city, for example) where the operators agree to "share" a subscriber. This situation may arise if one operator does not have coverage in a certain geographical area, and another does. As another possibility, the spotty coverage of IS-95 at this time may require that operators agree to support the mobile station roaming through non-CDMA areas, with the ability to shift back to analog operations, if necessary.

Of course, during these operations, the mobile station will determine if the system is an analog or CDMA operation. If it is analog, the mobile station will enter the conventional AMPS-type procedures. If it is a CDMA system, the mobile station will enter the pilot channel acquisition substate.

The pilot channel acquisition substate is the operation in which the mobile station acquires the pilot channel of the selected CDMA provider (System A or B). The station tunes to the channel number that it has stored in a variable called CDMACH and searches for the pilot channel. The station turns on a timer when it starts this operation (T_{20}) to ensure the operation occurs on a timely basis. If the pilot channel is acquired

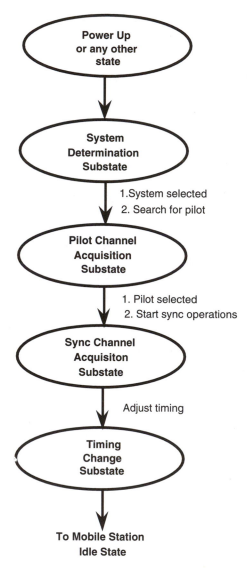

Figure 6–30 Mobile station initialization state.

within the timer period, the mobile station enters the sync channel acquisition substate.

In the sync channel acquisition substate, the mobile station receives a message on the sync channel containing information about configuration requirements and timing. Upon entering this substate, the mobile station sets its code channel for the sync channel (code = 32). During this process, the mobile station checks fields in the message to ensure the IS-95 version is compatible (the protocol revision level).

If the mobile station can accept the message (and it should be able to do so, since it can simply ignore any fields at the end of the sync channel message that are not part of the known protocol revision), it extracts and stores the following information in the message:

- Protocol revision level
- The system identification (SID)
- The network identification (NID), which identifies a network (or a part) of the SID's cellular system
- Pilot PN sequence offset (PILOT_PN), which is used to identify the base station
- Long code state (LC_STATE), which is used for scrambling on the forward channel and spreading on the reverse channel.
- System time (SYS_TIME), and optionally local offset from system time, and so on.
- Paging channel (PRAT) data rate

After these operations, the mobile station enters the timing change substate.

In the timing change substate, the mobile station uses the parameters in the sync channel message to adjust its timing and synchronize its long code timing and system timing to those of the base station. It uses the PILOT_PN, LC_STATE, and SYS_TIME values in this message for these operations. The mobile station synchronizes its long code timing to the network's long code timing based on LC_STATE, and its system timing based on the network's system timing based on SYS_TIME.

In addition, during this substate, the mobile station sets a value in a parameter called PAGECH to identify the paging channel. Also, the mobile station initializes several sequence number parameters that are used for sequencing different types of messages (which are used later).

The mobile station then enters into the mobile station idle state.

Idle State

The mobile station idle state entails the mobile station monitoring the paging channel to receive messages, receive incoming calls, and so on. Upon entering this state, it sets its code channel to PAGECH, and uses the PRAT to set its paging channel data rate. It then performs the ten procedures listed in Figure 6–31.

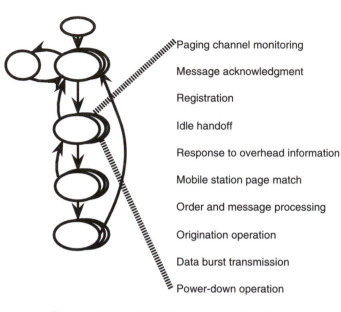

Paging channel monitoring

Message acknowledgment

Registration

Idle handoff

Response to overhead information

Mobile station page match

Order and message processing

Origination operation

Data burst transmission

Power-down operation

Figure 6–31   Mobile station idle state.

During this state, the mobile station can receive messages, incoming calls. It can also initiate a call, as well as transmit a message. Registration can also occur during the mobile station idle state.

Paging Channel Monitoring.   The paging channel monitoring procedures define how a mobile station monitors the paging channel. There are two modes of operation for this procedure. The non-slotted mode for this operation means that the paging slots are not assigned to the mobile station, which therefore must monitor all the slots. In contrast, the slotted mode of operation means that slots are specifically assigned to the mobile station and it need only monitor specific slots on the channel.

While operating in the slotted mode, the paging channel is monitored either one or two slots per slot cycle. The mobile station is also permitted to monitor additional slots to receive broadcast messages as another option.

Figure 6–32 shows an example of a mobile station monitoring slot number 6 on a slot cycle length of 1.28 seconds. The slot is identified to the mobile station during registrations or an operation such as the transfer of the origination message or a page response message. These operations permit the mobile station to specify its preferred slot cycle using a

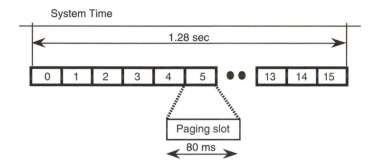

System Time

1.28 sec

| 0 | 1 | 2 | 3 | 4 | 5 | • • | 13 | 14 | 15 |

Paging slot

80 ms

Figure 6–32   The paging channel monitoring procedures.

field in the registration, origination, or page response message called the SLOT_CYCLE INDEX.

Since this example shows the mobile station monitoring slot 6, it is set up to monitor another slot, 16 slots later, which would be slot 22 (a value called SLOT_NUM) is used to number all the slots in a paging channel.

The paging channel can be coded with 19 different messages, such as page, channel assignment, order, and so on. The network sends the specific message, depending on specific circumstances. In turn, the mobile station responds to the specific message on the access channel.

Message Acknowledgment.   This procedure was described earlier when we examined layer 2 of IS-95. Therefore, we need not revisit it again.

Reregistration.   Even though a mobile station may have registered previously, when it is in an idle state certain timers may have expired or become disabled. In this case, the mobile station is required to initiate idle registration procedures. One of the uses of registration is for the mobile station to inform the network of its location. This eventually leads to reduced paging operations because all cells need not be paged when the system has information for the mobile station. There are two broad categories of the registration. Autonomous registration occurs when the mobile station initiates the registration. In contrast, non-autonomous registrations are initiated by the network.

Within the autonomous registrations, there are five categories of registration types (and these are all governed with rules in Section 6.6.5.5.2 of IS-95 specification, if more detailed information is needed).

Power-up registration is the first type and occurs when the mobile station first powers-up the system. *Power-down* registration occurs when the mobile station powers down. The third type of registration is *timer-based*. This situation can occur when a power-up or initialization timer has expired or is disabled. The fourth type of registration is called *distance-spaced registration* and the mobile station enters this procedure when its distance exceeds a certain threshold from the base station. Finally, *zone-based registration* occurs by the mobile station registering within a group of cells. This concept allows the system to send pages to a zone and then the zone will cover the cell or cells in which the mobile station is registered.

Non-autonomous registrations are categorized into four types. The *parameter-change registration* procedure is used for the mobile station to register with the system if certain parameters are changed in an operations. At any time, the network can use the second type of non-autonomous registration called *ordered registration*. As the name implies, the mobile station must register with the system when it is ordered to do so by the network. The third type of non-autonomous registration is called *implicit registration*. This is simply an ongoing registration that is performed by the network by receiving ongoing information from the mobile station, typically, in a page response message or in an origination message. The final type of non-autonomous registration is called the *traffic channel registration* and this registration occurs during the time the mobile station is actually assigned a traffic channel. Through the exchange of information between the mobile station and the network, these registration procedures occur.

Handoffs.   IS-95 defines four types of handoff. The first three listed here are performed when the mobile station is on a traffic channel. The fourth is performed when the mobile station is idle and monitoring the paging channel. They are: (a) hard handoff, (b) soft handoff, (c) softer handoff, (d) idle handoff.

The idle handoff procedure occurs when a mobile station moves from one base station coverage area to another while it is in the mobile station idle state (see Figure 6–33). The operation occurs when the mobile station detects a pilot channel from a base station that is stronger than its current base station.

The mobile station continuously searches for the strongest pilot channel within the assigned CDMA spectrum. This occurs while it is monitoring the paging channel. The search performance criteria is not defined in IS-95, but in IS-98, recommended minimum performance standards for Dual-Mode Wide-Band Spread Spectrum Cellular Mobile Stations.

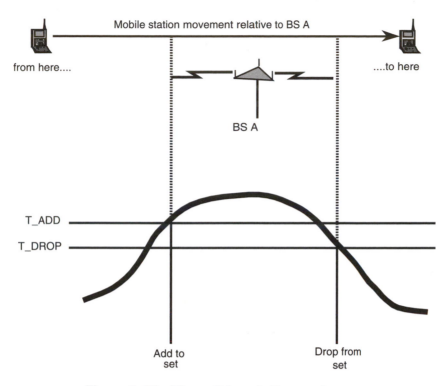

Figure 6–33   The soft handoff procedures.

The idle handoff procedures require that the mobile station operate in a non-slotted mode until it has received at least one valid message on the new paging channel. After that, it can move to a slotted mode of operation as discussed earlier in this seminar.

The new base station must be listed in a neighbor list message from the old base station in order for the mobile station to determine the actions needed to transition to the new base station. Otherwise, if this base station is not available in this list, the mobile station can perform handoff operation with other procedures.

Response to Overhead Information.   The mobile station may receive several overhead messages on the paging channel. These messages are (a) system parameters message, (b) access parameters message, (c) neighbor list message, (d) CDMA channel list message, (e) extended system parameter message, and (f) global service redirection message.

The mobile station's response to these messages vary based on the message. As a general statement, the purpose of these messages is to provide information to the mobile station regarding system parameters, neighbor lists, CDMA channel lists, paging channels, SID, NID, registration zones, base station identifiers, base station class, power up and power down parameters, base station latitude, base station longitude, various parameters for timers, power requirements for the ongoing operation, and authentication values.

The operations at the mobile station to process and react to these parameters vary widely in the seminar leader will take you through some examples during the discussion.

Mobile Station Page Match.   IS-95 defines three messages that are transmitted on the paging channel. They are (a) the page message, (b) the slotted page message, and (c) the general page message. These messages are used to support the mobile station page match operation, which is performed whenever the mobile station receives a paging message. If this message contains the mobile stations IMSI, the mobile station must transmit the page response message on the access channel. In addition, the mobile station may be configured to receive broadcast messages, in which case the mobile station must also search for a data burst message, and, if this is the case, the mobile station performs a broadcast page procedure described in EIA IS-637.

This operation entails a check to make certain that certain page match parameters are consistent between the network and the mobile station. One important operation is the mobile station comparing its IMSI with the MIN in each record of the page message. If MIN1 and MIN2 are present in a record and both MIN1 and MIN2 match the mobile station's storage for IMSI_S1 and IMSI_S2, a successful match has occurred.

Order and Message Processing.   During the mobile station order message processing operation procedures, the mobile station must process all messages except overhead messages and page messages, which were explained earlier. As discussed before, the mobile station performs the address matching and if the address matches, the mobile station must then process the message. Otherwise, the message is simply ignored. The message will contain information if it requires acknowledgment (also discussed earlier) in which case the mobile station will acknowledge the message. The following list is a description of the messages that can be received during this operation. The discussion of each of these messages is beyond our general overview. Some of the titles of the messages is descriptive enough to describe their functions. For a more information, the reader should refer directly to the specification in Section 6.6.2.2.4:

- Abbreviated alert order
- Audit order
- Authentication challenge message
- Base station acknowledgment order
- Base station challenge confirmation order
- Channel assignment message
- Data burst message
- Feature notification message
- Local order control order message
- Lock until power cycled order message
- Maintenance required order
- Registration accepted order
- Registration rejected order
- Registration request order
- Service redirection
- SSD update
- Unlock order

Origination Operation. The mobile station origination operation procedures are executed when the mobile station is activated by the customer to begin a call. When this occurs, the mobile station enters the update overhead information substate or the system access state, discussed in other parts of this seminar.

Data Burst Transmission. The data burst message procedures are optional. If this procedure is supported the mobile station reacts to the user directing it to transmit a data burst message. Once this is indicated to the mobile station by the user, the mobile station then enters the update overhead information substate of the system access state, discussed in other parts of this seminar.

Power Down. The mobile station power-down procedures are executed when the user of the mobile station directs the mobile station to power down.

System Access State

In this state, the mobile station sends messages to the base station on the access channel(s) and receives messages on the paging channel. During this state, the following substates are possible:

- Update overhead information substate: The mobile station monitors the paging channel until it has a current set of overhead messages.
- Mobile station origination attempt substate: The mobile station sends an Origination Message to the base station.
- Page response substate: The mobile station sends a Page Response Message to the base station.
- Mobile station order/message response substate: The mobile station sends a response to a message received from the base station.
- Registration access substate: The mobile station sends a Registration Message to the base station.
- Mobile station message transmission substate: The mobile station sends a Data Burst Message to the base station.

PUTTING IT ALL TOGETHER

Let us see if we can tie together some of the major aspects of IS-95 with several general examples. Figure 6–34 provides a summary of the operations and message exchanges that occur during a start up operation across the air interface. The mobile station seeks and acquires the pilot channel as shown in events 1 and 2. After successful acquisition of the pilot channel, the mobile station receives the sync channel and adjusts its timing parameters. These operations are shown in events 3 and 4. Next, the mobile station is ready to receive administrative and operations information, which is provided on a paging channel shown in event 5.

Upon receiving this information, if the mobile station wishes to make a call (which in this example it does), in event 6 it creates an origination message and sends this across an access channel in event 7. The network analyzes this message and creates the channel assignment message (event 8) and sends this across the paging channel in event 9.

Next, upon successful reception of the channel assignment message (in event 10) the mobile station begins sending on the reverse channel (event 11) the preamble pattern. Following the reception of the preamble pattern on the reverse traffic channel, in event 12, the base station creates an acknowledgment order message and forwards this in event 13 on the forward traffic channel. This prompts the mobile station to begin sending null channel data on the reverse channel as shown in events 14 and 15. Finally, in event 16, upon successful completion of event 15, the base station creates a service option order message and sends this message across the forward traffic channel in event 17.

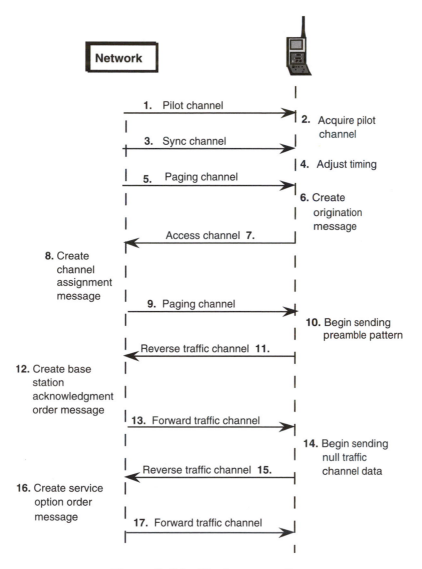

Figure 6–34   Startup operations.

This completes the initial startup operations for a call origination emanating from the mobile station.

Figure 6–35 shows the operations that occur when the mobile station receives a call. The events in Figure 6–34 are still relevant in regard to acquiring the pilot channel and synchronizing and receiving information on the paging channel. This figure assumes these events have occurred successfully. Thereafter, events 1 and 2 show that the network sends the mobile station an alert with information message that is sent

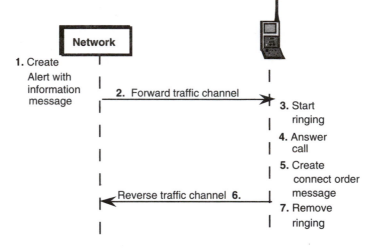

Figure 6–35   Call termination at mobile station.

on the forward traffic channel. Upon receiving this message, in events 3, 4, and 5 the mobile station starts ringing the terminal set.

If the user answers the call, the mobile station creates the connect order message and in event 6, sends this message onto the reverse traffic channel. About the same time in event 7, the mobile station removes the ringing from the handset. Upon receiving the connect order message, the network will then begin sending the user traffic to the mobile station.

STATUS OF CDMA IN THE MARKETPLACE

CDMA is now being installed in many locations throughout the world, and it is proving to be more of a challenge than many people thought. In the 1980s, CDMA advocates stated that CDMA would provide 40 times the capacity of AMPS. These figures were revised, and in the early 1990s, Qualcomm used the numbers between 10 to 20 times AMPS systems.

As systems came into place, experience shows (at least, at the present time) that these figures are still too optimistic. One of the earlier systems is in South Korea, which reports an increase of 6 to 8 times the capacity of AMPS.

In the United States, Lucent (summer, 1997) stated that the network operator should expect no more than 6-fold increase over AMPS. Other operators have reported the following:

- Sprint PCS: Experiencing 8 times the capacity of AMPS
- PrimeCo: Experiencing 8 to 12 times the capacity of AMPS
- Most are stating about 6 times AMPS in relatively sparse densities

But as of this writing, IS-95 is proving difficult to tune for good coverage. On 800 MHz systems, network operators report interference from neighboring AMPS channels. Some now think CDMA will require double the number of cell sites as stated in previous specifications.

The problem is not that CDMA is a poor technology. The problem of the overblown estimates means that carrier business plans are off by several orders of magnitude. Indeed, as the industry learns more about this relatively new technology, it is certain that the technology will become a dominant mobile wireless air interface.

SUMMARY

In the past few years, CDMA has gained a significant part of the second generation mobile wireless marketplace, especially in North America. CDMA's main problems stem not from its technical attributes, but from the fact that these attributes have not met their expectations and the fact that the theoretical capacity of CDMA has not matched its real capacity. That is not the fault of the technology; it is the fault of human expectations, and the marketing aspect goes along with any technology.

As we learn more about CDMA, and as we migrate to new CDMA generations, the furore will go away and CDMA will become a dominant air interface technology.

APPENDIX 6A   THE CDMA FAMILY

Although our primary subject for this chapter is IS-95, for the reader who is working on designing, marketing, or implementing a CDMA system, there are a number of other specifications, published by the Telecommunications Industries Association/Electronic Industries Association (TIA/EIA), that are also support IS-95. Table 6A–1 should be helpful to you. Some of the specifications in Table 6A–1 are also used with other air interfaces.

Table 6A–1   The CDMA Family from TIA/EIA

Specification Number	Title
IS-95	Mobile Station-Base Station Compatibility Standard for Dual-Mode Wideband Spread Spectrum Cellular System
IS-96	Speech Service Option Standard for Wideband Spread Spectrum Digital Cellular System
IS-97	Recommended Minimum Performance Standards for Base Stations Supporting Dual-Mode Wideband Spread Spectrum Digital Cellular Mobile Stations
IS-98	Recommended Minimum Performance Standards for Dual-Mode Wideband Spread Spectrum Cellular Mobile Stations
IS-99	Data Service Option Standard for Wideband Spread Spectrum Digital Cellular Systems
IS-124	Cellular Radio Telecommunications Intersystem Non-Signaling Data Communications
IS-125	Recommended Minimum Performance Standard for Digital Cellular Wideband Spread Spectrum Speech Service Option 1
IS-126	Service Option 2: Mobile Station Loopback Service Option
IS-127	Enhanced Variable Rate Codec, Speech Service Option 3 for Wideband Spread Spectrum Digital Cellular Systems
IS-634	MSC-BS Interface for Public 800 MHz
IS-637	Short Message Services for Wideband Spread Spectrum Digital Cellular Systems
IS-657	Packet Data Service Option Standards for Wideband Spread Spectrum Digital Cellular Systems
IS-658	Data Services Interworking Function Interface for Wideband Spread Spectrum Digital Cellular Systems
IS-683	Over-the-Air Service Provisioning of Mobile Stations in Wideband Spread Spectrum Digital Cellular Systems
SP 3383/ J-STD-019	Recommended Minimum Performance Requirements for Base Stations Supporting 1.8 to 2.0 GHz Code Division Multiple Access (CDMA) Personal Communications Systems
SP 3384/ J-STD-008	Personal Station Base Station Compatibility Requirements for 1.8 to 2.0 GHz Code Division Multiple Access (CDMA) Personal Communications Systems
SP 3385/ J-STD-018	Recommended Minimum Performance Requirements for 1.8 to 2.0 GHz Code Division Multiple Access (CDMA) Personal Stations
TSB 29	International Implementation of Cellular Radiotelephone Systems Compliant with ANSI/EIA/TIA-533
TIA/EIA 533	Mobile Station—Land Station Compatibility Specification
TIA/EIA 660	Uniform Dialing Procedures and Call Processing Treatment for Radio Cellular Telecommunications
TIA/EIA	Cellular Features Description

7

IS-41-C and IS-634

This chapter examines IS-41-C, the protocol that operates on the network side of North American mobile and wireless networks. The chapter begins with a description of the architecture of IS-41-C and its relationship to the Open Systems Interconnection (OSI) Model. This discussion is followed by a brief explanation of the bearer services (X.25 and SS7) that support the exchange of IS-41-C messages. The remainder of the chapter provides some examples of IS-41-C operations, just a few of the many possible features available in this protocol.

A large part of this chapter is devoted to the security/privacy aspects of IS-41-C, principally with authenticating the mobile station user. Authentication entails the exchange of messages between the user and the network. The goal is to verify that the user is who the user claims to be. In some situations, the network can also be authenticated. Since these IS-41-C operations are supportive of all North American air interfaces, I devote considerable space to this subject.

The later part of the chapter provides examples of how IS-41-C supports registration, roaming, call features, and other MAP procedures. The chapter concludes with an introduction to IS-634, a specification that defines the operations between the MSC and BS. This standard is quite new, and is just seeing deployment in the industry. For the air interface operations in this chapter, I use IS-54-B examples, unless otherwise stated.

One last point is made before we move into the material. IS-41-C specifies over 100 distinct operations, and all entail the transport of multiple messages between the MSCs and their associated databases. Our goal in this chapter is to understand the architecture of IS-41-C and its major operations. Therefore, my approach is to show several of these operations in a general way and encourage you to obtain the actual specifications for more details. The same approach is taken with IS-634.

THE IS-41-C SPECIFICATION

IS-41-C is published by the Telecommunications Industry Association (TIA). It permits the interworking of different vendor equipment (by placing the IS-41-C protocol suite in each vendor's product). IS-41-C was published originally in February 1988 as Revision A. It has since undergone revisions B and now C. With each revision, it has become more powerful and versatile. With the current release, it now supports the AMPS, IS-54-B, IS-136, and IS-95 air interfaces. For the reader who wishes to learn about the details of IS-41-C, Table 7–1 lists the specifications as published by the TIA/EIA.

THE IS-41-C MODEL

IS-41-C exhibits a topology and model that is quite similar to the network side of GSM. Figure 7–1 depicts the functional entities of

Table 7–1   The IS-41-C Specifications

IS-41-C.1	Cellular Radiotelecommunications Intersystem Operations: Functional Overview
IS-41-C.2	Cellular Radiotelecommunications Intersystem Operations: Intersystem Handoff Information Flows
IS-41-C.3	Cellular Radiotelecommunications Intersystem Operations: Automatic Roaming Information Flows
IS-41-C.4	Cellular Radiotelecommunications Intersystem Operations: Operations, Administration, and Maintenance Information Flows and Procedures
IS-41-C.5	Cellular Radiotelecommunications Intersystem Operations: Signaling Protocols
IS-41-C.6	Cellular Radiotelecommunications Intersystem Operations: Signaling Procedures

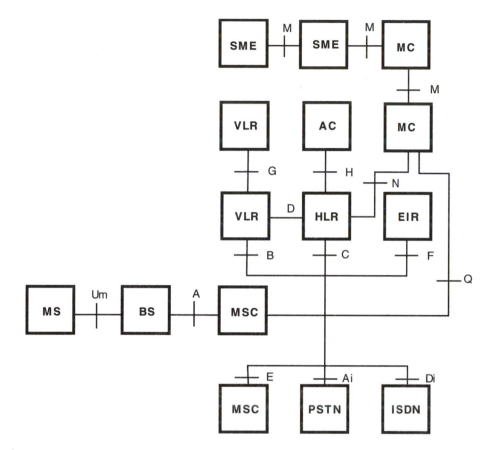

where:
AC   Access control
BS   Base station
CSS   Cellular subscriber station
EIR   Equipment identity register
HLR   Home location register
ISDN   Integrated services digital network
MC   Message center
MSC   Mobile switching center
PSTN   Public switched telephone network
SME   Short message entity
VLR   Visitor location register

Figure 7–1   IS-41-C entities and reference points.

IS-41-C and the associated interfaces (reference points) between the functional entities. This figure represents a conceptual model only and a piece of physical equipment may have several functional entities and reference points internal to the equipment. That being the case, these components are not required to adhere to the IS-41-C standard.

The terms in this figure are listed at the bottom of the figure. The reference points in Figure 7–1 labeled Um, A, B, and so on are used to describe the interfaces and procedures (protocols) between the IS-41-C entities, such as mobile switching centers (MSCs). This chapter concentrates on the B, C, E, and H interfaces. The Um interface is covered in other parts of this book pertaining to the operations between the mobile station and the network.

The A interface is not defined in IS-41-C. It is being defined in IS-634 and is covered later in this chapter.

TERMS AND CONCEPTS

In order to explain the operations of IS-41-C, we need to clarify and define a few terms and concepts. First, the term *anchor MSC* identifies the MSC that is designated as the initial contact point when an originating call is initiated by the mobile station or when a terminating call (to the mobile station) is received from the telephone network. For the duration of a call, this MSC remains the anchor point, even though the mobile station might be handed-off to other MSCs.

A *candidate MSC* is a MSC that is being requested to provide the next service during a handoff operation. This procedure entails the candidate MSC exchanging various messages with the current serving MSC to indicate the signal quality and to exchange identifiers. The intention of the process is to find an appropriate MSC for the roaming mobile station.

The *homing MSC* identifies the MSC that is the "owner" of the mobile system in the sense that it is the owner of a directory number from which the mobile station's MIN is derived. The homing MCS houses the mobile station's HLR records.

Next, the *serving MSC* is the MSC that is currently serving the mobile station at a cell site within a coverage area controlled by the MSC. Finally, the *target MSC* is the MSC that was selected from a list of MSCs as having the cell site that can service the mobile station with the best signal quality. The target MSC is selected from a list of candidate MSCs during the location request function, which will be described later in this chapter.

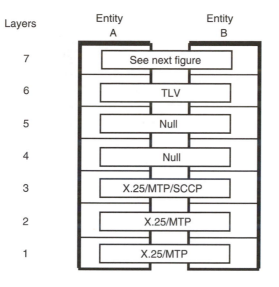

where:
MTP   Message transfer part
SCCP   Signaling connection control part (of SS7, class 0)
TLV   Type-length-value (a transfer syntax)

Figure 7–2 IS-41-C and Open Systems Interconnection (OSI) model.

THE LAYERED STRUCTURE OF IS-41-C

IS-41-C is organized around the OSI Model. It does not make use of all of the layers in the model. Those not used are labeled null[1] in Figure 7–2.

Since the publication of IS-41, the OSI Model has had changes made to the application and presentation layers. We will use the older IS-41 terminology, but correlate these terms to the current OSI terms. The lower three layers of IS-41-C can consist of the X.25 layers or the SS7 layers, known as the message transfer parts (MTPs) in SS7. The SS7 signaling connection control part (SCCP) class 0 is also part of layer 3 (and some of layer 4, not a clean OSI fit). Layer 6 uses the ISO/ITU-T transfer syntax (1984 = X.409; 1988 = X.209) to define the syntax and structure of the IS-41-C messages that are transported between the MSCs. Layer 7

---

[1]The term null is not completely accurate. A minimum core service is provided. A more recent term is "pass-through." The session and transport layers are pass-through layers.

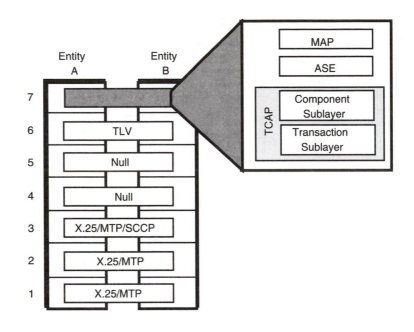

where:
   ASE   Applications service element
   MAP   Mobile application part of IS-41-C
   MTP   Message transfer part
   SCCP   Signaling connection control part
   TCAP   Transaction capabilities applications part
   TLV   Type-length-value

Figure 7–3   The layers of IS-41-C.

contains the conventional OSI service elements, which are explained in the next figure.

Layer 7 is shown in more detail in Figure 7–3. The IS-41-C mobile application part (MAP) can make use of an OSI layer 7 protocol called the association control service element (ACSE),[2] known more generally as an application service element (ASE).

If implemented, ACSE is used to "bind" two applications together. For example, ACSE sets up an association between (for example) entity A and entity B and permits the negotiation of various services and options, which are dependent upon the specific network and switches. In

---

[2]For the OSI expert, IS-41-C does not define the use of an ASE. Nonetheless, if the IS-41-C implementation is built on an OSI layer 7 architecture, an ASE is used. It is called the association control service element (ACSE).

essence, it is a housekeeping tool and is not invoked during ongoing transfer of IS-41-C messages. A variation of the OSI-based Remote Operations Service Element (ROSE) is invoked for this purpose, which is explained shortly.

The Bearer Services[3]

The IS-41-C bearer services are shown in more detail in Figure 7–4. The term bearer services refers to the lower three layers of the OSI Model. For IS-41-C, the bearer service can be X.25 or SS7. With both of these bearer services, the IS-41-C traffic resides in the data (information) field of the layer 2 protocol data unit (PDU), which is usually called a frame.

The X.25 bearer service uses X.25's link access procedure, balanced (LAPB) at layer 2, and the packet layer procedures (PLP) at layer 3. LAPB is a link layer (L_2) protocol and is responsible for the safe transfer of the traffic across the link. PLP sets up a virtual circuit between the MSCs and manages the transfer of IS-41-C traffic across the virtual circuit. This traffic is carried inside an X.25 L_3 packet, which is encapsulated inside the LAPB frame.

The SS7 bearer service uses message transfer part 2 (MTP 2) at layer 2, and MTP 3 at layer 3. MTP 2 is a link layer protocol and is responsible for the safe transfer of the traffic across the link. It has similar operations to X.25's LAPB, but it is more powerful in its link integrity operations. MTP 3 is responsible for the routing of IS-41-C traffic between the MSCs.

In addition, SS7 also provides the signaling connection control part (SCCP) for additional services, such as message distribution operations at the final destination (that is, determining which software module is to receive and process the incoming traffic) and address translations (for example, translating a mobile identifier to an address for MTP 3 to use for routing). See Table 7–2 for a review of how SCCP is used by IS-41-C.

The notation ⌐‾‾‾‾‾‾‾‾‾‾‾¬ in Figure 7–4 means the functions (and headers) of ROSE, the OSI L_6, and TCAP have been combined into TCAP. TCAP is an amalgamation of: (a) ROSE, (b) L_6 X.208, and (c) L_6 X.209. I mentioned earlier that X.209 defines the syntax of the IS-41-C messages, such as the order of the bits in the message and how they represent a value (integer, bit stream, etc.). X.208 is a compiler-independent language using

---

[3]For the reader who wishes more information on these bearer services (which is beyond the scope of this book), I refer you to (a) *ISDN and SS7*, a Prentice-Hall book by Uyless Black, and (b) *X.25 and Related Protocols*, an IEEE Computer Society book by Uyless Black.

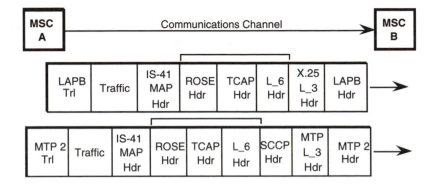

where:
LAPB   Link access procedure, balanced
MAP   Mobile application part of IS-41-C
MSC   Mobile switching center
MTP   Message transfer part
ROSE   remote operations service element (*Note:* TCAP assimilates many of ROSE
        functions)
SCCP   Signaling connection control part
TCAP   Transaction capabilities applications part

Figure 7–4   The IS-41-C bearer services.

Table 7–2   SCCP Support of IS-41-C

- SCCP Class 0 is used
- The subsystem numbers (SSN) are
      5   Mobile Application Part (MAP)
      6   Home Location Register (HLR)
      7   Visitor Location Register (VLR)
      8   Mobile Switching Center (MSC)
      9   Equipment Identity Register (EIR)
      10   Authentication Center (AC)
      11   Short Message Service
- The global title address information field is the 10-digit MIN (BCD coding)
- SS7 point codes, global titles, and SSNs must be supported by the IS-41-C MSCs

Abstract Syntax Notation.One (ASN.1). IS-41-C programmers use ASN.1 to code structures, which can be complied into C structures.

Use of the Layer 7 Remote Procedure Call (RPC)

IS-41-C was published when the layer 7 protocol ROSE was part of the ITU-T X.410 Recommendation. ROSE is now published in the X.200 recommendations. It is used with modifications in this technology and is now embedded into TCAP. This section provides a brief tutorial of ROSE and how it is used in IS-41-C. Figure 7–5 is a useful reference for this discussion.

The OSI Model supports a process for remote operations and remote procedure calls (RPCs). The remote procedure operation is based on a client server model and an asymmetric type of communications. Asymmetric means that a requester, such as a client, sends a request message to a process, identified as a server. It waits for an action to occur and receives a reply about the success or failure of the request. The client is not aware of the server's location (the server could be on a different machine in the network). This approach is in contrast to many of the OSI protocols and entities in which transfer is symmetric: Traffic flows in both directions at the same time. The ROSE model is ideal for IS-41-C, since operations between MSCs, VLRs, and HLRs, are asymmetric.

Result of Operation and Expected Report from Server

Success or failure, if successful, return a result
   If a failure, return an error reply.

Failure only, If successful, no reply
   If a failure, return an error reply

Success only, If successful, return a result
   If a failure, no reply

Success or failure, In either case, no replies

Class number	Definition
1	Synchronous: Report success (result) or failure (error)
2	Asynchronous: Report success (result) or failure (error)
3	Asynchronous: Report failure (error) only
4	Asynchronous: Report success (result) only
5	Asynchronous: Report nothing

Figure 7–5 Remote Operations Service Element (ROSE) operations.

TCAP is based on two principal concepts: sending a request for an operation to a server (an INVOKE message) and conveying the results of that operation to the client (a result message).[4]

The results of the operation can report on various combinations of success or failure. ROSE also uses class numbers to describe the result of the operation, either for synchronous or asynchronous communications processes. Figure 7–5 provides a summary of these aspects of ROSE. Be aware that vendors vary in how some of these ROSE attributes are implemented.

THE FIVE SECURITY/PRIVACY OPERATIONS

The next sections of this chapter explain the operations employed by IS-41-C to support security and privacy operations. These operations have two key goals: to give the network assurance that the user's identifiers (and the user's account) are not being used by someone else (which could lead to incorrect billing to the user), and to ensure that the user's voice conversation or data transfer is not being "listened to" by an unauthorized party.

To make certain that a user is actually the valid user, IS-41-C defines five procedures for the authentication of the mobile station. Remember from Chapter 1 that IS-41-C is used for all the North American air interfaces, and the authentication operations are basically the same for all these interfaces. Some minor differences exist but they are not significant enough to single out in this discussion.

The authentication operations entail the exchange of information between the network and the mobile station to ensure that the mobile station user is who the user *claims* to be. The idea is to use a secret key, called the SSD (for shared secret data), that is known only to the network and the mobile station. A successful authentication means the mobile station and the network: (a) have identical copies of the SSD stored in their internal memories, (b) use the SSD to generate other values that are exchanged to verify (authenticate) the identity of the mobile station and the network, and (c) encrypt (perhaps) the voice or data traffic.

This part of the chapter explains the five authentication and privacy operations used by IS-41-C in the order listed below. Each operation is

---

[4]For documentation purposes in IS-41-C and in this chapter, an INVOKE is noted in uppercase, and the reply is in lower case.

described with the (a) security and authentication parameters used for the operation, (b) examples of air side operations, and (c) examples of network side operations.

- Authentication of mobile station registration
- Unique challenge-response procedures
- Authentication of mobile station originating a call
- Authentication of a call to a terminating mobile station
- Updating the shared secret data (SSD)

The examples in this chapter show IS-41-C messages being exchanged between an MSC and a VLR. However, in most situations, the VLR is co-located with the MSC (directly attached), in which case these messages are not created.

AUTHENTICATION PARAMETERS

Before we examine the five operations, let us take a look at the parameters that are used in the overall authentication and encryption operations, shown in Figure 7–6. I mentioned the shared secret data (SSD) parameter earlier. It is a 128-bit pattern stored in the mobile station and network. It is divided into two parts: SSD-A and SSD-B, as shown in Figure 7–6a. SSD-A is used for authentication procedures and SSD-B is used for encrypting voice traffic and selected messages. Later discussions explain how the SSD is created and managed.

The random challenge (RAND) variable is 32-bit random number that is issued periodically (broadcasted) by the network in two 16-bit parts: RAND1_A, and RAND1_B. RANDC is an 8-bit number used to confirm the last RAND received by the mobile station; it is the 8 most significant bits of RAND.

The electronic serial number (ESN) is the hardware identifier of the mobile station handset. The mobile identification number (MIN) is a 34-bit representation of the mobile station's 10-digit directory telephone number. These parameters are described in Chapters 3, 4, and 5.

The A-key is a secret 64-bit pattern stored only at the mobile station and the authentication center (AC). If an AC does not exist, the key is stored at the user's HLR.

The shared secret data random variable (RANDSSD) is a 56-bit random number generated by the mobile station's home system. The unique

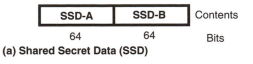

64   64   Bits

(a) Shared Secret Data (SSD)

(b) Random Challenge (RAND) and RANDC

ESN
32

(c) Electronic serial number (ESN)

MIN1
24

(d) Mobile identification number (MIN)

A-key
64

(e) A-key

RANDSSD
56

(f) Shared secret data random variable (RANDSSD)

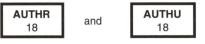

(g) Challenge authentication (AUTHR and AUTHU)

Figure 7–6 Security operations and parameters.

challenge authentication response (AUTHR & AUTHU) are 18-bit patterns generated by an authentication algorithm.

AUTHENTICATION OF MOBILE STATION REGISTRATION PROCEDURES

The Parameters

Registration authentication is the first type of authentication operation supported by IS-41-C. The basic concept behind registration authentication is shown in Figure 7–7. Both the network and the mobile station

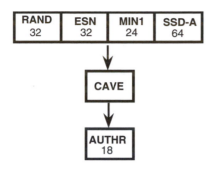

where:

AUTHR   Challenge authentication (response)
CAVE   Cellular authentication and voice encryption
ESN   Electronic serial number
MIN   Mobile identification number
RAND   Random value
SSD   Shared secret data

Figure 7–7 Computation of AUTHR for registration challenge.

execute a cellular authentication and voice encryption (CAVE) algorithm to create AUTHR.[5] As input to the CAVE algorithm, the mobile station and network use RAND, ESN, MIN1, and SSD-A. MIN1 is the Nxx-xxx part of the telephone number.

At the Air Interface

Registration operations at the air interface proceed in event 1 of Figure 7–8 by the network sending a system parameter overhead message with its contents indicating that the mobile station is to send a computed AUTHR to the network (an authenticate directive). In event 2, the mobile station executes the CAVE algorithm as shown in the previous figure and sends AUTHR and other parameters to the network, as shown in event 3. A count value (COUNT s-p) is also sent to the network, as is RANDC. The COUNT s-p parameter is explained later. The RANDC is used to confirm the last RAND received. This information is sent in (for IS-54-B) an RECC autonomous registration order message.

In event 4, the registration process is passed to IS-41-C, which is explained in the next section. For this example, after the authentication process occurs in event 4, the mobile station is informed of its results (in event 5). The sole purpose of these procedures is to compare the AUTHR

---

[5]The CAVE is not defined in IS-41-C. It is defined in other TIA specifications.

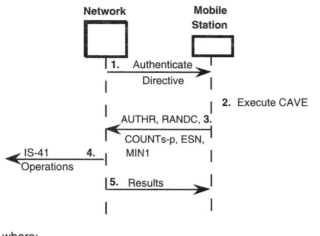

where:
   AUTHR   Registration authentication key
   CAVE   Cellular authentication and voice encryption
   ESN   Electronic serial number
   MIN   Mobile identification number
   RANDC   Random value (part of RAND)

Figure 7–8 Authentication of mobile station registration on the air side.

computed internally in the network to the value of AUTHR received from the mobile station.

On the Network Side

Figure 7–9 shows the registration authentication operations on the network side. The base station passes the mobile station's parameters to the serving MSC, which issues the IS-41-C AUTHREQ message to the VLR to initiate the authentication request operation (event 1). This information is passed to the mobile station's HLR (event 2) and then to authentication control (AC), event 3. The AC compares the received values for RANDC (and optionally COUNT s-p) with internally stored values associated with the received MIN1/ESN. If a match occurs, the AC executes the CAVE algorithm using the SSD-A value it has stored internally, as well as the other values shown for CAVE in Figure 7–7. The result of computation is AUTHR, which is compared to the mobile station's computed AUTHR. This result is returned to the HLR and MSC/VLR in the authreq message, shown in Figure 7–9 as events 4, 5, and 6.

The count value that was introduced earlier (COUNTs-p) is supplied by the mobile station and compared to a count variable at the AC.

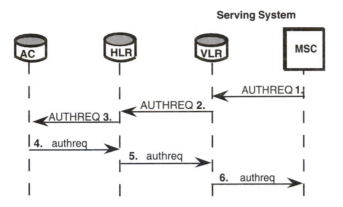

Figure 7–9 Registration authentication operations on the network side.

If they are equal, and the AUTHR values match, the AC accepts the authentication.

Encryption Capabilities. Two other values can be returned to the mobile station by the AC. The signaling message encryption key (SMEKEY) is used to encrypt messages, and the voice privacy mask (VPMASK) is used to encrypt voice traffic. The use of encryption capabilities is not a requirement in IS-41-C, nor in any of the air interfaces that are supported by IS-41-C.

UNIQUE CHALLENGE-RESPONSE PROCEDURES

The Parameters

The unique challenge is the second type of authentication supported by IS-41-C. Another parameter is computed for this operation. It is different from the authentication of mobile station registration just described because: (a) The network executes the CAVE algorithm first and sends a challenge (instead of the mobile station executing CAVE first); (b) if the authentication of mobile station registration operation fails, this operation can be invoked; and (c) the RAND value used in the authentication of the mobile station registration is broadcast to all mobile stations in the cell and updated periodically by the network. In contrast, the value used in the unique challenge is RANDU, which is 24-bit random pattern generated for a one-time unique challenge to a specific mobile station.

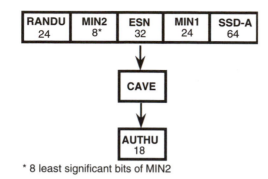

* 8 least significant bits of MIN2

where:
    AUTHU   Unique challenge key
    CAVE   Cellular authentication and voice encryption
    ESN   Electronic serial number
    MIN   Mobile identification number   **Figure 7–10 Computation**
    RAND   Random value   **of AUTHU for unique chal-**
    SSD   Shared secret data   **lenge.**

The network generates AUTHU as shown in Figure 7–10. It uses RANDU and the other parameters shown in the figure to compute AUTHU. As explained next, this value is sent to the mobile station as a unique challenge.

At the Air Interface

Figure 7–11 shows the operations for the unique challenge-response procedure for the air interface. It is similar to the authentication of mobile station registration procedure, discussed earlier, with the differences cited in the text associated with the previous figure.

On the Network Side

Figure 7–12 shows the operations for the unique challenge-response procedure on the network side. It is similar to the authentication of mobile station registration procedure, discussed earlier. This example shows that the operation is initiated by the AC. It may also be initiated by the VLR if the VLR and AC are both sharing the SSD.

The parameters used in this operation (and originated by the AC) are: (a) served MS MIN, (b) served MS ESN, (c) RANDU number generated to produce AUTHU, and (d) AUTHU, which is the expected MS response to this challenge. These parameters are passed to the HLR, then the VLR in events 1 and 2. The VLR adds the location area ID (LOCID)

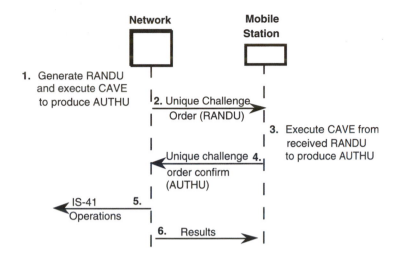

where:

AUTHU	Unique challenge authentication
CAVE	Cellular authentication and voice encryption
ESN	Electronic serial number
MIN	Mobile identification number

Figure 7–11   Unique challenge-response procedure on the air side.

to the message, if it is available, then forwards the message to the MSC (in event 3).

In events 4, 5, and 6, an empty authdir message is returned to indicate the directive has been accepted. These operations are shown as event 5 in Figure 7–11. This empty authdir message is sent if the MSC is not able to initiate a unique challenge to the mobile station at this time.

IS-41-C does not explain how the subsequent message transfer occurs. It must be inferred that the MSC does return a authdir message later to indicate success or failure of the authentication. This "double" response is possible with the use of TCAP's ability to allow multiple reply messages to one INVOKE message.

AUTHENTICATION OF MOBILE STATION ORIGINATING A CALL

The Parameters

The third type of authentication is executed when the mobile station originates a call. For this operation, the mobile station generates AUTHR,

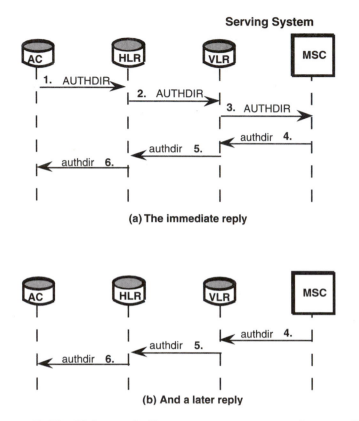

Figure 7–12   Unique challenge-response procedure on the network side.

as in the registration authentication procedure, described earlier, but the input to CAVE is slightly different (see Figure 7–13). In place of the MIN1 value, the last six digits of the dialed number are used. The mobile station sends AUTHR together with RANDC and COUNTs-p to the network, and these operations are shown in the next figure.

At the Air Interface

As just explained, when the mobile station is to originate a call, it must generate AUTHR from CAVE, with the input parameters of RAND, ESN, the last six digits of the dialed number, and SSD-A. This information is sent to the network in the authentication word C of the RECC origination message for IS-54-B. Figure 7–14 depicts this operation.

The network uses the received AUTHR to compare it against its own computation of AUTHR, once again using the same input to CAVE as the

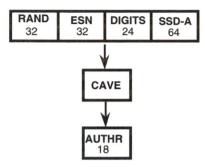

DIGITS are last 6 digits transmitted by mobile station

where:

AUTHR   Key for call origination
CAVE   Cellular authentication and voice encryption
ESN   Electronic serial number
RAND   Random value
SSD   Shared secret data

Figure 7–13 Computation of AUTHR for call origination.

mobile station. If both computed AUTHRs are equal, channel assignment procedures begin.

On the Network Side

On the network side for call origination authentication, the MSC receives the authentication message from the mobile station. Its job is to

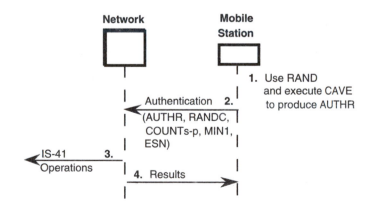

where:

AUTHR   Key for call origination
CAVE   Cellular authentication and voice encryption
RANDC   (8 most significant bits of RAND)

Figure 7–14 Authentication for call origination on the air side.

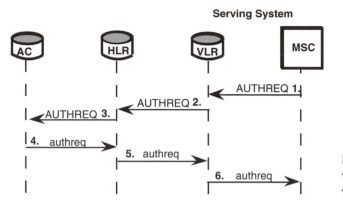

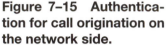

Figure 7–15 Authentication for call origination on the network side.

compare the received values of RANDC (and optionally the count value) with values stored internally that are associated with the received MIN1/ESN. The network also computes AUTHR with the same input described above and compares the computed AUTHR with the mobile station's computed AUTHR. If they match, the mobile station is assigned the necessary resources to set up the call, as well as the resources for the originating call itself.

Figure 7–15 shows the operations on the network side for a successful authentication where the SSD is not shared (that is, the mobile station is attempting a call origination on a serving system that is not sharing an SSD with the AC).

The serving MSC sends the AUTHREQ message to the VLR, which contains the AUTHR and the identity of the called party (the dialed digits). In events 1, 2, and 3, this information is forwarded to the AC, which determines that the mobile station is valid and sends the authreq reply message back to the HLR, the VLR, and the MSC. This message may also contain a CDMA private long code mask (if the air interface is CDMA). It may also contain SMEKEY and VPMASK, which were described earlier in this chapter. The authreq messages are shown in events 4, 5, and 6.

AUTHENTICATION OF A CALL TO A TERMINATING MOBILE STATION

The Parameters

The authentication for terminating a call to the mobile station is the fourth type of authentication and is similar to other operations described in this material, but with some variations (see Figure 7–16). First, the

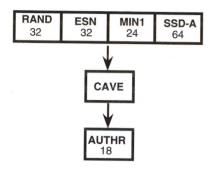

where:

AUTHR	Key for call termination
CAVE	Cellular authentication and voice encryption
ESN	Electronic serial number
RAND	Random value
SSD	Shared secret data

Figure 7–16 Computation of AUTHR for call termination.

computation of AUTHR is different in call termination (shown here) than call origination (shown in the last examples): The MIN1 is used instead of dialed digits. Otherwise, everything else is the same.

At the Air Interface

As illustrated in Figure 7–17, for call termination, the mobile station receives a page message. In an IS-54-B system, this message is conveyed in the system parameter overhead message. The mobile station executes the CAVE algorithm to create AUTHR and sends this value, along with RANDC and COUNTs-p, to the network in the (for IS-54-B) authentication word C of the RECC page response message.

The network receives this information and compares the received values of RANDC (and optionally COUNT) to those values associated with the MIN1 and ESN that were sent in the message. If the computed AUTHRs are equal, the station is assigned the necessary resources to manage the terminating set up of the call, as well as resources for the call itself.

On the Network Side

The message flow for IS-41-C for a call termination to a mobile station is the same as for call origination, but as just discussed, the AUTHR value is computed by CAVE with different input parameters. Figure 7–18 shows this operation.

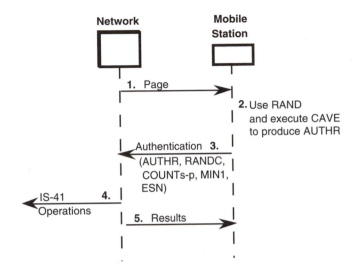

Figure 7–17 Authentication for call termination on the air side.

UPDATING THE SHARED SECRET DATA (SSD)

The Parameters

Updating the SSD is the fifth major security/privacy operation defined in IS-41-C. The SSD is generated from a key stored in the mobile station and at the AC. This key is called the A-key. The SSD is generated using the A-key upon an order from the network. This concept is similar

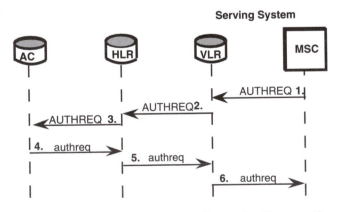

Figure 7–18 Authentication for call termination on the network side.

to the security measures in GSM, except that the North American systems do not define the use of the subscriber interface module (SIM) card. The AC generates a new SSD by executing the CAVE algorithm by using the subscriber's secret A-key, the ESN, and 56-bit RAND, which is called RANDSSD, see Figure 7–19a.

Another value, called AUTHBS, is used in the SSD update procedures. It is generated with CAVE and with the input parameters RANDBS, ESN, MIN1, and SSD-A_NEW. This later value was a result of the calculation in the top figure, which is then used as input to the CAVE calculation in Figure 7–19b.

At the Air Interface and on the Network Side

Figure 7–20 shows how the SSD values are updated. When the network creates the new SSD, it sends a message to the mobile station directing it to update the SSD by using the RANDSSD, shown as event 1. In turn, the mobile station generates the new SSD using its secret A-key, the ESN, and the RANDSSD. Next, the mobile station sends to the net-

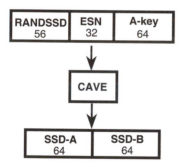

(a) Computation of shared secret data (SSD)

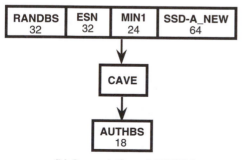

(b) Computation of AUTHBS   **Figure 7–19   SSD computations.**

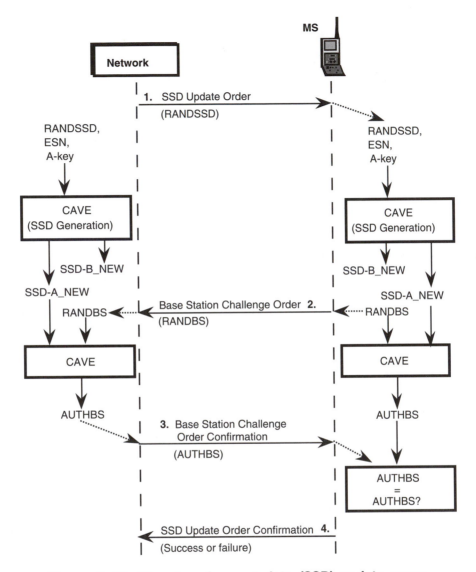

**Figure 7–20 The shared secret data (SSD) update opera-
tions.**

work a challenge using a 32-bit random number called RANDBS, shown
as event 2.

The mobile station generates an 18-bit AUTHBS value by once again
executing the CAVE algorithm with input as RANDBS and the new
SSD-A. The AC also performs the operation by executing CAVE with input

of: RANDBS and the new SSD-A. After this operation occurs, the network responds to the mobile station with the AUTHBS value, shown as event 3. If the two AUTHBS values match, the handset then accepts the new SSD and responds with an ACK to the network, shown as event 4.

One could ask, why all these operations just to update some security parameters? The answer is that these procedures allow the network to verify the mobile station, *and* they also allow the mobile station to verify the network. After all, the SSN Update Order in event 1 may not be from a legitimate party (the network). So, the mobile station verifies the network by the Base Station Challenge Order message in event 2. The RANDBS value, provided by the mobile station must be used by the network, in conjunction with SSD-A_NEW to compute AUTHBS, which is sent to the mobile station in event 3. The mobile station compares this AUTHBS with its own computed AUTHBS to determine if the network is legitimate.

The remainder of this chapter provides several more examples of IS-41-C operations, principally aspects of registrations with VLRs and service features such as call forwarding and call waiting. As stated in the introduction to this chapter, IS-41-C defines over 100 operations. This chapter represents a small sampling of IS-41-C capabilities. For more details, there is no substitute for the actual specifications cited earlier.

REGISTRATION IN A NEW SERVICE AREA

When a mobile station moves to a new location, IS-41-C is invoked to coordinate the updates between the old serving MSC and VLR, the new serving MSC and VLR, and the subscriber's HLR. Figure 7–21 shows how these operations occur on the network side.

After the serving MSC has determined that the mobile station is in its area, it sends a registration notification message (REGNOT) to its VLR (event 1). This message contains (at a minimum): (a) the 10-digit mobile identification number (MIN), (b) the 32 bit electronic serial number (ESN), (c) the qualification information code, (d) a system type code (a code that identifies the vendor type of system (Nokia, Motorola, etc.), and (e) the 3-digit identifier of the specific system, which includes the registered SID.

If the mobile station had registered previously with an MSC that is within the domain of the VLR, no further action is taken by the VLR except to make certain that the MSC serving the mobile station is correctly

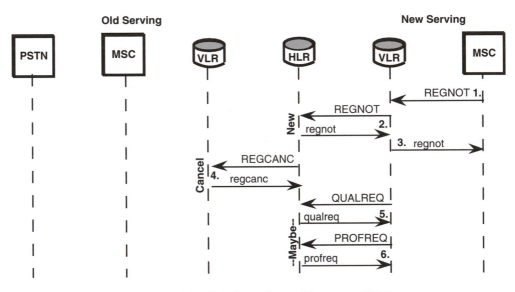

Figure 7–21   Registration with a new MSC.

recorded. In this example (event 2), the VLR sends a registration notification message to the subscriber's HLR. This message contains the MIN and the ESN. Upon receiving a response from the HLR, the new serving VLR sends a response back to the new serving MSC (event 3).

In event 4, the HLR sends a registration cancellation message to (REGCANC) the old serving VLR, if the station had been registered elsewhere. This message contains the same type of information that is in the registration notification message. This message can be sent by the HLR at any time after it receives the registration notification message from the new serving VLR.

Events 5 and 6 may or may not occur, depending on an actual implementation. The response to the qualification request (QUALREQ) will contain information pertaining to the origination of the call, subscriber-restricted calls (i.e., sent-paid), and parameters dealing with ancillary services (i.e., call forwarding and call waiting).

The messages invoked for mobile registration are the registration notification (REGNOT), the registration cancellation (REGCANC), the qualification request (QUALREQ), and the profile request (PROFREQ). These messages vary in how many fields (parameters) they carry, and the reader should study IS-41-C5 for more details. The message parameters for the registration operations are shown in Table 7–3.

Table 7–3   Message Fields

* *Mobile identification number:* The 10-digit representation of the mobile station's MIN.
* *Mobile serial number:* The 32 bit ESN of the mobile station.
* *Qualification information code:* Indicates the type of qualification needed during the registration, such as validation and profile, validation only, etc.
* *System my type code of VLR:* ID of vendor of mobile system.
* *MSC id of serving MSC:* Indicates the ID of a specified system. This three byte field contains a 2-byte SID and the 1-byte SWNO.
* *System my type code of HLR:* ID of vendor of mobile system.
* *Origination indicators:* Identifies the types of calls the mobile station is allowed to originate (local only, international, etc.)
* *Dialed digits:* The number of a station that is called.
* *MSC identifier:* Indicates the ID of a specified system. This three byte field contains a 2-byte SID and the 1-byte SWNO.
* *System my type code:* An identifier registered for each mobile equipment vendor. For example, this could contain a value of 5 for GTE equipment, 6 for Motorola equipment, 7 for NEC equipment, etc.
* *Billing ID field:* Contains the ID of the anchor MSC system, and it is initially assigned at the anchor system. Used principally for billing records but it can be used for identifiers as well. In addition to the anchor SID value, this field must also contain the anchor switch number as well as an ID number. The ID number is not required; but, the anchor SID and the anchor switch numbers are registered and are used in combination with the SWID.

CALLING AN IDLE MOBILE STATION

Figure 7–22 shows an example of a call made to a mobile station that is outside the serving area of the MSC that participates in the call origination. In this example, the mobile station is not busy (idle). The call is placed through the conventional PSTN (event 1) and is relayed to the originating system MSC through the identification of the mobile station's directory number. In event 2, the originating MSC sends a location request invoke message (LOCREQ) to the HLR that is associated with the mobile station.

The HLR performs several validity checks to make sure the subscriber is legitimate and that call forwarding is allowed. If all goes well, in event 3 the HLR sends a routing request invoke message (ROUTREQ) to the VLR that last provided information about the subscriber. This information had been provided earlier from this VLR through a registration notification message (REGNOT). The VLR then forwards this rout-

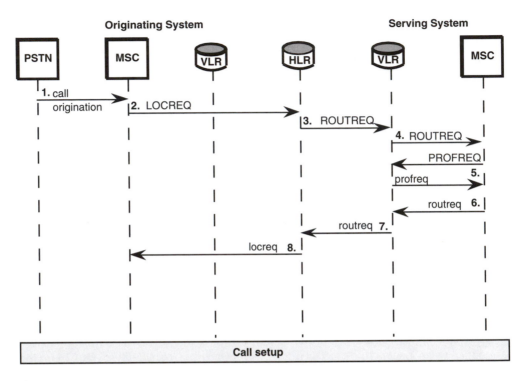

Figure 7–22   Calling an idle mobile station.

where:

    LOCREQ   Location request message
    PROFREQ: Service profile request message
    QUALREQ: Qualification request message
    ROUTREQ   Routing request message

ing request to the current serving MSC (event 4). The VLR must know that the mobile station may have roamed within the domain of the serving VLR and, if so, the station has already reported its new location to that VLR through the serving MSC.

If the MSC has not yet obtained information about this mobile station, it will obtain a service profile on the mobile station from its VLR. The service profile may already be known by the MSC; in which case, this information is not needed. This example shows the MSC sending a profile request (PROFREQ) to the VLR with the VLR responding with the result (event 5). In event 6, the MSC responds to the VLR with its profile request result that was requested in event 4.

Next, in event 7 the serving MSC VLR accesses a routing number for inter-MSC call routing and returns this information to the HLR in the routing request response message (routreq). Upon receiving this message, the HLR constructs a location request response (locreq) to give to the originating MSC (event 8). This operation is performed by placing the MIN and ESN values of the mobile station into the location request response message. Upon the originating MSC receiving this information from the HLR, it establishes a voice path to the serving MSC.

CALLING A BUSY MOBILE STATION

If the mobile station is busy when a call is directed to it, the operations proceed as described in the previous section (events 1–4), with the following alterations (shown in Figure 7–23). The serving MSC, upon checking its internal tables, determines that the mobile station is engaged in another call. This check results in the sending of the busy status message (of this mobile station) to the serving VLR (event 5) and then to the HLR in a routing request response message (event 6). The HLR looks at the profile of the mobile station and determines that (in this example) it does not have any special termination privileges (call interrupt, etc.) and returns a busy status signal to the originating MSC in the location

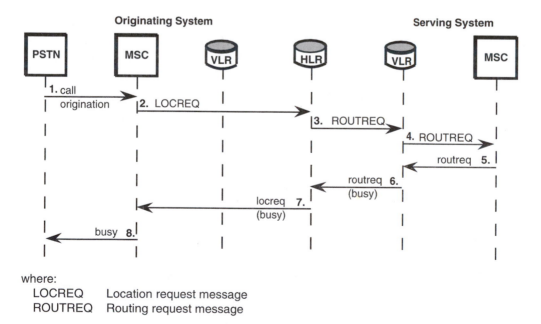

where:
    LOCREQ   Location request message
    ROUTREQ   Routing request message

Figure 7–23   Calling a busy mobile station.

request response (event 7), which means that the originating MSC must return a busy indication to the calling PSTN (event 8).

CALL FORWARDING

Figure 7–24 shows what happens when the called mobile system has subscribed to call forwarding. The term *unconditional call forwarding* refers to the mode in which the mobile station is never alerted or paged. It has designated the HLR to automatically (unconditionally) forward the call. Events 1 and 2 are the same as in previous examples. The location request message is sent to the mobile station's HLR. The HLR examines its files for the called party and finds that an unconditional call forwarding mode is in effect. It then returns the location request response to the originating MSC (event 3). The call forwarding number is in this response, which is coded in the message as the destination directory number. It is then the responsibility of the originating MSC to establish the call forwarding setup operations with the PSTN.

RECOVERY FROM AN HLR FAILURE

One hopes that the HLR suffers from few problems and even fewer failures. However, in the event of a failure at the HLR, operations are invoked to recover. In essence, the goals of these operations are to purge all

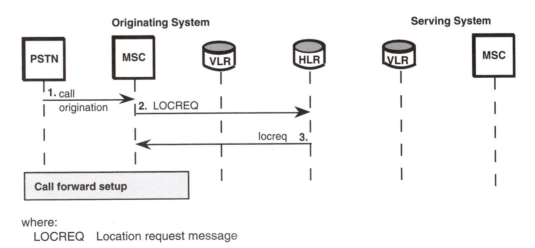

where:
    LOCREQ   Location request message

Figure 7–24   Call forwarding.

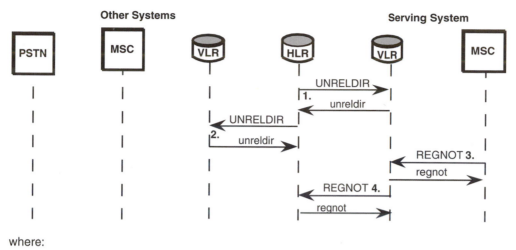

where:
  UNRELDIR   Unreliable roamer data directive

Figure 7–25   Recovery from failure at the HLR.

information from all the associated VLRs that are correlated to the failed HLR and, at a later time, locate the mobile station and update the HLR and VLRs accordingly. Figure 7–25 depicts the operations invoked to recover from an HLR failure.

In events 1 and 2, the HLR sends the unreliable roamer data directive invoke message (UNRELDIR) to all its associated VLRs. Upon receiving this message, the VLRs remove the record of all the mobile stations belonging to the home HLR and return the unreliable directory response to the HLR. In event 3, an MSC discovers the presence of a mobile station in its area that belongs to the subject HLR. It first sends a registration notification message (REGNOT) to its VLR. In turn, and in event 4, the VLR sends this information to the HLR. Obviously, this information allows the HLR to recover on a station-by-station basis as each mobile station is found within the system.

HANDOFF BETWEEN MSCs

A serving MSC can query its adjacent MSCs to determine if the mobile system should be relocated to another serving system (see Figure 7–26). This operation is achieved with the exchange of handoff measurement request messages. In event 1, the serving MSC sends to its adjacent MSCs the request of a measurement level on a specific channel. The

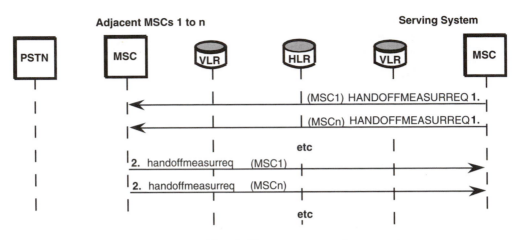

Figure 7–26   Handoff measurement request.

request message includes the station class mark (SCM) field of the subscriber station, the identifier of the serving cell site for the specific channel, the SAT color code, voice mobile attenuation code, and the channel number of the specific channel.

In event 2, the adjacent MSCs respond with the handoffmeasreq response, which contains the identifier of the responding cell site and the quality of the signal (signal strength) that is being received on the specific channel. The serving MSC examines each response to determine if a handoff is or is not appropriate.

HANDLING A CALL COLLISION

Figure 7–27 shows the operations for a call collision. As we have learned in other examples, the serving MSC informs the HLR of the call setup by the return of the routreq message to the HLR (in event 5).

Since the call has not actually taken place from the perspective of these originating entities, it is possible that the mobile station can become engaged in another call. The most common event is for the user in the mobile station to make a new call by going off-hook. It could also occur because of the arrival of another call setup from a previous ROUTREQ. During the call setup operation, the serving MSC discovers the mobile station is busy. In this example, we assume that call waiting is not available. Also in this example, we assume that the mobile station has call forwarding on busy activated. Therefore, the serving MSC in event 8 returns to the originating MSC a redirection request message (REDREQ) noting that the station is indeed busy. The reader should note

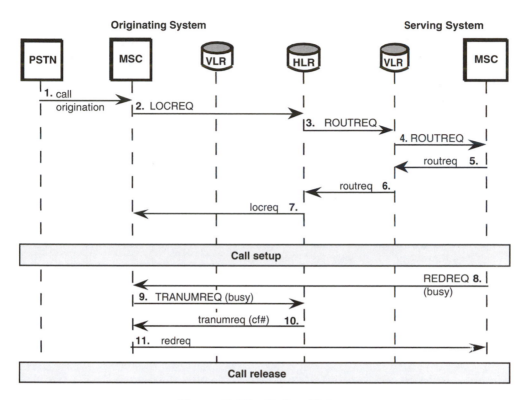

Figure 7–27   Call collision.

that this information flow is not passed through the HLR. In event 9, upon receiving this message, the originating MSC sends a transfer to number request message (TRANUMREQ) to the HLR indicating that the mobile station is busy and that it would like the HLR to return a call forwarding number. This request is honored in event 10. Finally, in event 11, the redirect request response is returned from the originating MSC to the serving MSC to complete the outstanding request message created in event 8. Thereafter, ongoing call forward and call release procedures are invoked as noted by a box in the bottom part of the figure.

CALL WAITING

Call waiting procedures are invoked in accordance with the operations shown in Figure 7–28. We pick up these operations in events 5, 6, and 7. We learned earlier that the MSC can discover that a mobile station is busy. Furthermore, by examining the service profile of that station it can determine if the station has call waiting activated. In event 6,

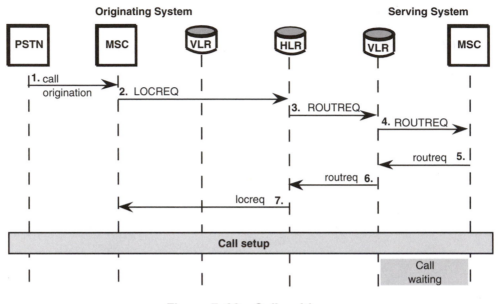

Figure 7–28   Call waiting.

the serving MSC returns this information to the HLR route request in a response message. In event 7, the HLR performs its own ongoing operations discussed in previous examples. The call setup takes place with conventional operations described earlier and when this second call arrives at the serving MSC, the mobile service receives the call waiting treatment from the MSC, shown at the bottom of Figure 7–28.

MOBILE STATION IS INACTIVE, THEN ACTIVE

A mobile station is often powered down when the mobile phone is not in use (see Figure 7–29). When the MSC sends page messages to the mobile station and receives no response, it notifies its VLR of this state through a CSS inactive message (CSSINACT), as shown in event 1. The VLR updates its records accordingly and responds to the MSC with a response. Next, in event 2, the same set of operations occur between the serving VLR and the HLR.

In this example, we assume that the mobile station is powered up once again and the MSC detects the presence of the mobile station through the procedures described in other chapters. In event 3, the MSC notifies its VLR of these events through the registration notification invoke message. Since the mobile system may have roamed while it was inactive, it is

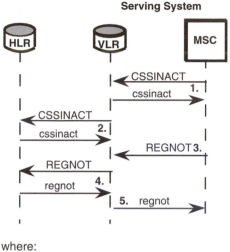

where:
CSSINACT   CSS inactive message

Figure 7–29   Mobile station is inactive, then active.

possible that the reporting MSC in event 1 is different from the reporting MSC in event 3. Whatever the case may be, the HLR will know about this roam because in event 4 the serving VLR sends the registration notification to the HLR. Thereafter, both the serving system and the HLR know that the mobile system is active and where it is located.

IS-41-C AND AMPS INTERWORKING

Figure 7–30 illustrates how the IS-41-C messages are used by the serving system to set up an AMPS connection with the mobile station. Events 1 through 5 have been described in previous examples. Events 6 through 9 were described in the AMPS chapter but warrant a few more comments here. The network uses a control channel to page the mobile unit in event 6. The mobile station accepts the page with the page response message in event 7. In event 8, the mobile station responds with the answer message in event 9.

INTERWORKING GSM AND IS-41

Due to the prevalence of GSM and IS-41[6] in many parts of the world, it has become necessary to interwork these systems. Several vendors

---

[6]The term IS-41-C is not used in this discussion since the operations support earlier versions of IS-41.

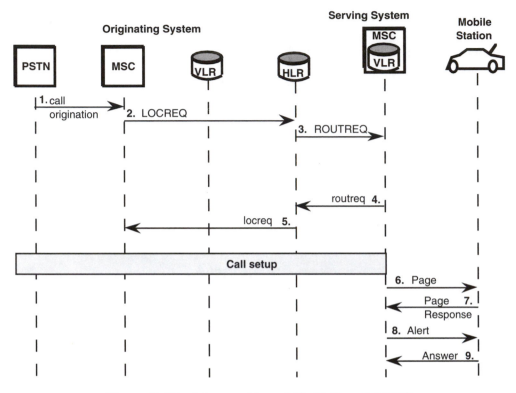

Figure 7–30   Interworking of IS-41-C and AMPS.

have developed gateways for this interworking operation. Our example in this discussion is Nortel's Internetwork Services Gateway (ISG).

As shown in Figure 7–31, the ISG operations operate as follows. When a GSM user roams into an IS-41 network, the ISG operates as an HLR to an IS-41 MSC/VLR. In turn, the ISG also acts as an IS-41 VLR to a GSM HLR. The ISG participates during call establishment to handle functions such as registration, authentication, and location updates, but it does not participate in the call itself.

A typical call delivery occurs as depicted in Figure 7–32. In event 1, a call is passed to the GSM network (to the gateway MSC) from the public switched telephone network. In event 2, the gateway MSC queries the HLR for routing information. In event 3, the HLR sends a roaming number request to the ISG (which we have just learned is acting as a gateway between the two systems). In event 4, a route request is sent to the IS-41 VLR. In event 5, the route response is returned with a temporary local directory number (TLDN). As a result of this query, in event 6 the ISG

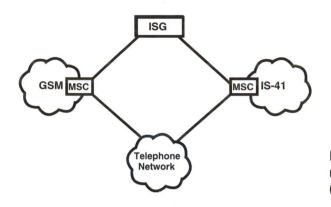

Figure 7–31 Nortel's Inter-network Services Gateway (ISG).

responds with the roaming number of the IS-41 MSC (where the subscriber was last registered). This allows the HLR to return the number to the GSM MSC, as depicted in event 7. Consequently, in event 8 the GSM MSC is able to deliver to the call to the IS-41 MSC.

The ISG is responsible for converting messages from an IS-41 VLR into GSM HLR messages and vice versa. It is transparent to the GSM and IS-41 systems. In order to provide these conversions, the ISG supports data storage, message and parameter mapping, and formatting functions for each of the systems.

Figure 7–33 shows the message flow involved in the internetworking process. The Nortel ISG hardware is an HP 9000 K server. The HP 9000/K260 can be configured to support 50,000 to 150,000 simultaneous active roaming subscribers.

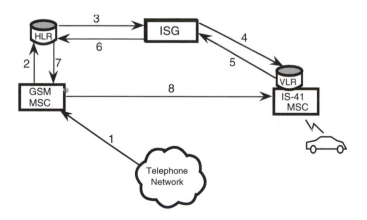

Figure 7–32   Interworking the GSM VLR and an IS-41 HLR.

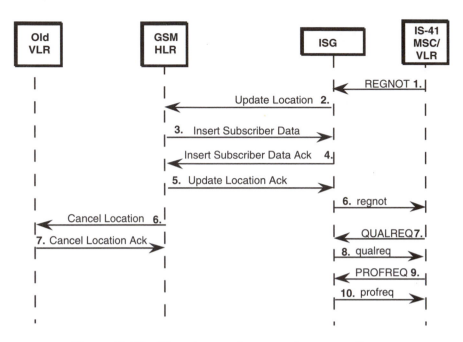

Figure 7–33   Mapping and conversion operations.

The ISG is in conformance with GSM MAP 9.02 (Phase II)-v 4.9 (with ITU-T White Book TCAP over ANSI SCCP/MTP), IS-41-A and IS-41-B (with ANSI TCAP over ANSI SCCP/MTP). IS-41-C is forthcoming. In addition, the operations are conformant with IS-129/TR-45.

IS-634

IS-41 (revisions A and B) is an old specification that was written initially to support an AMPS air interface operation and the operations between MSCs. During the past ten years, other air interfaces have come into existence, and the operations at the network side of a mobile system have evolved. In recognition of these facts, IS-634 has been published. It is designed to support a 800 MHz air interface and defines the operations between the BS and MSC (the A interface in Figure 7–1).

IS-634 supports the following air interfaces by defining physical layers, channel structures, message types and contents, and overall operating procedures:

- ANSI/TIA/EIA-553   AMPS
- EIA/TIA IS-54-B   Dual mode MS

- EIA/TIA IS-91   BS compatibility
- EIA/TIA IS-95   BS compatibility for wideband spread spectrum

IS-634 is organized in layers and partitions, as shown in Figure 7–34. The upper partitions are called functional planes, and are responsible for:

- Transmission facilities management: Manages the transmission media
- Radio resource management: Supports links between BS and MSC and handoffs
- Mobility management: Manages databases and subscriber location data
- Call processing: Manages call control and telecommunications services

SUPPORT OF THE IS-95 AIR INTERFACE

Figure 7–35 provides an example of how IS-634 supports the IS-95 air interface operations. This example shows a call originating from the mobile station. In event 1, the mobile station transmits an origination message with the stipulation that a layer 2 acknowledgment is required.

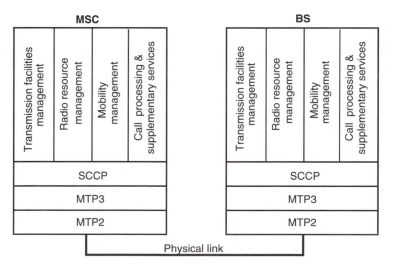

Figure 7–34   IS-634.

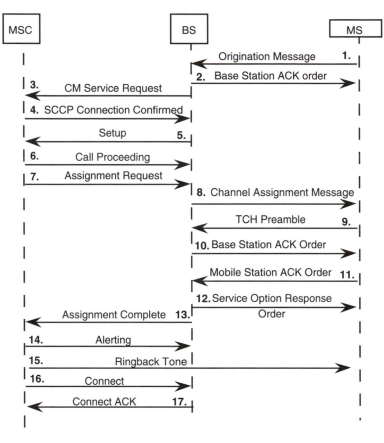

Figure 7–35   Supporting the IS-95 air interface.

This message is sent over the IS-95 access channel to the base station. In event 2, the base station acknowledges the receipt of the origination message with the base station ACK order message. After interpreting the message from the mobile station, in event 3 the base station creates the connection management (CM) service request message and places it into the layer 3 information message. It then sends this message to the MSC.

In event 4 the MSC responds with an SCCP connection confirm message to indicate the completion of an establishment of a signaling channel connection. Upon receiving the SCCP message, the base station transmits a setup message to the MSC, which is depicted in event 5. The setup message must contain all information required to set up a call to the terminating station. Other parts of this book have described the information that is required in the setup message; for example, the called party number and parameters associated with the call. In event 6, the

MSC returns a call proceeding message to the BS to indicate that the call establishment has been initiated toward the called party and that additional information is not needed from the mobile station.

In event 7 the MSC sends and assignment request message to the BS. The purpose of this action is to notify the BS to assign radio resources, and since this request from the mobile station is for a voice connection, event 7 entails the request for the assignment of a traffic channel for the speech transmission. Since the connection is based on an IS-95 air interface, the message will contain information pertinent to this specific interface.

In event 8 the base station uses the IS-95 paging channel to send a channel assignment message to the mobile station. In effect, this event initiates the establishment of a radio traffic channel.

In event 9 the mobile station receives the channel assignment message and begins sending the traffic channel preamble over the designated reverse traffic channel. Assuming that all goes well, in event 10 the base station has acquired the reverse traffic channel and it in turn sends back to the mobile station the base station acknowledge order. For this example, this information stipulates that a layer 2 acknowledgment is required. Consequently, in event 11 the mobile station acknowledges the reception of the base station order by sending back the mobile station acknowledge order message.

In event 12 the base station sends to the mobile station the service option response order message which specifies the service configuration for this call. The information contained in this message defines how the mobile station will begin the processing of traffic.

In event 13 it is assumed that the terrestrial circuit has been established for the call. That being the case, the base station sends to the mobile station an assignment complete message. Eventually, the called party will be rung as a result of these operations. When the MSC receives back from the network that the called party is indeed being rung, the MSC sends the alerting message to the BS as depicted in event 14. Since the systems in place today use a combination of older in-band tone signaling and the new out-of-band message signaling, the network may send back (in event 15) a ring-back tone. For this particular example, the ring-back tone is available on the audio circuit path toward the mobile station.

If the called party answers the call (as shown in event 16), the ring-back tone is removed and the MSC connects the terrestrial circuit to the called party. In so doing, it sends a CONNECT message to the base station and the base station (in event 17) acknowledges the connect message by sending a connect acknowledge back to the MSC.

SUMMARY

IS-41-C uses the information at the air interface to manage the network side of the cellular call. It uses the information from the telephone network to manage the network side of the cellular call. IS-41-C relies on the principles of layered protocols and uses the trusted workhorses X.25 and SS7 for its bearer services. IS-634 is a newer standard for the network side that will support BS-MSC operations for four different North American air interfaces.

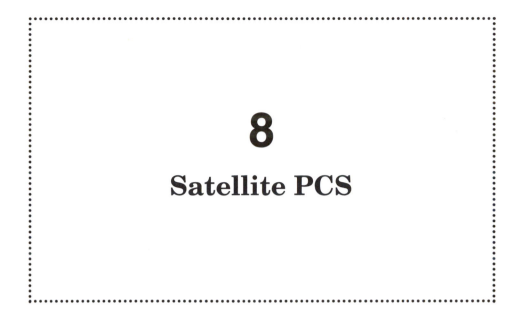

8

Satellite PCS

Second generation mobile wireless networks are being deployed in both land-based systems and satellite-based systems. These satellite systems, called satellite PCS, are the focus of attention of this chapter. The first part of the chapter provides an overview of older satellite systems and a brief history of how these systems evolved into the present technology. Next, satellite PCS technology is explained and several commercial systems are compared.

THE ALOHA LEGACY

While ALOHA is an old concept, it is included in this chapter because it was the forerunner to satellite TDMA. In the early 1970s, Norman Abramson at the University of Hawaii devised a technique for uncoordinated users to effectively compete for a common channel. The approach is called the ALOHA system; it is so named because the word ALOHA is an Hawaiian greeting without regard to whether a person is arriving or departing.

The premise of ALOHA is that users are acting on a peer-to-peer basis in that they all have equal access to the channel. As shown in Figure 8–1, a user station (an earth station) transmits whenever it has traf-

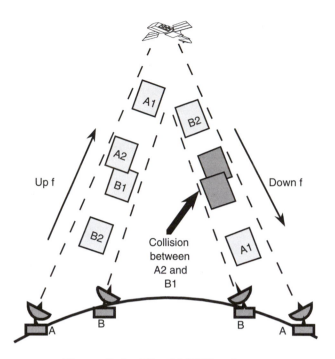

Figure 8–1   The ALOHA scheme.

fic to send. Simultaneous transmission results in the signals interfering and distorting each other as the separate signals propagate up to the satellite transponder. These "collisions" necessitate the retransmission of the damaged frames for data (and ignored for voice/video). Since the users of the satellite link know exactly what was transmitted onto the up-link channel and when it was transmitted, they only need listen to the down-link channel at a prescribed time to determine if the broadcast packet arrived without damage.

If a packet is damaged due to a collision, the stations are required to retransmit the damaged packet. In essence, the idea is to listen to the down-link channel one up-and-down delay time after the packet was sent. If the packet is destroyed, the transmitting site is required to wait a short random period and then retransmit. The randomized wait period diminishes the chances of the competing stations colliding again, since the waiting times will likely differ and result in retransmissions at different times. When traffic increases, the randomized waits can be increased to diminish the collisions.

Figure 8–1 depicts a typical ALOHA system using satellite communications. Stations A and B are transmitting packets on a shared channel. The down-link channel shows that packet 1 (A1) from station A is transmitted up and down safely; packet 2 (B2) from station B is also transmitted without error. However, the second packet from A (A2) and the first packet from B (B1) are transmitted at approximately the same time. As the transmissions of the two stations are narrowcasted up to the satellite station, the signals interfere with each other, resulting in a collision.

The satellite station is not responsible for error detection or error correction; it transmits what it receives from the up-link. On the down-link, stations A and B note the packets have collided and, upon waiting a random period of time (usually a few milliseconds), attempt to retransmit. This approach is quite effective when the users are uncoordinated and are sending traffic in bursts, such as from data from keyboard terminals or database accesses.

Random ALOHA experiences considerable degradation of throughput when the channel is heavily utilized. However, it should be kept in mind that what is transmitted across the channel is all end-user traffic. ALOHA uses no polls, selects, or negative responses to polls. Only end-user information is transmitted. Nonetheless, the pure random scheme can be improved by adapting a more efficient strategy for using the uncoordinated channel, called slotted ALOHA.

Slotted ALOHA requires that common clocks be established at the earth stations and at the satellite (see Figure 8–2). The clocks are synchronized to send traffic at specific periods. For example, the clocks may require that packets are transmitted only on 20 ms increments. In this example, the 20 ms increment is derived from a 50,000-bit/s channel and 1,000-bit packets (1,000 /50,000 = .020 second).

The 20 ms increment is referred to as the packet duration, which is the time in which the packet is transmitted on the channel. All stations are required to transmit at the beginning of a slot period. A packet cannot be transmitted if it overlaps more than one slot.

The slotted ALOHA approach increases throughput substantially on the channel, because if packets overlap or collide, they do so completely; at most, only one slot is damaged. However, like pure random ALOHA, slotted ALOHA does offer opportunities for collisions. For example, if two stations transmit in the same clock period, their packets collide. As in the pure random ALOHA approach, the stations are required to wait a random period of time before attempting to seize a slot for retransmission.

Another refinement to slotted ALOHA is slotted ALOHA with non-owner. The channel slots are combined into an ALOHA frame. The

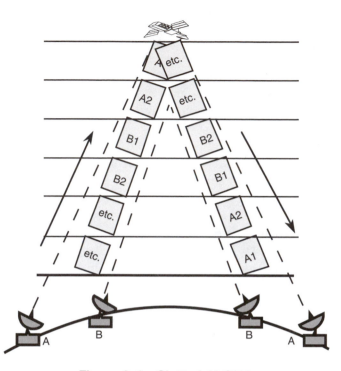

Figure 8–2   Slotted ALOHA.

ALOHA frame must equal or exceed the up-and-down propagation delay. This relationship is defined as:

$$AFL \geq PD$$
$$\text{or}$$
$$NSL * SLT \geq PD$$

where: AFL = ALOHA frame length; PD = the up-and-down propagation delay; NSL = number of slots in an ALOHA frame; and SLT = time interval of a slot.

Consequently, a 1000-bit packet lasting 20 ms would require a minimum of 12 slots to make up the ALOHA frame: 12 slots × 20 ms = 240 ms. The 240 ms. period represents the minimum up-and-down propagation delay (120 ms (up) × 120 ms (down) = 240 ms).

Another variation of slotted ALOHA is slotted ALOHA with owner. The slots of each frame are now owned by users. The user has exclusive use of its slot within the frame as long as it has data to transmit. In the event that the user relinquishes the slot, it so indicates with an established code. The slot becomes empty and is available for any other user to seize it. Once another user has seized the slot, it has exclusive rights to the use of the slot, until the original owner seizes the slot. The rightful owner can claim the slot at any time by beginning transmissions within its designated slot in the frame. The relinquishment is required when the rightful owner transmits. Obviously, the first time the owner transmits in its slot a collision may occur. On the subsequent frame, the rightful owner retransmits. The relinquishing station then must look for another free slot or go to its own slots if it has them. This refined approach of ALOHA is classified as a peer-to-peer priority structure, since some stations can be given priority ownership over other stations.

These operations should look familiar, since they form the basis for many of the TDMA operations that are now in existence in mobile wireless systems.

TDMA ON SATELLITES

COMSAT initiated work on TDMA in the mid-1960s. Since then, scores of TDMA systems have been implemented worldwide and earlier chapters explain their use in earth-bound wireless systems. TDMA shares a satellite transponder by dividing access into time slots. Each earth terminal is designated a time and its transmission burst is precisely timed into the slot. Our example of TDMA is an earlier system on satellite, which is chosen to allow the reader to compare this "old" system with the new systems covered later.

This version of TDMA assigns slots as needed. However, unlike the ALOHA system, the slots are assigned by a primary station called the reference (REF). The reference station accepts requests from the other stations, and based on the nature of the traffic and available channel capacity, the REF assigns these requests to specific frames for subsequent transmission. Every 20 frames, the reference station is assigned to each transponder of the system. The REF is like the base station controller in a wireless land-based system. This technique (introduced in Chapter 1), is now called extended TDMA (E-TDMA).

A LOOK AT THE GEOs

In the past, most of the satellite communications that "touched" the end user employed geosynchronous earth orbital satellites, or GEOs. The most common example (especially in rural areas) are the television programs that are broadcast to customers that have a GEO receiving antenna. We take a look at this technology here, and later compare it to a new technology called satellite PCS.

GEO satellites are in a geosynchronous orbit (see Figure 8–3). They rotate around the earth at 6900 (11040 Km) miles/hour and remain positioned over the same approximate point above the equator. Thus, the earth stations' antenna can remain in one position since the satellite's motion relative to the earth's position is fixed. Furthermore, a single geosynchronous satellite with nondirectional antenna can cover about 30% of the earth's surface.

The geosynchronous orbit requires a rocket launch of 22,300 miles (35680 Km) into space. Geosynchronous satellites can achieve almost worldwide coverage with three satellites spaced at 120° intervals from each other.

GEOs are attractive because of their wide coverage, but they have several disadvantages. First, the long distances between the satellite and the earth station create propagation delay of the signals, which can cause problems with applications that need low delay capabilities. Second, the

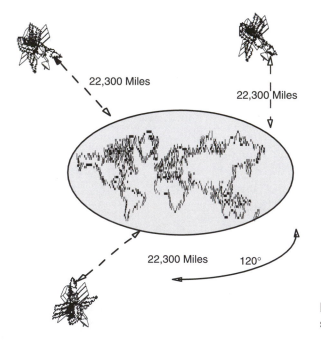

Figure 8–3 Geosynchronous satellites.

long distances require the transmitters to use relatively high-powered signals, which makes it difficult, expensive, and awkward to install in a compact, low-cost mobile phone. Third, the nature of the signals preclude the use of a small antenna that is required on a mobile handset.

Figure 8–4 provides two examples that illustrate the problems with using GEOs (Source: "Trends in Mobile Satellite Technology," by Gary Comparetto and Rafols Ramirez, *IEEE Computer,* February, 1997). The examples assume the following operating parameters:

- Transmit power: 1W
- Antenna diameter: 0.33 M
- Antenna noise temperature: 750 k
- Operating frequency: 2 GHz
- Other link losses: 6 dB

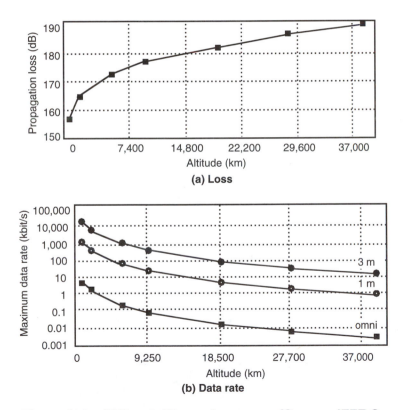

(a) Loss

(b) Data rate

Figure 8–4   GEO satellite performance. (*Source: IEEE Computer,* February 1997.)

- Required signal-to-noise ratio: 10 dB
- Link margin: 3 dB

Figure 8–4a shows that signal loss is much greater for GEOs than for LEOs. Figure 8–4b shows the maximum data rate that can be achieved in relation to the satellite altitude, using three types of antennas: (a) 1-meter parabolic, (b) 2-meter parabolic, and (c) a cellular-like omni antenna. Increased altitude poses a difficult problem because the data rate decreases as a function of satellite altitude.

However, the GEO does not require the earth station to track the satellite across the sky since its relative position is fixed, and this is a significant advantage in that it greatly simplifies the earth terminal.

With this background information behind us, let us now examine the technology that is designed to support the mobile wireless technology, with the orientation toward voice support.

LEO AND MEO SATELLITE SYSTEMS FOR VOICE TECHNOLOGY

Recall that GEO satellites rotate around the earth, and in relation to the earth's rotation, they appear to be stationary. In contrast to GEO systems, LEO satellites rotate around the earth at a low orbit of a few hundred miles (the distance varies, depending on the system). They are not stationary relative to the earth's rotation, but are moving at a speed of over 10,000 miles per hour. Another notable feature of one of the LEO PCS satellite systems is its ability to relay calls from satellite to satellite.

The low orbit has its advantages and disadvantages. Its principal advantage is its low power requirements, due to the short distance between the sender and the receiver. This arrangement permits the use of hand-held terminals. Additionally, the short distance translates into a small propagation delay between the terminal and the satellite. The required signal power between a transmitter and receiver decreases with the square of the distance between the systems. For example, reducing the distance from 36,000 km to 10,000 km translates into a 13-fold increase in the signal strength.

The major disadvantage of LEO technology is that the low orbit means that a satellite has a small coverage in relation to the earth's surface. Consequently, many satellites are required to provide for worldwide coverage. This arrangement also means that a LEO system is expensive (many satellites are to cover a large area on the earth). At an orbit of

10,000 km, the satellite circles the earth about every six hours, and "sees" a small part of the earth's surface. Moreover, due to the need to concentrate power between the mobile and satellite stations, the satellite must transmit narrow spot beams to the earth.

One attribute that has its advantages and disadvantages is the relaying of the call between satellites, without the need to send the call back-and-forth between intermediate earth nodes. This process is efficient but it is expensive and requires that considerable intelligence be built into the satellite.

Figure 8–5 shows one aspect of satellite technology: the distance the satellite is positioned above earth. This distance is the orbit the satellite travels as it circles earth. Generally, the orbits are described as: (a) LEO, for low earth orbit, with an orbit of 500–1,500 miles above earth;

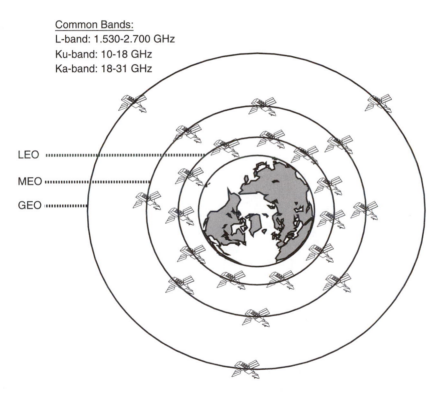

where:

LEO	Low earth orbit	500–1,500 miles
MEO	Medium earth orbit	6,250–13,000 miles
GEO	Geosynchronous earth orbit	22,300 miles

Figure 8–5   Satellite technology.

(b) MEO, for medium earth orbit, with an orbit of 6,250–13,000 miles above earth; and (c) GEO, for geosynchronous earth orbit, with an orbit of 22,300 miles above earth.

The higher the distance, the greater the coverage on the earth's surface. As stated earlier, the GEO orbit can cover most of the earth's surface with three satellites, whereas the LEO orbit needs about 40 to 60 satellites. The number of satellites vary, based on antenna design, the amount of overlap of the satellites' footprint on the earth's surface, and other factors. Conversely, the farther away from the earth, the greater power needed for the system. The distant satellites also suffer from signal propagation delay.

The frequency bands differ also. The L-band (1.53–2.7 GHz) provides robust signals, with long wave lengths. The Ku-band (10.7–18.1 GHz in Europe, 11.7 GHz–17.8 GHz in North America) has been used for some time and provides considerable bandwidth with acceptable quality. The Ka-band (fostered by excellent work by the U.S. agency, NASA) operates at very high frequencies (about 18–31 GHz). As a result, there is considerable bandwidth available at this spectrum, but these short wavelengths are subject to severe attenuation from water, foliage, and so on.

MOBILE BASE STATIONS

The satellite PCS system is like a conventional earth-based mobile wireless system in that both operate with cells. But the handoffs are more complex with satellites. Consider the Iridium system. The handoff of a user is performed between Iridium satellites (they are *mobile* base stations), as illustrated in Figure 8–6. In addition, the user's handset can be mobile, but that aspect of the handoff is like an earth-based operation.

The Iridium satellites route traffic. The earth station transmits a message to the satellite, which uses routing tables to relay the traffic to another satellite, yet to another, and eventually to the called party. For example, if the called party is not in view of the anchor satellite, the call is passed to another satellite, and so on.

The other systems do not support satellite cross-links, just described. Instead, these systems use a gateway on earth to relay the signals to and from the satellites. This approach is much simpler, but it restricts the flexibility to reach anyone, anytime. A user can gain access to this type of system only when the satellite over the user is also over a gateway. The idea of this approach is not to support worldwide coverage but to target a specific part of the world.

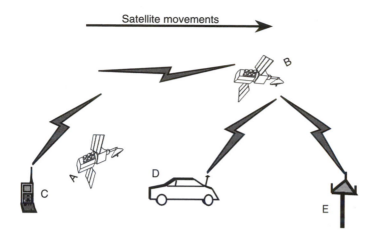

Figure 8–6   The mobile base stations.

EXAMPLES OF VOICE-ORIENTED SATELLITE PCS DEPLOYMENTS

This section highlights several satellite PCS systems. As of this writing, 12 systems are being launched, with most systems slated for operations before the year 2000.

Iridium

One of the more interesting satellite PCS systems is called Iridium, introduced in the last section. In the early 1990s, Motorola created the Iridium project, a satellite-based technology for PCS (as it is now called). The idea is to have enough satellites in the sky to cover any spot on earth, with continuous line-of-sight coverage. The satellites communicate directly with each other for control signaling and the passing off of calls. Iridiums "homing" capabilities will allow anyone to be tracked down— whether in a city or in a remote part of the world. It is expensive, but its potential is enormous. We shall have to wait to the end of this century to see if it will be successful.

Originally, the Iridium engineers considered 77 satellites (now reduced to 66). The project was named for the chemical element iridium, which has 77 electrons.

Iridium plans to have the service fully operational in the latter part of 1998. The system has a 20 GHz range, with each satellite at an orbital plane of 780 km. As of 1998, the estimated cost is $3.4 billion to implement the system.

Each of the 66 satellites is capable of handling about 1100 simultaneous calls. The satellite has a life span of eight years, based on the amount of fuel it consumes.

Figure 8–7a shows the Iridium satellite constellation, which consists of 66 satellites. They operate in six different 780 km (468 mi) planes.

(a) Orbits

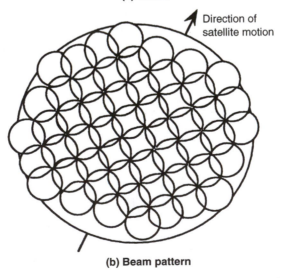

(b) Beam pattern

Figure 8–7   The Iridium satellite orbits and beam pattern.

Each plane contains eleven satellites spaced equidistant from each other. This constellation provides worldwide coverage on a continuous basis. Each satellite covers a circular area (a footprint) of 4600 km (2720 mi).

As seen in Figure 8–7b, the beams form a hexagonal pattern on the earth's surface. Iridium uses TDMA for its channel utilization scheme and reuses the TDMA channels with a seven-cell grouping. These groupings are geographically fixed on the earth's surface. Communications is performed with one satellite at a time, and the satellite is responsible for handing off the call as it leaves the subscriber's cell.

The mobile uplinks and downlinks use the same frequency band with time division duplex (TDD) operations. The mobile stations transmit 8.28 ms bursts in every 90 ms frame. The signal is modulated with quadrature phase shift keying (QPSK). Each TDMA frame is divided into four transmit and four receive time slots and the carriers are spaced at 41.67 kHz intervals in the frequency band.

The satellites are networked together with 22 and 33 GHz. Each satellite uses four 25 Mbit/s channels to communicate with four adjacent satellites. Two of the satellites are in its own orbit and one in each of the adjacent orbits.

Iridium is a very sophisticated and complex system. It supports worldwide coverage with satellite cross-links described earlier. It provides three types of links: (a) mobile uplinks and downlinks, (b) fixed earth station (FES) uplinks and downlinks, and (c) inter-satellite links. Table 8–1 provides a summary of the frequencies and access schemes used by Iridium.

Table 8–1   Characteristics of Iridium

Frequencies (GHz):	
Mobile uplinks	1.62–1.63
Mobile downlinks	1.62–1.63
FES uplinks	19.4–19.6
FES downlinks	29.1–29.3
Inter-satellite links	23.2–23.4
Multiple access:	
Scheme	TDMA
Spot beams/satellite	48
Approximate spot beam area	350,000 km
Channels per beam	23
Channels per million km	66

Globalstar

The Globalstar is a joint venture between Qualcomm of San Diego and Loral Aerospace Corp. in Newport Beach. Its reported cost is about $2.6 billion, and its bandwidth will be sold through local operators. Consequently, we can anticipate dual-mode handsets being developed to use traditional cellular and mobile satellite services.

The Globalstar system is made up of 48 satellites operating in eight planes at 1414 km (484 mi) altitude. Six satellites operate in each plane. Coverage on the globe is provided from two satellites at the same time. This approach is used to avoid shadowing and takes advantage of CDMA soft handover techniques.

As Figure 8–8 illustrates, each satellite's coverage is split into 16 beams and the same frequencies are reused in every beam. This approach is quite different from Iridium and allows the same frequencies as the satellite passes over users.

The up-and-down link channels are frequency division duplexed into two different bands. Both bands are divided into thirteen 1.25 MHz CDMA channels.

Globalstar does not employ cross-links between satellites, which simplifies the system, but restricts its availability. This restriction is considered by Globalstar to be an advantage: The manner in which the satellites cover the earth and the deployment of an inclined orbit of 52 degrees with respect to the equator (in contrast to Iridium's 86.5 degrees translates into a system that has little or no coverage beyond 70 degrees latitude in either hemisphere. In other words, Globalstar goes where

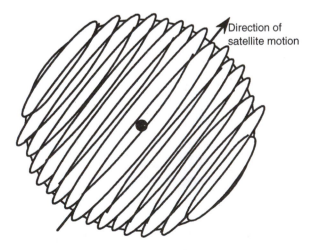

Direction of
satellite motion

Figure 8–8   Elongated spot beams (Globalstar).

Table 8–2   Characteristics of Globalstar

Frequencies (GHz):	
Mobile uplinks	1.61–1.63
Mobile downlinks	2.48–2.50
FES uplinks	5.09–5.25
FES downlinks	6.70–7.08
Inter-satellite links	None
Multiple access:	
Scheme	CDMA
Spot beams/satellite	16
Approximate spot beam area	2,900,000 km
Channels per beam	175
Channels per million km	61

population resides. Table 8–2 provides a summary of the Globalstar frequency usage and access schemes.

ICO

Like the other satellite PCS systems, ICO is a joint project. It is jointly owned by Inmarsat and Hughes. ICO consists of a ten-satellite constellation with five satellites in two orbits. It operates as a MEO (see Figure 8–9). The up-and-down links will operate in the 2 GHz band with the uplink occupying 1.98–2.01 GHz and the downlink occupying 2.17–2.20 GHz. ICO will use a four-cell reuse pattern and, like Iridium, will use TDMA channel sharing techniques.

ICO provides a robust link between the handset and the satellite. It deploys 160 spot beams on each satellite and uses digital processors and an array of radiating elements to form the spot beams. The end result is a complex and power-consuming system that provides high-quality signals. Table 8–3 provides a summary of the ICO frequency usage and access schemes.

LEO, MEO, AND GEO SATELLITE SYSTEMS FOR DATA TECHNOLOGY

Another market in the PCS satellite arena focuses on the support of data and video applications. These systems have not yet been launched and are still in the planning stages. Nonetheless, as Table 8–4 shows, a

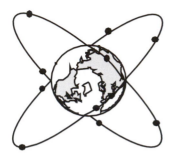

Figure 8–9   ICO constellation orbits.

number of vendors and operators are planning to launch these systems. Some systems will operate in LEO, others in MEO, and still others in the GEO orbits. Some will launch satellites that will use more than one of these orbital planes.

Because of the frequency congestion that exists in the current geosynchronous bands, most of these systems will operate in the Ka-band. As discussed earlier, the Ka-band represents a technical challenge because the small wavelength of about 1 to 1.5 centimeters means that the signals are severely attenuated by rain. Nonetheless, the engineers working with these systems believe that availability for the satellite link can reach 99.99%.

Of these systems, the Teledesic technology is the one that has aroused the most interest (it is also the most expensive but then it is being financed partially by Microsoft, so this probably is not an issue). The Teledesic system will launch 288 satellites at an altitude of

Table 8–3   Characteristics of ICO

Frequencies (GHz):	
Mobile uplinks	1.98–2.01
Mobile downlinks	2.17–2.20
FES uplinks	6.5
FES downlinks	3.6
Inter-satellite links	None
Multiple access:	
Scheme	TDMA
Spot beams/satellite	163
Approximate spot beam area	950,000 km
Channels per beam	28
Channels per million km	29

Table 8–4 Data-Oriented Personal Communications Satellite Systems

	Astrolink	Celestri	Cyberstar	Spaceway	GE*STAR	Morning-star	Teledesic
Company	Lockheed Martin	Motorola	Loral	Hughes	G.E. American	Morning Star	Teledesic
# of Active Satellites	9	63 LEO/9 GEO	3	20 MEO/16 GEO	9	4	288
Orbit Planes	Equatorial (0°)	7 inclined (48°); 1 Equatorial (0°)	Equatorial (0°)	4 inclined (98°); 1 Equatorial (0°)	Equatorial (0°)	Equatorial (0°)	12 inclined (98°)
Orbit Altitude (km)	GEO	1,400 (LEO) and GEO	GEO	10,352 (MEO) and GEO	GEO	GEO	1,375 (LEO)
Estimated Satellite Capacity (Gbit/s)	6.0	1.5	9.0	4.4	4.7	0.5	10.0
Estimated Capital Investment (in Billions $)	4.0	12.9	1.6	6.4	4.0	0.82	9.0

Source: "New Satellites for Personal Communications," *Scientific American*, April 1998.

1400 kms. This system, like some of the other systems in this technology, will offer a wide range of data and multimedia services with connections to the Internet and intranets. In addition, most of these systems will offer high bandwidth capabilities ranging from at least 64 kbit/s up to a megabit range, probably 1.55 Mbit/s. The estimated cost for the Teledesic system is $9 billion.

An even more expensive system that is comparable in complexity to Teledesic is Motorola's Celestri system. This operator will launch 63 satellites at an altitude of 1400 km. It will also deploy 9 geosynchronous satellites. The GEOs will be used for subscribers with applications not sensitive to delay caused by the geosynchronous orbit.

Other systems are less ambitious, less complex, and do not cost as much. For example the Loral and Morningstar technologies will provide limited coverage with only 3 or 4 satellites targeting the more highly populated areas of the world.

LITTLE LEOs

Due to the progress made in antenna design, a new type of satellite is being launched to support mobile communications with low data rates (100–300 bit/s) and low frequencies (below 1 GHz). An example of a little LEO is Orbital Sciences Corporation's OrbComm. It will support two-way messaging, paging, position location, and data collection.

The system will consist of 26 to 36 satellites weighing only 85 pounds. These satellites will have a lifetime of about four years. The up-link will be at the 148–150.5 MHz spectrum; the down-link will be 137–138 MHz.

The handset will operate with TDM bursts with a receive rate of 4.8 kbit/s and a send rate of 2.4 kbit/s.

WHAT IS NEXT?

Even though the Ka-band systems are still in the planning stages, several companies are planning systems that are operating beyond the Ka-band. Hughes and Motorola have filed for licenses from the FCC to launch systems that operate at wavelengths at approximately 6–8 millimeters. This band is the so-called Q/V band, which (at this time) severely tests the limits of technology.

Notwithstanding the challenges of the technology and the additional aspect that there may be too many operators for the market to support, it is obvious that within the next few years an individual may be able to directly communicate to any point in the world with a cellular phone. Like it or not, the combination of the satellite technology and the second generation mobile-earthbound technology will allow us to stay in touch at any time.

SUMMARY

Satellites are cost-effective systems for voice, data, and video applications. The early systems used ALOHA and slotted ALOHA schemes to manage traffic on the channel. The TDMA technology was used on satellite channels long before it appeared on land-based wireless systems.

The satellite PCS technology holds great promise, but the number of licensed operators that will go into service may saturate the market and lead to commercial failures. Some will survive, and another tool is emerging for the instant, stay-in-touch communications world.

9

Data Operations

This chapter is devoted to the discussion of data communications operations on second generation mobile wireless systems. After a look at the forecast for the growth of data traffic over mobile wireless systems, the use of the ITU-T I, X, and V series standards is examined. This part of the discussion explains the terminal adaptation (TA) operation, including the support of asynchronous and synchronous bearer capabilities.

The chapter also describes the short message service (SMS) and the cell broadcast service, both of which are used in Europe and North America on the GSM-based systems, with SMS also employed on IS-136.

The chapter also discusses the Cellular Digital Packet Data (CDPD) system, a data communications network built to operate on AMPS interfaces, widely used in North America.

No discussion would be complete if the TCP/IP suite of protocols were excluded, and this chapter explains how TCP/IP is employed in a mobile wireless network. In addition, an introduction to Mobile IP is provided at the end of the chapter.

Also, a review is provided of new data initiatives that is taking place on TDMA systems, including High Speed Circuit Switched Data (HSCSD), V.42 bis, GSM General Packet Radio Service (GPRS), and the 14.4/28.8 kbit/s service.

MARKET FORECASTS

Various studies predict a steady growth in the mobile PC user market. Figure 9–1 shows the forecasts the worldwide market through the year 2000. One might question the relatively small numbers, especially in light of the very large growth rate of the data communications market. One reason is that it is difficult and dangerous to operate a data terminal in a moving vehicle and awkward to use with pedestrian mobility.

This forecast was provided by Intel at the IBC Data over GSM Conference (July 1 and 2, 1997), The Royal Garden Hotel, London. As keypads and notebook computers become more user-friendly and drop in price, and as the wireless phone reaches further into the population, the data market might be greater than this study predicts. But the very nature of user-network interaction with a data terminal will always limit the deployment of data communications applications in mobile cellular networks.

Nonetheless, data over wireless represents an attractive market for the service provider. One reason for this statement is the long holding times for many data-related calls and the added income that can result from the longer connects.

The data over wireless market growth rate is slow because it is new, and current techniques limit most transmissions to only 9.6 kbit/s. But products are emerging (and the standards bodies are putting together specifications) that provide more throughput across the air interface.

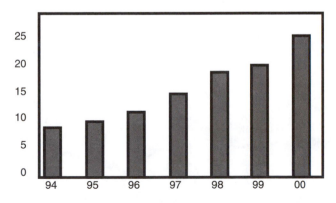

Figure 9–1 Worldwide mobile PC users (in millions).

CONNECTION OPTIONS

As the data over wireless market emerges, several connection options are becoming available to users. These are shown in Figure 9–2 as options 1, 2 and 3. Be aware that these options may not be available in some countries, due to regulations and the state of the data communications technology.

The first option is to use the public switched telephone network (PSTN) for the transit system between the mobile user and the user's home network (an intranet), although the session could just as easily be a session to a server in the Internet. In the long run, this option is the least desirable, because it consumes resources of a network (the telephone network) that is not designed for data transport. I say "in the long run," because this approach is certainly effective, but until the telephony infrastructure evolves to an asynchronous, statistical multiplexing architecture, this option will remain suboptimal. However, in some locations in the world, it is the only way to transport data over wireless.

Option 2 is the bypassing of the telephone with a direct access to the mobile user's communicating partner. Examples are private microwave systems and satellite systems. In some instances, this option takes the form of using non-telephone service providers; for example, in the United States, the Ardis and RAM service providers or the Cellular Digital Packet Data (CDPD) network that is deployed in most large U.S. cities.

Option 3 makes use of the Internet. In many installations, this option still takes the traffic through the public telephone network, at least through a local end office. At this end office, a "front-end processor" may be installed to divert data traffic from the conventional voice-oriented cir-

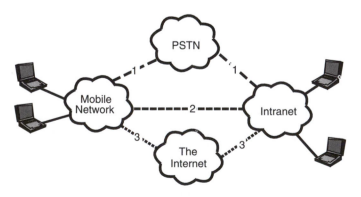

Figure 9–2   Connection options.

cuit switch to a packet switch and/or directly to an Internet Service Provider (ISP). This option is only as effective as the telcos and ISPs' capabilities.

Figure 9–3 shows the layers and the names of the layers that are invoked across the interface between the mobile and land station for a wireless, data configuration. We will be using this figure throughout these explanations to illustrate how data traffic is exchanged between the two stations. The next few paragraphs provide an overview of these layers.

The lowest layer in the model is called the *physical layer*. The physical layer is responsible for activating, maintaining, and deactivating a physical circuit between communicating machines. The physical layer's most common operations deal with the creation and reception of physical signals. For example, conventions may exist to represent a binary one with a plus voltage and a binary zero with a minus voltage. Of course, in the mobile environment, the data communications physical layer must be integrated with the air interface physical layer.

The *data link layer* is responsible for the transfer of data across *one* communications link. It delimits the flow of bits from the physical layer. It also provides for the identity of the bits. It usually (but not always) en-

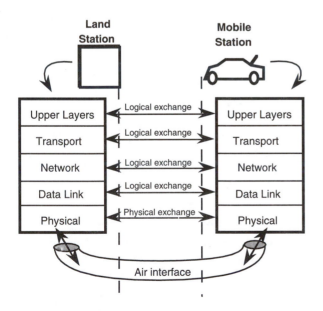

Note: Invocation of network, transport, and upper layers at a land station varies. Each vendor offering should be examined.

Figure 9–3 The mobile air data interface.

sures that the traffic arrives safely at the receiving machine. It often provides for flow control to ensure that the machine does not become overburdened with too much data at any one time. One of its most important functions is to provide for the detection of transmission errors and many data link protocols provide mechanisms to recover from lost, duplicated, or erroneous data. If this operation is supported, traffic is accounted for by the exchange of positive acknowledgments (ACKs) or negative acknowledgments (NAKs) between the sending and receiving stations.

The *network layer* specifies the interface of the user into a network, as well as the interface of two machines with each other through a network. It may allow users to negotiate options with the network and each other. For example, the negotiation of throughput, delay, and acceptable error rates are common negotiations. The network layer defines switching/routing procedures within a network. It also includes the routing conventions to transfer traffic between networks (internetworking). The network layer support varies from system to system. For example, the X.25 features are quite different from the Internet Protocol (IP) features.

The *transport layer* provides the interface between the data communications network and the upper three layers (generally part of the user's system). The transport layer provides for the end-to-end accountability of user traffic across more than one data link. It also is responsible for end-to-end integrity of users' data in internetworking operations. Therefore, it is a vital layer for sending traffic to users that are attached to different networks.

THE TERMINAL ADAPTATION (TA) MODEL[1]

The mobile wireless technology was designed primarily for the support of voice traffic at both the air interface and in the network. However, provisions have been made for the support of non-voice traffic, principally data and facsimile (fax). The transmission rates for these systems are modest, with a peak rate of 9.6 kbit/s.

Notwithstanding the relatively slow speeds, some systems provide a wide variety of configuration and interface options for the support of data and fax. These options are based on the Integrated Services Digital Network (ISDN) model, with modifications made for a mobile, wireless system.

---

[1]The TA model's use varies between the mobile wireless standards. The reader should check the specific air interfaces specification for the details.

Figure 9–4 illustrates the mobile wireless adaptation of the ISDN model. The terms and phrases in this figure are identical to ISDN, except the term MT (mobile termination) replaces the ISDN term NT (network termination). The MT is the MS's interface across the air interface (Um) to the network. It has a number of responsibilities:

- Rate adaptation (accommodating different data rates between the network and the MS)
- Flow control and data integrity of user traffic
- End-to-end synchronization between terminals
- Filtering status information from the user
- Terminal compatibility checking
- Loopback testing across the air interface

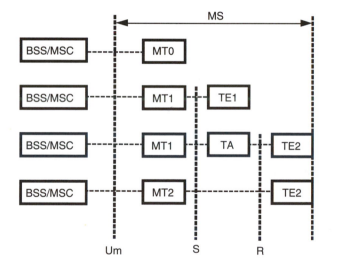

where:
BSS	Base station system
MSC	Mobile switching center
MT	Mobile termination
R, S, Um	Reference points
TA	Terminal adapter
TE1	Terminal equipment type 1 (ISDN native equipment)
TE2	Terminal equipment type 2 (non-ISDN equipment [X or V terminal])

Figure 9–4   Model for terminal adaptation.

The TA is a terminal adapter, which performs the rate adaptation operations cited above and acts as an interworking device between ITU-T X or V Series type terminals (terminal equipment type 2 [TE2]) and the network. In this regard, the TA may perform protocol mapping operations.

The TE1 operates in the native mode of the network (the operations at the BSS/MSC) and does not need the intervention of the TA.

Finally, the R, S, and Um reference points the define points of interconnection of the MT, TA, and TE entities, and a description of the protocol operations that occur between them.

TA Support Services

The terminal adapter operations support four major types of services, which are listed in Table 9–1. All services, including the short message service (SMS) and the cell broadcast service (CBS), rely on the use

Table 9–1   Interfaces and Protocols Supported

Asynchronous Bearer Capabilities

- V.14
- V.21 interface
- V.22 bis interface
- V.23 interface
- V.32 interface
- I.420 interface
- V.25 bis signaling procedures

Synchronous Bearer Capabilities

- V.22 interface
- V.22 bis interface
- V.26 ter interface
- V.32 interface
- X.21 interface
- X.21 bis interface
- X.25 procedure
- X.32 procedure
- V.25 bis procedure
- I.420 interface

Short Message Service (SMS)

Cell Broadcast Service (CBS)

of the X and V Series Recommendation (standards) published by the ITU-T.

The term interface in this figure refers to the conventional DTE/DCE interface (data terminal equipment/data circuit terminating equipment); for example, a DTE work station that interfaces with a DCE modem. In most systems, the DTE/DCE usually refers to the terminal adapter function (TAF). The "interface" is between the TE (a DTE) or TA (a DTE) and the MT (a DCE). This interface requires the implementation of subsets of the V or X Series Recommendations. This rather simple statement (as just stated, a requirement in the specifications) means a great deal: The interface is standardized with well-understood and tested procedures (and available in off-the-shelf packages).

The SMS operations define how the MT and TE cooperate with each other to transfer and store messages. The CBS operations define how cell broadcast services and SMS operations interwork with each other in relation to the TE and MT interface. Figure 9–5 shows the SMS operations, as defined in the North American GSM-based specifications. Several options are provided to the user. For example, messages can be held at the

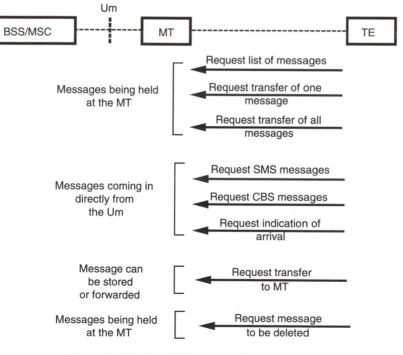

Figure 9–5   The SMS and CBS operations.

MT and reviewed by the mobile user. Then, the user can decide which messages to release. As well, messages can be held or deleted, all at the discretion of the user.

Upcoming Capabilities

By the time this book is in print, the reader will have access to handsets that use the TA/MT operations to support a wide range of sophisticated services. For example, work is underway to place Java capabilities in the handset and support the downline loading of applets to the MS.

TCP/IP ON MOBILE WIRELESS SYSTEMS

Scores of books are available on the Internet and TCP/IP, and this series will have books on the advanced features of the Internet. I will not waste your time on yet another description of this technology, but will provide a general overview of the pertinent aspects of TCP/IP in relation to mobile wireless systems.

Figure 9–6 provides a brief summary of the functions of the Internet layers. The dashed lines indicate the logical flow of the traffic in the layers, which is actually the exchange of protocol control information (PCI) between peer layers, and at the application layer, the exchange of user traffic.

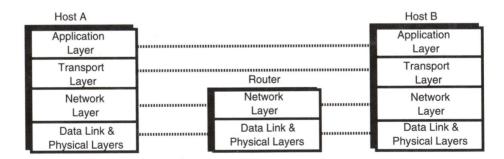

Functions of Layers:
   Application: User traffic transfer (files, E-mail, browsing, etc.)
   Transport: Safe delivery of traffic across the Net
   Network: Routing of traffic, as well as route discovery
   Data link: Traffic management on each link
   Physical: Signaling of bits across air interface

Figure 9–6   Example of Internet layer operations.

The application layer is responsible for the transfer of user traffic, such as files, E-mail, browsing messages, and so on. An Internet usually has scores of application layer protocols, and the sole purpose of the layers below the application layer is to support the delivery of application layer traffic between computers.

The transport layer is responsible for the safe delivery of traffic across the network. Thus, it provides mechanisms for acknowledging traffic between two end machines, such as two workstations or a workstation and a server. In case traffic is lost or discarded in the network, the transport layer is able to recover by resending the traffic. Other options at the transport layer do not provide for end-to-end acknowledgment, if the end user does not need this level of integrity (say, for voice traffic).

The network layer is responsible for the routing of traffic and for route discovery; that is, finding a route in the network between the two end stations.

The data link layer is responsible for traffic management on each link. It can also be configured to provide acknowledgments, but only on one link. Links on local area networks usually do not perform these acknowledgments, due to their inherent reliability and the overhead that is necessary to institute these operations. Most Internet point-to-point links use the Point-to-Point Protocol (PPP) at the link layer. PPP provides a wide array of options for negotiating features like authentication, compression, as well as loading IP addresses.

The physical layer is responsible for the signaling of the bits and other functions such as the timing of the signals between machines, the stipulation of the voltages, current flow, and so on. Usually, the end user implementation of the physical layer is through the well-known modem.

Figure 9–7 shows a typical invocation of common protocols in the layers to deliver traffic from one user machine to another. Once again, the dashed lines indicate the logical flow of the traffic in the layers, which is actually the exchange of protocol control information (PCI) between peer layers, and at the application layer, the exchange of user traffic. In this example, the traffic is data in the file transfer protocol (FTP) messages.

At the transport layer, the transmission control protocol (TCP) is responsible for the end-to-end management of the traffic between the host computers. This entails: (a) acknowledging traffic, (b) resending lost or errored traffic, (c) controlling the flow of traffic between hosts, and (d) identifying the applications resting above TCP that are sending and receiving the traffic. An other transport layer is called the user datagram protocol (UDP), which does not perform acknowledgment functions.

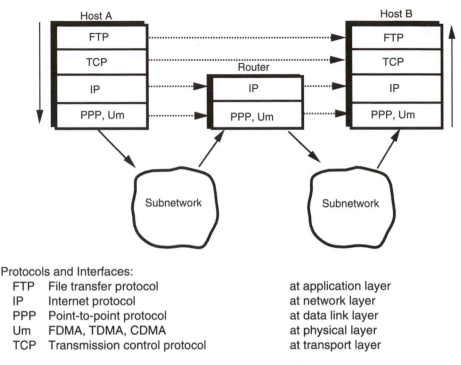

Figure 9–7   Internet protocol operations.

PPP operates at the data link layer, and the physical layer is the mobile wireless Um specification on the air interface. However, on the network side, the physical layer is usually a T1 or SONET link.

TRAFFIC MANAGEMENT AND INTEGRITY ISSUES

The issue of data integrity in a mobile wireless system raises issues that do not exist in wire-based systems. The first issue pertains to the relatively error-prone RF channel in contrast to a relatively error-free wire-based channel. The second issue pertains to the variability in transmission times in a mobile environment due to the roaming of the mobile station and the transport of the mobile station's traffic across (potentially) many intermediate nodes.

Figure 9–8 shows one approach to providing data integrity in a mobile wireless system. As suggested by the solid arrow operating at the data link layers, error detection, acknowledgments, and retransmissions are provided at the air interface itself. Therefore, conventional layer 2

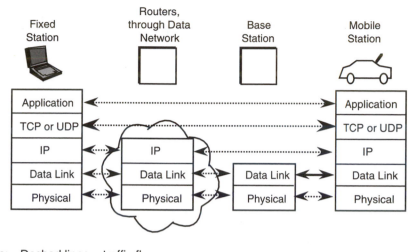

Notes: Dashed lines = traffic flow
Solid arrows = traffic flow and ACKs
UDP not invoked if ACKs needed

Figure 9–8   Approaches to data integrity: Option 1.

protocols such as adaptations of the link access procedure for the D channel (LAPD_ or the point-to-point protocol [PPP] can be utilized).[2] The advantage to this option is that it corrects the problem shortly after it is detected. In addition, retransmissions, if needed, occur only on the RF channel. Consequently, duplicate data units are not introduced into other components and links in the overall system.

The disadvantage to this approach is that traffic integrity is provided only at the air interface and there is no assurance that the traffic arrives correctly at the remote host. Link layer operations are capable only of error control measures on a specific link. To illustrate, assume that the traffic is delivered safely to the land node attached to the mobile link and is acknowledged by that node. The original transmitting mobile station receives the acknowledgment and deletes its copy of the traffic. Subsequently, if the acknowledging node fails (software bug, memory hit, etc.) then the traffic is lost from the standpoint of the data link (L2) protocol.

---

[2]PPP would be a very good choice for layer 2 because of its negotiation and encapsulation features. However, it would have to be modified if retransmissions of errored traffic are required. Currently, PPP uses the HDLC unnumbered information (UI) operation, which does not support retransmissions. However, it is a straightforward task to run PPP over another retransmission layer 2 protocol, such as a modified LAPD, which provides for retransmissions.

Another option for providing data integrity is to execute acknowledgments and retransmissions between the host machines themselves. Figure 9–9 shows the approach is performed through the layer 4 protocol, the Transmission Control Protocol (TCP). The advantage to this approach is that it provides end-to-end integrity since the acknowledgments and possible retransmissions are performed by the TCP modules that reside in the two host machines, the mobile station and the fixed station.

The disadvantages to this approach are as follows. First, the retransmission timers are more difficult to manage in a mobile network than in a fixed network due to increased variability in the transmission schemes. The second disadvantage results from the fact that while an error might occur at one specific node or specific link, the retransmitted traffic is reintroduced on each link and through each node. If errors are frequent, the retransmissions through the entire system will affect throughput and performance.

Another option for providing data integrity, depicted in Figure 9–10, is to place TCP at the base station and map two TCP connections. The first connection exists between the base station and the mobile station, and the second connection exists between the base station and the other host. This approach does not eliminate the problems associated with the

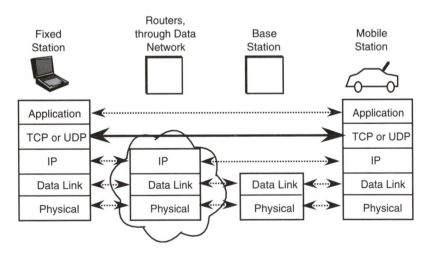

Notes: Dashed lines = traffic flow
         Solid arrows = traffic flow and ACKs
         UDP not invoked if ACKs needed

Figure 9–9   Approaches to data integrity: Option 2.

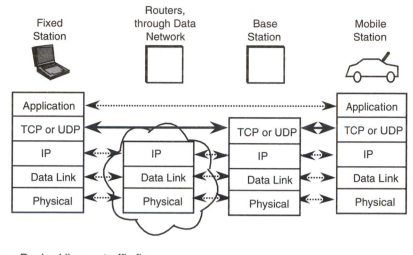

Notes: Dashed lines = traffic flow
         Solid arrows = traffic flow and ACKs
         UDP not invoked if ACKs needed

Figure 9–10   Approaches to data integrity: Option 3.

option just discussed (option 2) but the initial implementations of this option indicate that overall performance is improved in comparison to option 2. This concept is known by several terms in the industry. One of its original descriptions was *data link switching* (DLS). Some implementations call this approach *packet interceptions*.

The packet interception approach isolates the stream transmissions in the mobile cells from those in an internet and do not affect the overall operations of the internet traffic. This approach also simplifies and optimizes buffer management and reduces computational overhead in the mobile station.

For the reader who wishes more information on pros and cons of traffic integrity in a mobile environment the following paper is an excellent introduction: "Reliable Stream Transmission Protocols in Mobile Computing Environments," by Kevin Houzhi Xu, from *Bell Labs Technical Journal on Wireless,* 2 (3), Summer 1997.

THE CDPD NETWORK

In 1993, several mobile carriers published a specification for a wireless extension to the existing AMPS network. It is named the Cellular

Digital Packet Data System Specification (CDPD). Its goal is to provide a wireless packet data connectivity to mobile communications users.

The intent of CDPD is to utilize the unused voice capacity of the existing Advanced Mobile Phone Systems (AMPS) to support data transmission. Moreover, CDPD specifies the use of existing data communications protocols, such as the Connectionless Network Layer Protocol (CLNP), the Internet Protocol (IP), the OSI transport layer, and the Transmission Control Protocol (TCP).

In effect, existing protocols running at layers 3 and above use CDPD, which operates at the lower two layers. CDPD also specifies a wide variety of upper-layer protocols for directory management, electronic messaging, home location management, and so on. Many of these services are OSI- and Internet-based, such as X.500, X.400, and the Domain Name System (DNS), although not all these services are available.

Typical CDPD Topology

CDPD's architecture is OSI-based and is derived from ISO 7498 and the ITU-T's OSI X.200 Recommendations. The developers have used OSI concepts and terminology wherever possible, but the protocol stacks that have been implemented thus far are based also on the TCP/IP and related protocols. This section describes both protocol suites.

As seen in Figure 9–11, each CDPD service provider supports three interfaces: (a) the airlink interface (A): the interface between the service provider and the mobile subscriber; (b) the external interface (E): the interface between the service provider and external networks; and (c) the inter-service provider interface (I): the interface between cooperating CDPD service providers.

Two basic network entities exist in this architecture. The mobile end system (M-ES) is the user device, which is called a host in Internet terminology. Each M-ES must be identified with at least one globally unique Network Entity Identifier (NEI). During the handshake the NEI is verified, otherwise the M-ES cannot decode the data sent from the CDPD network.

The intermediate system (IS) is an internetworking unit, which is called a router in Internet terminology. In addition to supporting conventional protocols, such as TCP/IP, the IS also runs a CDPD-defined operation called the Mobile Network Location Protocol (MNLP), which provides location information in the system.

The other device is called a Mobile Data Intermediate System (MD-IS). The MD-IS is the only entity that has any knowledge of the mo-

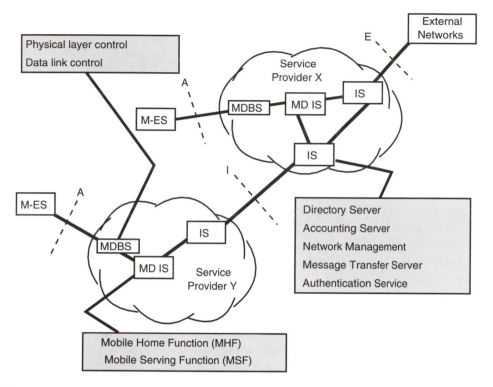

where:

A	Air interface
I	Inter-service provider interface
E	External interface
IS	Intermediate system
M-ES	Mobile end system
MD-IS	Mobile data intermediate system
MDBS	Mobile database station

Figure 9–11   The Cellular Digital Packet Data Specification (CDPD).

bility of the ESs. It provides mobility management through two routing services. The Mobile Home Function (MHF) provides a packet forwarding function and supports a database for its serving area (its "home" ESs and ISs). Each M-ES must belong to a fixed home area, and MHF keeps track of this information. The Mobile Serving Function (MSF) handles the packet transfer services for visiting MSs. Like most mobile systems, a visiting M-ES must register with the serving MD-IS, which notifies the visiting ES's MD-IS of its current location.

The mobile database station (MDBS) supports the air interface to the M-ES. It resides at the AMPS cell site, and uses the AMPS transmit and receive equipment. It must translate the data from the M-ES into packets and forward them to the MD-IS for further routing.

Sharing the AMPS Voice Channels

As mentioned earlier, CDPD shares the AMPS channels and equipment at the cell site. It uses these channels for a forward channel and a reverse channel. The forward channel is from the MDBS to the M-ES. The reverse channel is from the M-ES to the MDBS. The forward channel is broadcast from the MDBS to all the M-ESs in the cell or cell sector. It is always available and, since it is being sent from the MDBS, it is contentionless. In contrast, the reverse channel must be shared by more than one M-ES. Therefore, it has a contention protocol running on it to manage the traffic. This protocol is discussed later in this chapter.

In earlier chapters, we learned how TDMA channels are dynamically shared through the real-time allocation of time slots. CDPD is a TDMA technology that uses short time slots on an AMPS voice channel when there is no speech activity on that channel. Therefore, data traffic occupies a channel only when a voice system does not need the channel bandwidth.

The MDBS broadcasts the CDPD forward channel on an idle voice channel. Furthermore, when the MDBS detects that this voice channel is becoming active, the MDBS shuts off the forward channel and hops to an idle channel. In turn, the M-ESs are informed that the forward channel has been moved to another channel. This allows the M-ESs to tune to the particular channel, synchronize their activities, and continue ongoing communications.

Figure 9–12 provides a general view of how these activities are coordinated between the MDBS and M-ES, and Figure 9–13 shows the movement of the data transmission to different AMPS channels. In event 1, the M-ES is sending its data on AMPS channel number 5, shown as event 2. The MDBS, in turn, is monitoring all channels through a channel sniffing procedure. During this activity, the MDBS detects that an AMPS voice connection is starting to use this channel, which is occupied by CDPD traffic. As a result, the MDBS gives the direction through event 3 to the M-ES to hop to a different channel. This hop occurs in event 4.

Channel hopping requires that the M-ES resynchronize its signal and then commence sending data on another channel. This activity is de-

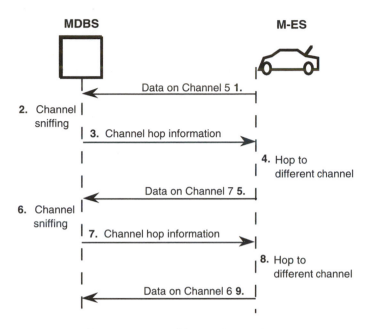

Figure 9–12   Channel hopping.

picted in event 5 where the M-ES has hopped to channel 7. Events 6 through 9 show yet another channel hop.

The MDBS detects the beginning of voice activity by "sniffing" low-level radio frequencies on the transmit side of the AMPS channel. Obviously, the MDBS must work within very tight time constraints since it may be analyzing all the calls in the cell or all the calls in a sector. The

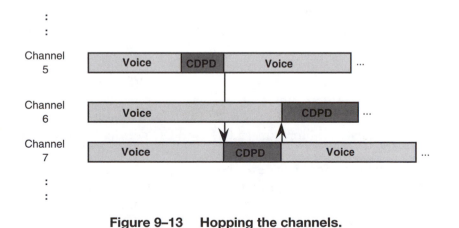

Figure 9–13   Hopping the channels.

sniffers can be either narrowband or wideband devices. A narrowband sniffer scans each 30 kHz channel, one at a time; whereas, the wideband receiver analyses all radio frequencies in the 12.5 MHz spectrum. In either implementation, the job of the MDBS is to allocate the data traffic to unused voice channels. In this example, the M-ES is hopping from channel 5 to channel 7 and then to channel 6. This allows the intermixing of both the ongoing AMPS voice traffic and the CDPD data traffic.

The M-ES and MDBS have slightly different methods of ramping up and ramping down during channel hops. For the forward RF channel, the MDBS has a ramp-up and ramp-down time of 10 ms. For the reverse channel, the M-ES has a ramp-up and ramp-down time of 2 ms.

Planned and Forced Channel Hops

A forced channel hop is the type of hop we just examined. A planned channel hop occurs at a time specified by the MDBS. Typically, the timer is set to a value less than an AMPS user's perception that the CDPD traffic is interference, which would result in the channel being taken out of use ("sealed").

Since the M-ES and MDBS may be hopping frequently, tight controls are needed for the off-to-on and on-to-off carrier switching. For example, in the off-to-on M-ES operation, the ramp-up time to the desired level is 1.979 ms.

Messages for Channel Configuration and Hopping

In Figure 9–14 some of the major operations between the MDBS and its associated M-ESs were explained. Although this figure shows four serial events, these events do not have to occur in the exact order shown in this figure. The figure does, however, represent a typical invocation of the events. In event 1, the channel identification message is sent by the MDBS to notify all M-ESs of the identity of the serving cell, the current channel stream, and the service provider network that is responsible for the cell. The fields in the message give the M-ESs information on the channel capacity, which indicates if there is spare capacity to support new mobile stations. The message also contains a channel stream identifier (CSI), the local cell identifier (LCI), and the service provider network identifier (SPNI). It also contains the local service area identifier (LSAI) field. All these identifiers are described shortly.

In event 2, the MDBS sends a channel configuration message to associated mobile stations. The purpose of this message is to provide information for the mobile stations for channel hopping and cell transfer. The

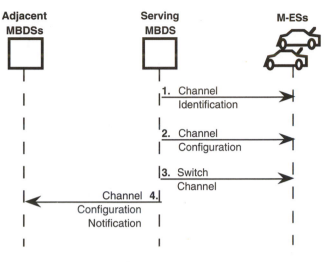

Figure 9–14   Configuration operations.

message contains information on the current cell or an adjacent cell as well as a list of channels currently in use for CDPD and the identified cells. It also contains the local cell identifier and an area color code. This color code is used to determine whether the referenced cell is served by the same MD-IS as the current cell. The message also contains an indication if the associated RF channel is dedicated for CDPD or must be used by AMPS as well. The RF channel numbers are also contained in this message.

In event 3, a channel message is sent to the mobile stations to give them information on the channel to which they should switch. In the message are a list of terminal end point identifiers (TEIs) that identify each mobile station that is required to process the message. Obviously, the message must also contain the RF channel fields to which the mobile station is to switch. Finally, in event 4, a channel configuration notification message is sent to other MDBSs to bring their information up to date on channel hops or to present new information if a channel stream is brought on-line or taken off-line. This message must be sent to each MDBS controlling an adjacent cell in which a change has occurred.

Mobility Management

Mobility management is responsible for the maintenance of location databases and the routing of the protocol data units to the M-ES. It works in conjunction with radio resource management, which is tasked with the selection and use of the optimal radio channel to the M-ES. Mobility management is organized around several key components, which are illustrated in Figure 9–15. The CDPD network service is provided through domains, areas, and cells. The cell, of course, is defined by the geographic area that is covered by either the mobile base data station (MBDS) or, if the cell is sectored, by the coverage area within the sector. An MBDS may control multiple cells.

An MBDS is under the control of a single mobile data intermediate system (MD-IS) and the combined coverage of all the MDBSs under the control of a single MD-IS defines a routing area subdomain. This area may cover multiple cellular geographic service areas (CGSA) or only one CGSA. The CDPD domain is defined by a cohesive set of MD-ISs that are operated and controlled by one CDPD service provider.

A single geographic service area defined by an MD-IS corresponds to the ISO definition of routing domains, which can be obtained in ISO-TR-9575 titled, the "OSI Routing Framework" and ISO-10589, titled "the IS-IS Intradomain Routing Protocol." Consequently, the MD-IS can be classified as a level 1 intermediate system because it routes directly to the end systems within its own area and it also routes to a level 2 IS when the destination is located in a different area.

The decision made to perform cell transfer, either within an area or between areas, is based on the local cell identifier (LCI), the channel stream identifier (CSI), and the channel stream color code, which is made of the cell group color and the area color. All cells in the same routing area are assigned the same area color code and the comparison of

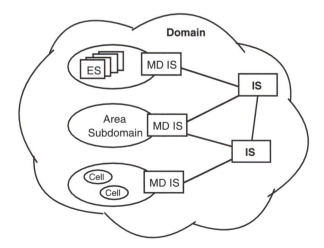

Figure 9–15 CDPD routing architecture.

these parameters on the previous RF channel to the current RF channel reveals one of three possible conditions:

1. There is no change in the cell group color or area color or the LCI or CSI; therefore, a channel hop has been performed and no further action is required.

2. The area color is the same, but the LCI and CSI is different; therefore an intra-area cell transfer is performed.

3. Different area colors exist, which means that a inter-area cell transfer procedure must be performed.

CDPD uses several identifiers in many of its messages between the various entities. Each cell is given a local cell identifier (LCI). The LCI must be unique among the cell and all the adjacent cells and it must be unique over all cells controlled by the same MDBS.

The channel stream identifier (CSI) is a unique 6-bit number for all channel streams on the cell. The LCI and CSI are concatenated to form a unique identifier for all channel streams on any given cell or its adjacent cells.

Each CDPD service provider network is identified by a 16-bit value called the service provider network identifier (SPNI). The SPNI must be unique among all CDPD service provider networks. The purpose of the SPNI is to allow the M-ES to identify the service provider network.

Finally, the local service area is identified by a 16-bit number called the local service area identifier (LSAI). This value must be unique among all local service areas in the CDPD network.

Intra-Area Cell Transfer

Figure 9–16 shows the operations involved for an intra-area cell transfer; that is to say, from one cell to another cell that is controlled by the same MD-IS. Since this activity involves only the transfer of the M-ES to another physical channel, these operations are transparent to the layers above the physical an data link layers. The M-ES decides to exit a cell if it detects an extended loss of channel synchronization and/or an unacceptable error rate. To assist the M-ES in locating a channel, the MDBS periodically broadcasts the RF channel number in use or as candidates for use in the adjacent cells.

After the M-ES has exited the old cell and made contact with the new cell and its MDBS, it then forwards a link layer receive ready (RR), shown in even 1, to the serving MD-IS. The MD-IS then acknowledges

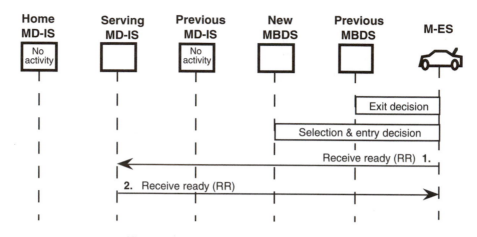

Figure 9–16   Intra-area cell transfer.

this frame by receive ready back, which is shown in event 2. This activity allows the MD-IS to update the physical media association for the M-ES.

Inter-Area Cell Transfer

In the event that the mobile station travels across cells, CDPD provides a set of procedures for the M-ES to re-register into a new MD-IS. These operations are shown in Figure 9–17. The first three boxes labeled exit decision, selection and entry decision, and data link establishment have been described in previous examples in this section. We pick up this discussion with the M-ES sending an end system hello (ESH, shown in event 1) to the new serving MD-IS. The function of this hello message is to inform the new MD-IS of the presence of the mobile station and to register the mobile station's addresses at the new MD-IS. The message must contain the unique address of the M-ES, which is known as the NEI. The NEI is either an OSI network layer address or the conventional Internet IP address. Upon receipt of this message, event 2 shows the new serving MD-IS sends to the home MD-IS the redirect request protocol data unit (RDR). This message contains the source address of the M-ES as well as a forwarding network address. This latter address is the address of the forwarding entity and the serving MD-IS and this is a direction to the home MD-IS to tell it where messages should be redirected. In event 3, the home MD-IS returns the request redirect confirm message to the new serving MD-IS and this tells this receiver if registration has been successful. In event 4, the new serving MD-IS returns to the mobile end system the intermediate system hello confirm (ISC), which is to confirm that

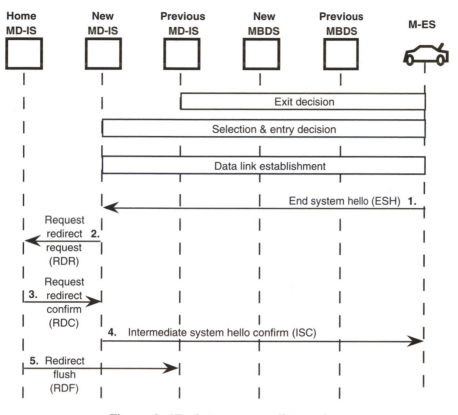

Figure 9–17   Inter-area cell transfer.

registration has indeed occurred. The final activity shown in event 5, is the redirect flush (RDF PDU), which is sent by the home MD-IS to notify a previous serving MD-IS that messages would no longer be forwarded to that location.

The CDPD Layers

Figure 9–18 illustrates one possibility of a full protocol layer stack operating at the mobile end station (M-ES), the mobile database station, the various intermediate stations and the end stations. We will use this figure to explain the functions of the layers, which will go a long way toward explaining some of the major features of CDPD.

For ease in this analysis I will discuss these layers from the physical layer and work up to the transport layer. The physical layer differs between the forward and reverse channels. We learned earlier that the forward channel is contentionless and the backward channel is contention-oriented. The data link on both physical channels operates at 19.2 kbit/s. The modems employ Gaussian-minimum shift keying (GSMK) with a modulation index of 0.5. The forward channel uses a Reed-Solomon encrypted packets of 378 bits in length. The format for this traffic is explained later in this section.

The ME-S and the MDBS operate with two layer 2 (data link) protocols: the mobile data link protocol (MDLP) and a MAC layer protocol designated in this figure as CDPD-MAC. The MAC layer is designed to provide frame delimiting of the traffic and also provides for error correction and detection on both the forward and backward channels. The MDLP sublayer is derived from HDLC.

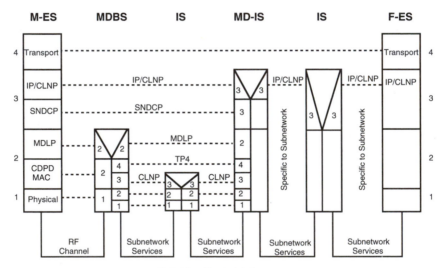

Dotted lines Denote data flow

where:

CDPD	Cellular digital packet data system
CLNP	Connectionless network protocol
F-ES	Fixed end system
IP	Internet protocol
IS	Intermediate system
M-ES	Mobile end system
MAC	Media access control
MD-IS	Mobile data intermediate system
MDBS	Mobile database station
MDLP	Mobile data link protocol
SNDCP	Subnetwork dependent convergence protocol
TP4	Transport layer protocol, class 4

Figure 9–18   Example of CDPD layers and data flow.

The subnetwork dependent convergence protocol (SNDCP) performs several functions. It is responsible for compression operations and also segments traffic into a preconfigured segment length. It is also responsible the encryption of the traffic at the transmit side and the decryption of the traffic at the receive side. Obviously, at the receive side, it is also responsible for reassembly of the segments and for performing decompression on the traffic.

At layer 3 rests either the Internet Protocol (IP) or the ISO connectionless network protocol (CLNP). These protocols provide CDPD with destination and source addresses. For IP, these are the well-known Internet addresses consisting of 32-bits that are registered through the Internet structure. For CLNP, the address varies but is usually derived from the OSI-based address defined in ITU-T recommendation X.200.

Finally, at the transport layer rests either the Internet's transmission control protocol (TCP) or the ISO/ITU-T transport layer protocol known as transport layer protocol class 4 (TP4). One of the major functions of these protocols is to provide end-to-end flow control and end-to-end acknowledgment of traffic.

The implementation of the layers within various subnetworks is not defined. For example, the physical layer, data link layers, and some transport services are unique to a specific subnetwork. Since we are dealing with an air interface in this chapter, those layers need not concern us.

Intended Services

Since CDPD is relatively new and deployment and development are still in their embryonic states, not all services have been developed. But it is important to keep in mind that if CDPD meets its goals of a nationwide connectivity, services will be quite important, just as they are in the fixed Internet.

Eventually, the intent is for the service provider to provide a number of "servers" for its domain. These servers reside in an IS and are called fixed end systems (F-ESs). The servers perform the operations that are summarized in the next paragraphs. Most of the services are based on layer 7 of the OSI Model. As a practical matter, more Internet-based layer 7 services are used in the industry, so the initial thrust of CDPD has concentrated on offering Internet applications. Figure 9–19 shows an abstract view of where the services can be provided. Bear in mind vendors vary in the placement (or inclusion) of these services. In addition, network providers vary in how these services are distributed and/or combined.

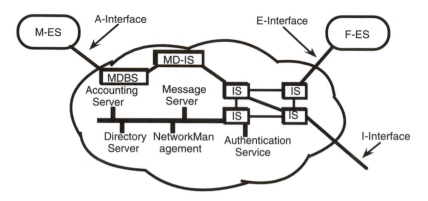

Figure 9–19   Service provider network fixed end systems (F-ES).

The directory server provides X.500 directory services for name-to-address translation, information on subscribers, and other "yellow" and "white" page functions. Lower layer access to a directory server must adhere to a specific CDPD protocol, ISO's Connection Oriented Transport Service (COTS), and optionally, ISO's Connectionless Network Service (CLNS), X.25, PVC frame relay, point-to-point, or a LAN profile.

The accounting server provides a repository for accounting information, including the collection and distribution of this information to interested (and authorized) parties. Lower layer access to an accounting server must adhere to the same conventions as the directory server.

Network management provides network management services through the use of either common management information protocol (CMIP) or simple network management protocol (SNMP). The ITU-T/OSI system management functional areas (ITU-T M.3400) must be supported (fault management, configuration management, accounting management, performance management, security management). Lower layer access to network management must adhere to the same conventions as the directory server.

The message transfer server provides an electronic messaging service through the use of ITU-T's X.400 Recommendation. Lower layer access to the message transfer server must adhere to the same conventions as the directory server, except ISO's connectionless network service (CLNS) is not allowed.

The authentication service provides an authentication service for a home MD-IS to verify a M-ES's credentials by the use of secret key encryption and decryption. The authentication protocol must run on top of

OSI's association control service element (ACSE, X.217) and the remote operations service element (ROSE, X.219). Authentication is explained in more detail later.

CDPD Layer Relationships

CDPD provides a wide variety of services at the various layers of a conventional OSI Model. Figure 9–20 shows the layers as well as the protocol entities residing in the layers. The subnetwork subprofiles include conventional layer 1 and layer 2 protocols such as X.25, frame relay, point-to-point, and of course the CDPD MAC physical layer. The lower layer subprofiles include several combinations of connection-oriented and connectionless services residing at the network and transport layers. The upper layers contain the services described earlier in this chapter.

Network Management Profiles. The CDPD network management profiles are illustrated in Figure 9–21. The I subprofile refers to an OSI-based protocol stack and the A subprofile refers to the Internet protocol subprofile. Due to the overhead in the OSI stacks, initial implementations have focused on the A subprofile.

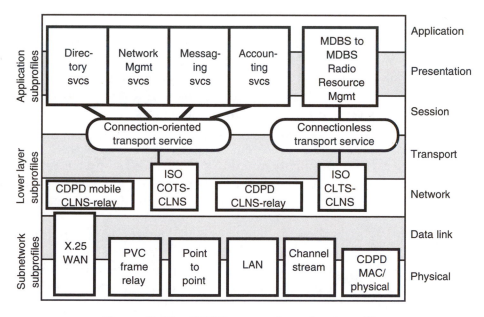

Figure 9–20   CDPD support services profiles.

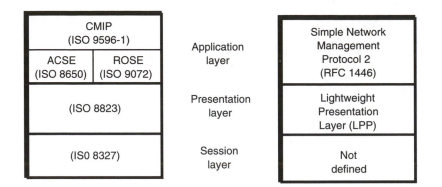

Figure 9–21   CDPD network management I & A subprofiles.

The OSI stack runs the common management information protocol (CMIP) over the association control service element (ACSE) and the Remote Operations Service Element (ROSE). CMIP performs conventional management operations such as the issuance of GET and SET messages to an agent. The agent, in turn, responds to these messages in accordance with the rules of the protocols and additional information stored in a management information base (MIB). ACSE is somewhat of a housekeeping protocol in the sense that it sets up an association between two CMIP entities in two different machines. After ACSE performs these functions, it is no longer invoked until the association is to be taken down. ROSE is a remote procedure call specification and is described in Chapter 8, therefore we shall not repeat this description in this chapter. The presentation and session layers are the conventional ISO, or ITU-T protocols. They are bound closely to the activities of the application layer and support syntax transfer and session management.

The Internet network management profile is much simpler. The simple network management protocol, version 2 (SNMP2) is used at the application layer. It too performs function such as GETs and SETs. It operates over a sparse presentation layer known as the lightweight presentation protocol (LPP). It does not invoke any session layer functions at this time.

Both protocols also allow an agent to send messages to a managing process. CMIP calls this message an event report and SNMP calls the message a trap. Generally, the protocols are similar in how they perform functions except CMIP is object-oriented allowing the use of inheritance, managed object classes, and the creation and deletion of instances of objects. SNMP is not object-oriented.

The Internet Profiles. Figure 9–22 shows a more commonly implemented protocol stack that uses the Internet specifications. The network layer contains the Internet Protocol (IP) and the Internet Control Message Protocol (ICMP). The transport layer contains the well-known Transport Control Protocol (TCP).

Physical Layer Interfaces

The unit transmitted over the channel stream is a fixed length block of 378 bits (see Figure 9–23). This burst is interleaved with a variety of control and synchronization bits, which are encoded using a systematic Reed-Solomon error correcting code. The encoding operation generates 47 6-bit symbols and a parity field of 16 6-bit symbols, yielding a block of 378 bits.

Each channel stream is assigned an 9-bit channel color code. This code has two fields: The 5-bit cell group color identifies a cell group and the 3-bit area color identifies a set of cells controlled by a given MD-IS. The color code is used by an M-ES to detect co-channel interference from a remote MDBS or to note that a cell transfer has involved a change of

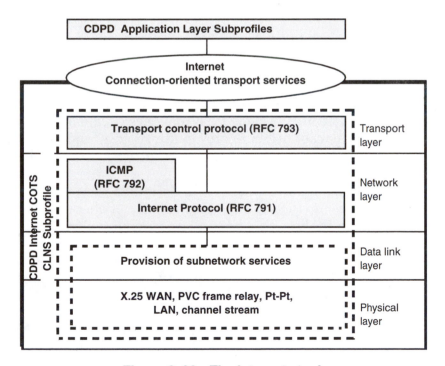

Figure 9–22 The Internet stack.

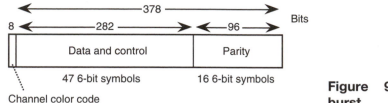

Figure 9–23 The CDPD burst.

MD-IS. The MDBS uses it to detect co-channel interference from a remote M-ES.

Data Flow Example

Figure 9–24 shows the flow of data from the network layer through the sublayers down to the physical layer. The figure shows where compression occurs, where encryption and decryption operations are implemented, as well as where segmentation operations are performed. Note that the names of the layers and sublayers are shown on the right side of the figure. The illustration is self-explanatory.

NEW INITIATIVES

When first generation mobile wireless systems were first conceived, there was not much interest in the support of data applications across the air interface. At about the same time that these systems began to be deployed, the data market began to grow quite rapidly, and with the advent of easy-to-use Internet interfaces, more attention has focused on mobile station data transfer capabilities.

The major problem is that these earlier systems were designed only for modest data rates, up to 9.6 kbit/s. This rate is not adequate for many applications, especially those that have a large amount of traffic to transfer, such as a file transfer.

To ameliorate this situation, the standards groups (and I highlight GSM) have been working on four techniques, all of which are designed to provide more bandwidth for data in GSM. They are: (a) data compression, (b) the High Speed Circuit Switched Data (HSCSD) method, (c) the GSM General Packet Radion Service (GPRS), and (d) the 14.4 kbit/s service. Table 9–2 lists these techniques and the associated bandwidth pro-

Packet Transformation Data Flow

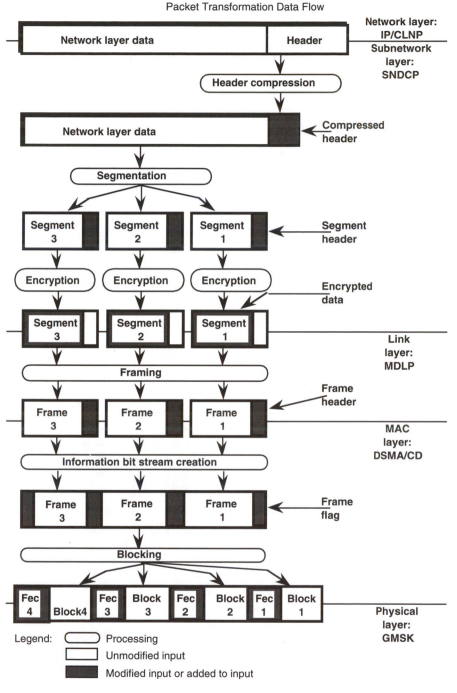

Figure 9–24   CDPD CLNS-relay subprofile.

311

Table 9–2   New Initiatives for Data Support

Method	Bandwidth Provided
• Data compression (using V.42 bis):	~38.4 kbit/s
• High Speed Circuit Switched Data (HSCSD):	Up to 64 kbit/s
• GSM General Packet Radio Service (GPRS):	Up to ~170 kbit/s
• 14.4 kbit/s service	14.4 kbit/s (28.8, with dual slots)

vided through their use. This part of the chapter discusses these techniques.[3]

V.42 has aroused considerable interest in the user community because it addresses three major problems that have developed with the increased use of asynchronous devices (and especially asynchronous personal computers): (a) an asynchronous-to-synchronous conversion protocol and a more sophisticated error-detection process for asynchronous systems than exists with simple echo checks and parity checks. V.42 is designed to perform code conversion as well as error detection and retransmission of damaged data. V.42 bis is an optional feature of V.42 and is the culmination of several years of efforts by CCITT, working in conjunction with users and vendors.

During the work on V.42, which was completed in 1988, the CCITT (now ITU-T) study group XVII decided that a data compression enhancement was needed to further the performance of error correcting modems. Consequently, a number of existing schemes were analyzed, notably British Telecom's BTLZ, Hayes' System, Microcom's MNP5 and MNP7, and the ACT Formula. The decision was made to use the BTLZ algorithm, which we examine shortly. V.42 bis was not published in the *Blue Book*, but has undergone rapid development and, as of this writing, is now an approved standard.

Compression attempts to make better use of a potentially overused resource, the communications channel. The following discussion illustrates this point.

Practically all symbols generated and used by computers are comprised of a fixed number of bits coded to represent a character. The codes (for example, ASCII) have been designed as fixed length because comput-

---

[3]Part of this material is sourced from the "Data over GSM" Conference, held in London (July 1–2, 1997) and sponsored by IBC Technical Services, Ltd., London, UK. Other sources are from my work on the V Series specifications: *The V Series Recommendations*, McGraw-Hill, 2nd edition.

ers require a fixed number of bits in a code to efficiently process data. Most machines use octet (8-bit) alignment.

The fixed-length format requirement means all transmitted characters are of equal length, even though the characters are not transmitted with equal frequency. For example, characters such as vowels, blanks, and numbers are used and transmitted more often than consonants and characters such as a question mark. This practice can lead to considerable link inefficiency.

One widely used solution to code and channel utilization inefficiency is to adapt a variable-length value (code) to represent the fixed length characters. In this manner, the most frequently transmitted characters are compressed, represented by a unique bit set smaller than the conventional bit code. This data compression technique can result in substantial savings in communications costs.

To gain an understanding for the need for data compression capabilities, consider that a normal page of text contains 1920 characters. Assuming an 8-bit code is used to represent a character, a total of 15,360 bits will be transferred across a communications link (this number is significantly understated because it does not include start/stop bits and other control functions). Therefore, the use of a conventional V.22 *bis* 2400 bit/s modem can cause significant throughput and response time problems for certain types of transmissions.

The V.42 bis data compression recommendation has a compression ratio of 3:1 to 4:1 (based on the use of ASCII text). Figure 9–25 illustrates the V.42 and V.42 bis model.

The recommendation requires approximately 3K of memory. The dictionary size for the characters and strings can be as little as 512 bytes and up to 2048 bytes. The designer must analyze the trade-offs between smaller and larger dictionaries and must consider the fact that the larger dictionaries provide better performance with higher compression ratios even though they consume more memory. Readers should keep in mind

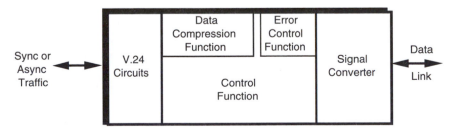

Figure 9–25   The V.25 and V.42 bis model.

that V.42 bis permits the same software to be used on different size dictionaries.

As depicted in Figure 9–26, the V.42 bis compression algorithm works on strings of characters. It does not work on character substitution, but encodes a string of characters with a fixed length code word. The system also uses a dictionary to store frequently occurring character strings along with a code to represent these character strings.

Figure 9–27 provides a general view of the operations of the transmit modem and the receive modem. The "argument" character string is matched against the directory on the transmit side and an attempt is made to match this character string to a string existing in the dictionary. If a code word is found that matches (for a previous match it could be CON but not CONE) a code word is created for CON, sent to another buffer for assembly with other previously matched code words. The code words are placed in the LAPM frame and transmitted to the receiving modem.

The bottom of this figure shows the operations at the receiving modem. The code words are used to perform a lookup in the receiving modem's dictionary. The code word value reveals a particular string. This permits the code word to be mapped back to the original character string.

The dictionaries must be updated in both modems. Consider the transmit side first. When the dictionary detects the first character in the data stream that does not match an entry in the dictionary, it forwards

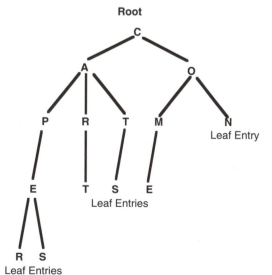

Figure 9–26   The V.42 bis tree.

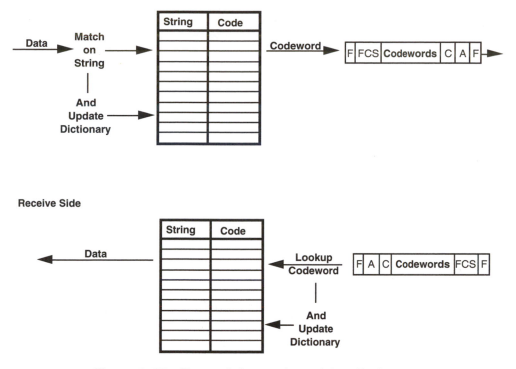

Figure 9–27   Transmitting and receiving dictionary.

the character string that did match with the appropriate code word and then uses the unmatched character to produce one more concatenated string in the dictionary. In this example, it sends the code word for CON and adds the CONE as a new string entry and with an appropriate code word.

The High Speed Circuit Switched Data Service (HSCSD)

The high speed circuit switched data (HSCSD) data feature is a recent addition to the European standards bodies to enhance the data capabilities of GSM. As shown in Figure 9–28, HSCSD allows a user to burst into several TDMA time slots on the radio interface. Since these bursts occur in one frame, the user is provided with more bandwidth.

HSCSD is designed for the network to dynamically allocate the time slots for the user. In addition, asymmetric allocation is provided, which allows the up-link and down-link capacity to vary.

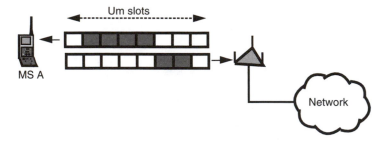

Figure 9–28   High Speed Circuit Switched Data (HSCSD).

HSCSD also is designed to provide a guaranteed throughput and fairly constant delay. The technique does require a relatively long setup time, typically entailing several seconds.

GSM Packet Radio Service (GPRS)

The GSM general packet radio service (GPRS) is yet another GSM Phase 2+ specification (see Figure 9–29). This technique is designed to transmit small amounts of frequently sent data or large amounts of infrequently sent data. The user reserves channel capacity only when the user application needs for sending or receiving traffic. At other times, the user is placed in a standby mode. The system uses different coding schemes based on the channel quality, therefore the data rate can vary from approximately 10 kbit/s up to approximately 170 kbit/s. GPRS also

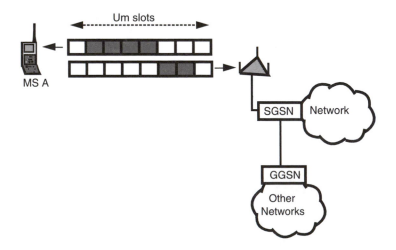

Figure 9–29   GSM Packet Radio Service (GPRS).

allows a single user to transmit simultaneously in several TDMA time slots. Channel reservation and bandwidth allocation varies depending on the number of simultaneous users requesting bandwidth.

Two additional components are placed in a GPRS network, principally to separate the GSM data and speech traffic. The first component is called the serving GPRS support node (SGSN) and the second component is called the gateway GPRS support node (GGSN). The SGSN typically connects to several BSSs and acts as a decision point for diverting the traffic to conventional voice networks or to data networks. The GGSN acts as the connecting point to the operator's SGSNs and to outside networks such as Internets, intranets, frame relay, and packet networks.

The SGSN and GGSN are routers configured for these operations and configured with mobility-aware software. The GPRS system works in conjunction with the overall GSM map protocols to support location information pertaining to the users.

As shown in Figure 9–30, the GPRS architecture is defined with interfaces and reference points. The SGSN also interfaces with the GSM MSCs and VLRs through the Gs interface. Information is exchanged with HLRs through the Gr interface. The other G interfaces are designed to support the exchange of registration and data traffic between the various components shown in the figure.

GPRS distinguishes between different types of mobile stations. These stations are designated as classes A, B, or C. Class A stations support both circuit switched and packet switched traffic simultaneously. Class B stations can attach simultaneously to circuit switched and packet switched systems and monitor both. Transfer is supported on both

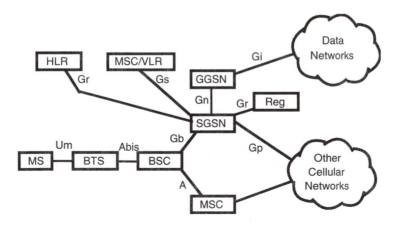

Figure 9–30   GPRS interfaces and reference points.

services but not simultaneously. Class C stations do not support simultaneous attachment nor the monitoring of traffic. A circuit switched or packet switched service must be selected manually or through preprovisioned settings.

12.0 kbit/s Operations

The 12.0 kbit/s service for GSM has been in operation for several years. Figure 9–31 shows a functional diagram for the service. The 12.0 kbit/s rate is supported through the conventional 20 ms time slices as input into the block coder. The 1/2 rate convoultional coder produces a 489-bit stream that is input into a puncturing process. The puncturing operation reduces the number of bits to a 456-bit stream, which is then block interleaved into the TDMA slots. The result of the process is the transmission of the 12 kbit/s rate over the conventional 22.8 GSM channel.

The 14.4 kbit/s Service

The 14.4 kbit/s service uses a different channel coding scheme that is basically a new puncturing scheme, as shown in Figure 9–32. The system supports both synchronous and asynchronous services and, through the simultaneous use of two time slots on the air interface, the 28.8 kbit/s service is also supported. This data rate is quite attractive since many

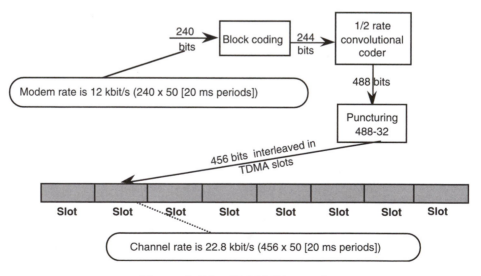

Figure 9–31   12.0 kbit/s service.

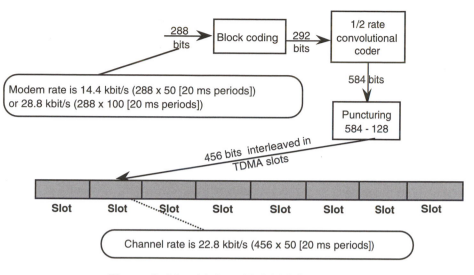

Figure 9–32   14.4 or 28.8 kbit/s service.

modems in operation today use the V.34 modem specification, which defines transmission rates up to 28.8 kbit/s.

The standards for the 14.4 kbit/s and 28.8 kbit/s rates are not finished. If the reader needs more information on this topic, the following papers are recommended:

1. Pirhonen, R.P., Ranta, P.A., "Single Slot 14.4 kbit/s Service for GSM," submitted to the Seventh IEEE International Symposium on Personal, Indoor and Mobile Radio Communications, October 15–18, 1996, Taipei, Taiwan.

2. Pirhonen, R.P., Ranta, P.A., "Single Slot 14.4 kbit/s Data Service for GSM," submitted to the Seventh Nordic Conference on Digital Mobile Radio Communications, DMR VII, October 2–4, 1996, Copenhagen, Denmark.

MOBILE IP

It is obvious from the material in this chapter that TCP/IP plays a big role in data communications systems operating with mobile-wireless technology. One of the principal challenges in applying TCP/IP to a mobile-wireless environment is accommodating the user's IP address. This address is a fixed address designed to identify the point-of-attachment of a user device (host) to a specific network or subnetwork.[4] Consequently, when the mobile station and its user roam into another network, some technique is needed to properly identify the roaming host that is now attached to a different network.

The purpose of mobile IP is to enhance the conventional Internet protocols to support the roaming of nodes wherein the mobile station can receive datagrams no matter where they are located. Without the use of mobile IP, a mobile station node would have to change its address whenever it moved to a new network (that is, whenever it changes its point of attachment). Additionally, without the use of mobile IP, routes specific to the host would have to be propagated into the networks that are concerned with supporting this host. Obviously, these two operations are not efficient and would create tremendous housekeeping problems for the network. In addition, due to the nature in which IP addresses are used to identify higher-layer connections (sockets into the applications themselves), it becomes an impossible task to maintain this relationship if the IP address changes.

The requirements for any type of system that supports the mobility of an IP node are summarized here:[5]

- The mobile station must be able to communicate when it moves to another point of attachment without having to change its IP address.

- The mobile station must be able to communicate with non-mobile-IP nodes. This should require no enhancements to conventional hosts or routers.

- Authentication must be provided to protect against security breaches.

- Overhead traffic flowing across the air interface must be kept to a minimum in order to reduce complexity and cut down on the power requirements for "continuous" transmission of overhead messages.

- The IP address must be the conventional IP address currently used in Internets.

- There must be no additional for these procedures requirements (for example, for the allocation of special addresses).

---

[4]I make no distinction between network and subnetwork in this discussion.

[5]For a more thorough description I recommend *Mobile IP: Design Principals and Practices,* an Addison Wesley book by Charles E. Perkins.

Hereafter, the term mobile node is used to describe any device that changes its point of attachment from one network to another network. The mobile node is typically a mobile station, but it could be a more elaborate device, such as a router. Home network refers to the original point of attachment that the mobile node made when it received its IP address. At the home network the home agent (typically a router) is responsible for sending traffic to the mobile node when it is away from the home network. This home agent is also responsible for maintaining location information on the mobile node. Another device involved in the process is called the foreign agent. This device is typically a router attached to the visited network that acts as a conduit of traffic coming from the home agent to the mobile node.

Let us use these concepts to show an example of how mobile IP operates. In Figure 9–33, a mobile node has moved from its original point of attachment (its home address) to another subnetwork. The operations involved to support this movement require that two IP addresses are made available. One IP address is used to locate the mobile node and another is used to identify the endpoint of the mobile node.

If the mobile node is attached to its home network, then the IP operations are the same as with any Internet routing. However, if the mobile node has roamed to another network, then the datagram that is sent to this node is tunneled inside another datagram. This datagram has a different address—called the "care-of address"—in its header.

The changing of the address of the datagram for routing to the other network is known as readdressing. In addition, once the traffic has ar-

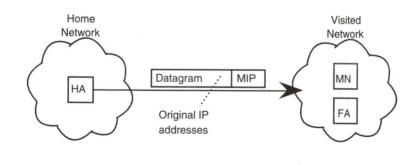

where:

FA   Foreign agent
HA   Home agent
MIP   Mobile IP header (contains the "care of address")
MN   Mobile node

Figure 9–33   Example of mobile IP operations.

rived at the mobile node's point of attachment, an operation called inverse readdressing occurs. Inverse readdressing entails the transformation of the datagram so that the care-of address is replaced by the original address in the datagram.

Mobile IP has many features beyond this general discussion. For the interested reader, I refer you to the Perkins book cited in the footnotes and to another book in this series titled *Advanced Features of the Internet*. Mobile IP is new and will play a big role in interworking fixed mobile Internets.

SUMMARY

Data communications networks and their associated market is a high-growth industry. The mobile network operations intend to exploit this market, but in order to do so, the bandwidth of the air interface must be increased. Efforts such as the GPRS are steps in the right direction.

The data protocols that manage the data traffic are in place and borrowed from fixed-wire networks. The TCP/IP suite and OSI's CLNP and IS-IS are the preferred protocols at this time.

10

The Wireless Local Loop (WLL)

This chapter describes the wireless local loop (WLL). The topologies for WLL are discussed first. Next, the LMDS and MMDS are explained as well. The chapter also includes a discussion on the DECT technology as a possible choice for a WLL protocol.

We highlight the DECT technology because (as of this writing) it is experiencing success in WLL. It is a leading technology for WLL with extensive implementations in Europe, China, South Africa, Egypt, Turkey, and Italy. It also has seen implementation in many parts of the former Soviet Union, Australia, Mexico, and almost all countries in South America.

In addition, the United States has defined a standard for low-power PCS that uses DECT as the foundation for Personal Wireless Telecommunications (PWT). Several manufacturers have worked together to define DECT for U.S. use. Currently, PWT is slated to operate at the unlicensed 1910–1930 MHz band and the licensed PCS band of 1850–1990 MHz. The RF power classes provide for 2mW and 90mW in unlicensed and 200 mW and 500 mW in licensed bands. The U.S. modulation technique is DQPSK yielding an approximate 825 kHz bandwidth.

While the development of DECT was a European initiative and has a European focus, we can see that it has become a worldwide technology. The European Telecommunications Standards Institute (ETSI) has decided that UMTS will be the only European part of UMT-2000. DECT is one technology that is being cited for accessing UMTS. (UMT-2000 and UMTS are covered in Chapter 11).

TOPOLOGY OF WLL

WLL access in the local loop provides yet another access alternative for the user. WLL both complements and competes with fixed wire access, such as telephone twisted pair (TTP), coaxial cable, and optical fiber. To see why, Figure 10–1 shows several WLL configurations.

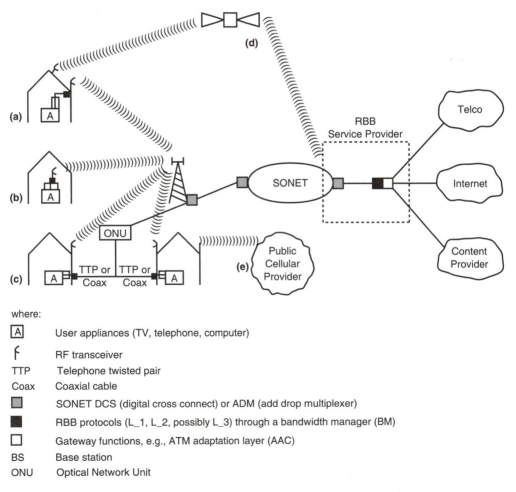

where:

A	User appliances (TV, telephone, computer)
ſ	RF transceiver
TTP	Telephone twisted pair
Coax	Coaxial cable
▪	SONET DCS (digital cross connect) or ADM (add drop multiplexer)
■	RBB protocols (L_1, L_2, possibly L_3) through a bandwidth manager (BM)
□	Gateway functions, e.g., ATM adaptation layer (AAC)
BS	Base station
ONU	Optical Network Unit

Figure 10–1   A wireless local loop topology.

Connections to the customer dwellings are made through the wireless base station (BS). The RF transceivers at the customer's site may be antennas located outside or inside the dwellings. Direct attachments to the dwellings eliminate the need for external wiring to the homes (options a and b in Figure 10–1) and thus compete with the fixed wire offerings such as HFC and TTP/ADSL.

With option c, the wireless part of the loop extends into the neighborhood to an RF transceiver, which acts as a conduit to the dwellings. This option competes with fiber in the loop, yet provides a means to extend fiber (with SONET) into the distribution plant.

Option c retains the TTP/coax, which at first glance appears to be a redundant configuration. However, the wireless part of the system may be a one-way broadcast in the downstream direction, which necessitates using the TTP/coax for upstream communications. Notwithstanding, if the RF bandwidth is configured as two-way (which is technically feasible in LMDS, for example), then the requirement for the TTP/coax is eliminated.

Option d is the direct TV (DTV) system. It can deliver 150 channels but is designed as a one-way system. The downstream direction uses the DTV media, but the upstream channel must use TTP on the POTS loop.

WLL VERSUS FIXED WIRE ACCESS

WLL's attraction over its fixed wire alternative is due to lower costs, design flexibility, and time-to-market. Figure 10–2 compares the costs to deploy wireless and wireline systems, based on subscriber per km. For an access system in the distribution plant, the wireless alternative is the clear choice.

A wire-based system requires the service provider to dedicate substantial resources to upgrade the system as traffic demand increases, as shown in Figure 10–3. The tasks of laying more cable, installing more underground conduits, and so on are quite labor-intensive and very expensive.

Wireless systems can be upgraded in a more incremental fashion. As traffic demand grows, wireless capacity can be added vis-à-vis the traffic demand. The time-to-market aspect of the comparison stems from the fact that wireless systems can be deployed faster than their wire-based counterparts.

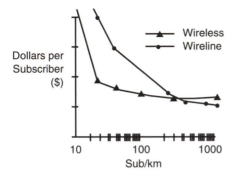

Figure 10–2 Capital costs for wireless and wireline.

WLL OPTIONS

WLL is different from cellular because it is designed for the local loop and mobile cellular is not so designed. This discussion will focus on WLL with emphasis on LDMS and MMDS and DECT.

Local Multipoint Multichannel Distribution Service (LMDS) and Multipoint Multichannel Distribution Service (MMDS)

MMDS has been in place for several years, and operates between 2.150 GHz and 2.682 GHz, and provides for 33 analog video channels. MMDS extends a cell to about 25 to 35 miles, depending upon the geographical region. It is a one-way technology and requires a separate channel (copper wire, for example) to communicate with a headend.

The LMDS technology uses smaller cells than MMDS (up to 5 miles for the cell radii). It supports two-way broadcast video, video-on-demand, data, and telephony services. The proposed bandwidth spectrum for LMDS is 27.5–28.35 GHz. This frequency band provides much bandwidth, but at

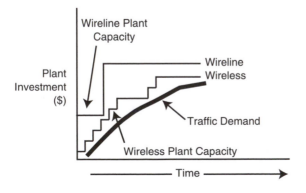

Figure 10–3 Adding plant capacity.

Table 10–1   LMDS and MMDS

Technology	Band	Pros	Cons
LMDS	27.5–28.35 GHz	• Bandwidth • Deployment ease	• Line of sight • 28 GHz electronics • Interference
MMDS	2.150–2.682 GHz	• Long range • Low cost • Deployment ease	• Spectrum is not contiguous • Interference

these high frequencies, the radio wavelengths are very short and more susceptible to attenuation than waveforms operating at lower frequencies. Therefore, many LMDS systems employ digital repeaters to expand the distance of the cell. Line-of-sight is required for LMDS.

Both LMDS an MMDS are attractive for their bandwidths and their ease of installation. However, their deployment depends on the amount of co-channel interference that may occur between nonadjacent cells using the same frequency. To help solve this problem, some operators are looking to spread spectrum and code division multiple access (CDMA), which allow adjacent cells to share the same spectrum spaces.

As mentioned earlier, LMDS operates in the 27.5–28.31 GHz spectrum, providing 850 MHz of bandwidth. An additional band has been allocated between 29.1 and 29.25 GHz for 150 MHz of bandwidth.

As just stated, these high frequencies are severely attenuated by foliage, and a line-of-sight installation requires antenna at hubsites at least 75 to 90 feet above ground. As stated earlier, these technologies also suffer from co-channel interference, and the FCC stipulates a 35-mile protection zone between MMDS service providers. Since LMDS cells are closely located, the LMDS service provider must deal with adjacent cell interference.

The advantages of LMDS and MMDS are the simplicity and ease of deployment and installation, especially in comparison with HFC systems. In addition, LMDS offers comparable capacity to HFC without the installation headaches. The *big* problem is the line-of-sight requirement. Table 10–1 provides a comparison of LMDS and MMDS.

DECT: AN ALTERNATIVE FOR WLL

As we will see in this section, DECT provides a flexible and efficient wireless technology for WLL. In North America, the TIA Personal Wireless Telecommunications Standards (PWT) are based on DECT and use the same MAC layer and frame structure of DECT (discussed shortly). The North American version uses a different physical layer to meet U.S. regulatory requirements.

In the United States, PWT operates in the unlicensed band at 1910–1920 MHz. PWT/Extended (PWT/E) is an extension into the 1850–1910 and 1930–1990 MHz spectrum.

DECT Architecture[1]

The Digital European Cordless Telecommunications (DECT) standard was initiated by the CEPT in the mid-1980s as a method to move to a second generation cordless telephone system. Several alternatives were evaluated by the CEPT in 1987, and eventually a technology known as Digital European Cordless Telephony was chosen. Later, the name was retitled to the Digital European Cordless Telecommunications standard to reflect that it supported not only voice traffic, but also data traffic. With the formation of ETSI in 1988, the responsibility for DECT standardization was passed to this organization. In 1992, DECT became a formal European common air interface standard known as the European Telecommunications Standard, ETS 300-175. The approval test standard is published in I-ETS 300176. It is now "enforced" as a standard by the European Commission Directive 91/287.

The original DECT specification uses ADPCM 32 kbit/s for speech coding, in accordance with ITU-T G.721. Twelve slots share each physical channel, as illustrated in Figure 10–4. Each slot contains 320 information bits. DECT uses TDD with 10 ms periods for two frames (fixed-to-mobile and mobile-to-fixed). Since each user has 320 bits per slot, and 100 10 ms slots per second, the channel capacity is 32 kbit/s (100 ∗ 320 bits = 32,000). The control channel (C channel) operates at a rate of 4 kbit/s (100 ∗ 40 bits = 4000).

Similar to other systems previously described in this book, the DECT frame contains various control fields, sync fields, and guard band time.

---

[1]This material was prepared from the DECT specifications and a conference titled: "DECT '98," in Barcelona, Spain 27-29 January 1998, sponsored by IBC UK Conferences LTD., London England.

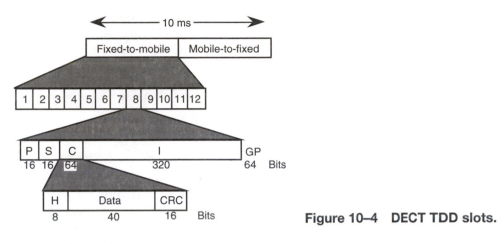

Figure 10–4   DECT TDD slots.

Support of Data

DECT does not restrict itself to voice transmission only. It is also designed to support data applications (see Figure 10–5). For data transmission, DECT uses the layered protocol stack based on the OSI Model and the IEEE 802 standards. The physical medium access control (MAC) and logical link control (LLC) layers are employed. A gateway examines the addresses contained in packets and routes the packets accordingly. This routing entails the relaying of the traffic to attached LANs, other gateways, or attached cordless devices (such as workstations, printers, fax machines, servers, etc.).

It is envisioned that most traffic will be carried with a connection-oriented procedure based on the DECT standard, although (technically)

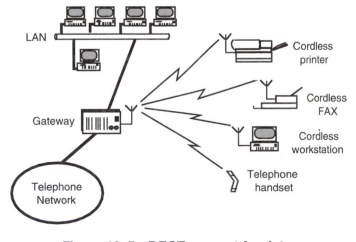

Figure 10–5   DECT support for data.

traffic can be sent in a connectionless mode. In addition, the gateway provides connections for voice traffic between workstations, telephones, and the telephone network.

DECT ARCHITECTURE

The structure of the DECT architecture is organized around the lower layers of the OSI Model. Figure 10–6 illustrates this architecture. The physical layer concerns itself with the radio interface. This interface operates with time division multiple access (TDMA) on multiple RF carriers. The MAC layer operates at both the physical and data link layers and is responsible for selecting physical channels and managing the connections on these channels. It is also responsible for multiplexing and demultiplexing information into slot-sized packets. The MAC functions provide for three types of services: (a) a broadcast service, (b) a connection-oriented service, and (c) a connectionless service.

The data link control layer (DLC) is a conventional layer 2 protocol that is responsible for the reliable transmission of traffic across the radio interface. It is divided in two planes of operation, the C-plane and the U-plane. The C-plane is applicable to all applications and is responsible for the transmission of internal control signaling and a limited amount of user information. This procedure is provided with a protocol called link access procedure for the C-plane (LAPC). The U-plane is specific to a ap-

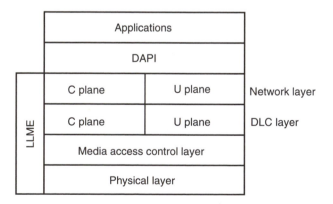

where:
   DAPI   DECT Application Programming Interface
   DLC   Data link control
   LLME   Lower layer management entity

Figure 10–6   The DECT layered architecture.

plication although the services can be tailored for a particular need of service. For example, the U-plane can offer unacknowledged and unsequenced transfer for speech traffic. It also offers options for circuit-mode and packet-mode data transmission.

The network layer operates at the OSI layer 3. It has many functions similar to the ISDN layer 3 protocol called Q.931. Its principal function is the establishment and release of connections between two devices, although we shall see that it also provides other services such as a connectionless service and a variety of supplementary services.

Finally, the lower layer management entity (LLME) is used to manage local MAC, DLC, and network layers. By local, I mean that the operations are not made visible outside the machine on which LLE operates.

Figure 10–7 shows the C plane of the network layer. The C plane of the network layer is invoked through service access points (SAPs). The SAPs are used to move the traffic into and out of specific entities in the C plane. At the top of the C plane are the following SAPs (and services):

CC   Call control: Management of circuit switched calls.

CISS   Call independent supplementary services: Support of all calls.

COMS   Connection oriented message service: Support of connection-oriented messages.

CLMS   Connectionless message service: Support of connectionless messages. The SAR entity will segment and reassembly traffic, if necessary.

MM   Mobility management: Support of location updating, and authentication, and key allocation.

The link (also called layer) control entity (LCE) routes messages to the appropriate data link layer endpoints through the SAPs shown at the bottom of the figure. It also routes the traffic up to the proper entity with a protocol discrimination function and a transaction identifier. Each of the entities is identified with a unique protocol identifier (e.g., CC messages = 2, MM messages = 5, etc.). The transaction identifier distinguishes multiple activities associated with one portable terminal (PT).

Figure 10–8 shows an example of how layer 3 of DECT sets up a connection. From a brief glance, you can deduce that DECT uses procedures that are similar to GSM 900, DCS 1800, and PCS 1900; that is, all use a version of Q.931.

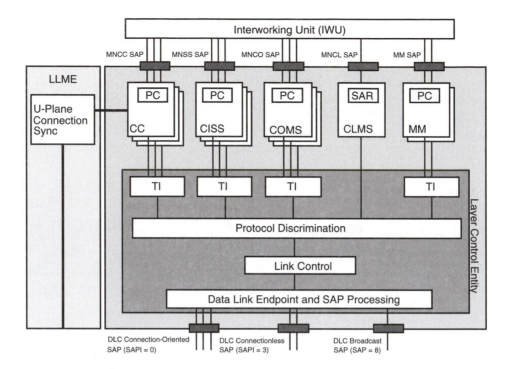

where:
    CC   Call control
    CISS   Call independent supplementary services
    CLMS   Connectionless message service
    COMS   Connection oriented message service
    MM   Mobility management
    MN   Mobile network
    PC   Protocol control
    SAP   Service access point
    SAR   Segmentation and reassembly
    TI   Transaction identifier

Figure 10–7   Network layer at the C plane.

I have added another aspect of layer 3 to this example: the use of states. Connection-oriented interfaces use states and state tables to control and govern how a connection is established and released. In addition, timers (not shown here) are turned on when the machine sends a message. Typically, when the machine sends a message, it progresses from one state to another (and turns on a timer). If the other machine does not respond with a specific message within the maximum bound of the timer,

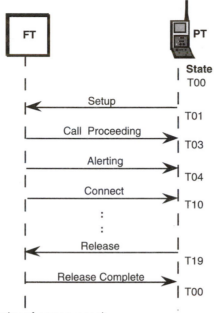

Message Contents (in order of appearance):
Protocol Discriminator: CC, CISS, MM etc.
Transaction ID   For each connection (activity)
Portable ID   ID of PT
Fixed ID   ID of FT
Basic services   For example, normal, emergency, etc.
Other   Optional fields

where:
FT   Fixed terminal
PT   Portable terminal

Figure 10–8   Example of a connection setup (and state transitions).

the machine takes remedial actions (usually, sending the message again, or invoking some other error-correction procedure).

This figure shows the states and state transitions on the mobile side (called a portable terminal [PT]) as it interworks with the base station (called as fixed terminal [FT]) to set up and clear down a connection.

The data link layer C plane (see Figure 10–9) is divided into three protocol entities, LAPC, Lc, and Lb. Taken as a whole, LAPC + Lc are accessed through the S SAP and provide for three classes of service:

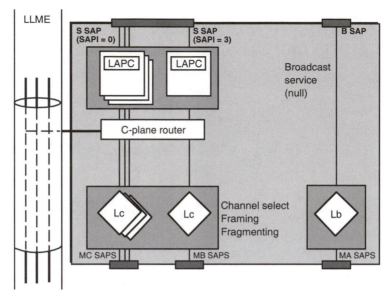

Figure 10–9   The data link layer at the C plane.

- Class U: Unacknowledged service
- Class A: A single frame acknowledged service
- Class B: A multiple frame acknowledged service

LAPC provides for the following types of service:

- Provisioning of one data link
- Control of one data link
- Error detection and error recovery
- Flow control
- Suspending or releasing the connection

Lc provides for the following types of service:

- Provisioning of one or more data links
- Frame delimiting
- Checksum generation and checksum checking
- Frame fragmentation (if appropriate)
- Frame routing to and from logical channels
- Connection handover

Lb is a broadcast service. The major aspect of the data link layer U plane (see Figure 10–10) is its use of link user plane (LU) service access points (SAPs). These are used to provide for the following services:

LU1 TRansparent UnProtected service (TRUP)
This is the simplest service, designed for speech transmission.

LU2 Frame RElay service (FREL)
Support of single user service data unit (SDU); very simple with no ACKs or NAKs.

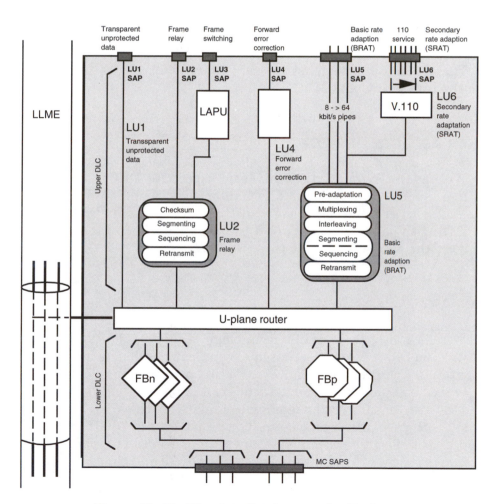

Figure 10–10   The data link layer at the U plane.

LU3   Frame SWItching service (FSWI)
       Supports a full, conventional data link protocol, such as
       ACKs, NAKs, sequencing. It is based on the V.42 protocol,
       which is an HDLC-based protocol.

LU4   Forward error correction (FEC)
       When finished, this will perform forward error correction op-
       erations.

LU5   Basic Rate adapTation service (BRAT)
       Used for ISDN interworking, it supports the continuous send-
       ing of data at 8, 16, 32, or 64 kbit/s.

LU5   Secondary Rate adapTation service (SRAT)
       Based on ITU-T V.110, this is also used with ISDN interfaces,
       and supports conventional V Series rates (50–19200 bit/s).

The U plane router is an internal router that routes traffic to and
from the upper DLC and MAC.

OTHER ASPECTS OF DECT

We have only touched on the basic aspects of DECT. It has many
features, such as encryption, ISDN interfaces, mobility management,
message services, and operation with the Point-to-Point Protocol (PPP).
The ETSI has published 121 specifications on DECT. For more information go to the ETSI website: http://www.etsi.fr.

SUMMARY

Wireless local loop (WLL) technology is in its infancy. The use of
high-frequency wave lengths presents significant problems because of severe attenuation problems. However, WLL operations employed inside a
building or between unobstructed senders and receivers is very effective.
    DECT is considered the leading candidate for the WLL air interface
as well as the network components. The proponents of DECT state that it
is more cost-effective to employ than a comparable wire-based system.
The final play out of WLL technologies like DECT and the traditional cellular systems is unknown. The best guess is that the technologies will
converge in the third generation mobile wireless technology, which is discussed in the next chapter.

11

Third Generation Mobile Systems (TGMSs)

This chapter provides an overview of the third generation mobile systems (TGMSs). Most of the formal, standardized efforts to define the TGMSs are being conducted in Europe. Our focus is to give you a general picture of these European efforts.

A VISION OF THE FUTURE

Figure 11–1 shows the development of radio technologies and systems that have contributed to intelligent networks since 1985, and the prediction of where they will be at the turn of this century. By 2005 it is envisioned that many systems will migrate to third generation mobile systems (TGMSs). This figure is a creation of British Telecom and several standards groups, amplified with some author's views.

Paging has been implemented in different countries by a variety of systems. One of the more popular networks is called POCSAG (Post Office Code Standardization Advisory Group). It is a third generation system and is employed in several countries in Europe. It operates in the 150–170 MHz frequency band (depending on the country). The pan-European digital paging system is called ERMES, which stands for Euro-

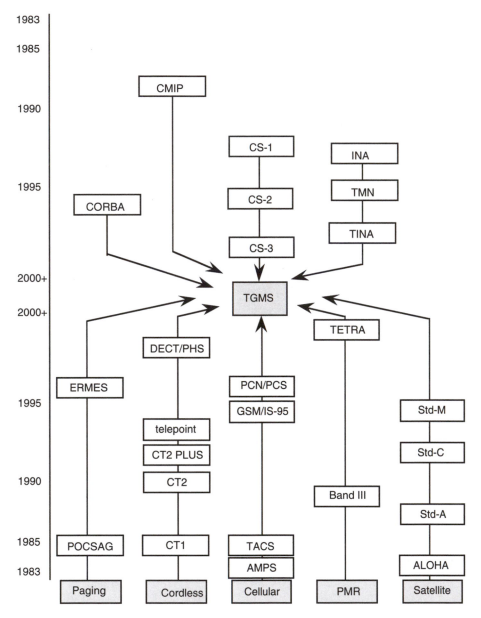

Figure 11–1   Vision of the future.

pean Radio Message System. This technology is supported throughout the European Community (EC).

Cordless telephony (CT) has enjoyed some success in various parts of the world. Initially this technology was intended for private wireless PBX applications. It led to the development of the telepoint technology, which was targeted for the mass market. Telepoint has not been very successful because (a) it relied on an existing population of CT2 handsets and CT2 has not been very successful, and (b) interest was beginning to surface in higher frequency digital services.

The DECT technology evolved about the same time as CT2. It was originally called Digital European Cordless Telephony and is now renamed Digitally Enhanced Cordless Telephony. Its principal goal is to support a high-density subscriber population typically found in offices and campuses and to support higher bit rates for data applications. It also operates over the 1880–1900 MHz band.

Cellular telephony was introduced worldwide in the early 1980s (for example, 1983 in the United States, 1985 in the United Kingdom). The U.S. deployment was with the Advanced Mobile Phone System (AMPS). The U.K. system is based on AMPS and is called TACS (Total Access Communications System). These analog-based systems operate in the 900 MHz range and are known as first generation mobile wireless systems.

The second generation mobile wireless systems are known as either personal communications network (PCN) or personal communications services (PCS). These systems are based on the Global System for Mobile Technology (GSM) and the IS-95 standard. Unlike AMPS and TACS, these systems are digital and operate in the 1800–1900 MHz bands. However, a number of systems are in operation that use GSM or IS-95 on the conventional 900 MHz band.

Private mobile radio networks (PMRs), as the name implies, are not part of a national pubic communications network, although they are regulated by the respective telecommunications administrations within each country. Initially, PMR systems were analog-based but they are evolving to the digital technology with the adoption of a European-wide standard called TETRA (TransEuropean Trunked Radio).

Finally, mobile satellite systems are seen as both a complement to the systems just described or in some cases as a competitor. Considerable interest has focused recently in what are called satellite PCN (Personal Communications Networks) or satellite PCS (Personal Communications Services). Their unique attribute is their use of low-earth orbits (LEOs), which requires the deployment of many satellites to cover the earth, yet allows the use of relatively inexpensive low-power mobile handsets. They also employ elaborate switching techniques in the satellites to support a user connection end to end, without the need to transport the signals on any terrestrial switching points until the signal reaches the called party.

The vision for the third generation mobile system is the convergence of the somewhat disparate technologies into a common interworking architecture. This architecture is forecasted by network planners to provide broadband services, bandwidth-on-demand, multimedia services, and asymmetrical bandwidth. In other words, it is designed to provide the same type of user services as its wire-based counterpart known as broadband ISDN (B-ISDN) or simply broadband networks.

The top part of the figure shows the role that network management and intelligent networks are playing and will be playing in TGMS. The Common Management Information Protocol (CMIP) was the first worldwide effort in developing a standardized network management platform. CORBA (the Common Object Request Broker Architecture) was developed in the late 1980s and implemented in the 1990s to prove a procedure for defining how objects interact in a distributed environment. It is used in many network management systems that are object-oriented with the use of well-known object request brokers.

Bellcore has provided extensive research leading to the information network and architecture (INA), which led to the subsequent development of the Telecommunications Management Network (TMN), published in the ITU-T M.3010. These specifications have provided a worldwide framework for developing a unified network management system, which in turn has contributed to the Telecommunication Networking Architecture (TNA).

Intelligent Network (IN) software will play a role in TGMA, with the emphasis on the work done by Bellcore and ITU-T. The evolution of the world wide IN standards have taken place through capability sets. It is anticipated that in the near future, capability set 3 (CS-3) will provide the final glue (of course, with revisions throughout) to the ITU-T view of the intelligent networks. As Figure 11–1 suggests, it is anticipated (and being planned by the Europeans) that these technologies will eventually contribute to the TGMS.

THE UNIVERSAL MOBILE TELECOMMUNICATIONS SYSTEM (UMTS)

The Universal Mobile Telecommunications System (UMTS) is considered a third generation system. It is intended to complement GSM and at the same time provide a path to improved technologies. Its principal aims are to provide:

- Common provisioning for all subscribers, either fixed or mobile (which translates into common supplementary services with common protocols to operate these services)
- Universal subscriber identifiers to support portable telephone numbers (this concept is more of a focus in the United States than in other countries)
- The switching network by ATM-based architecture
- Services for mobile and fixed subscribers by common call-processing procedures

The UMTS planes emphasize that UMTS will not replace GSM, but will supplement GSM capabilities, at least for the near future.

Figure 11–2 shows a possible migration path to UMTS. The approach is to provide a separate service layer for support of customized supplementary services. This service layer is currently being developed under the CAMEL (Customized Application for Mobile Networks Enhanced Logic) project. The integration of CAMEL and GSM provides an avenue to UMTS.

In Europe, where much of this architecture is being developed, it is anticipated that UMTS will not be available until around 2005. It is also anticipated that UMTS will be introduced in a phased approach by placing the services in the areas of highest demand and where population is dense. Wireless mobile operators predict that by 2005 (they also hope) that second generation systems will have reached a penetration rate of at least 50% of the population in industrialized countries.

THE UMTS ARCHITECTURE

The previous section dealt principally with the role of GSM in the third generation technology. The goal is to provide interfaces other than GSM. Indeed, the goal is to provide a generic interface which supports both TDMA and CDMA technologies. Figure 11–3 provides an example of the third generation architecture that is known as the Universal Mobile Telecommunications System (UMTS) and the International Mobile Telecommunications 2000 (IMT-2000). The architecture shown in Figure 11–3 is being defined by the European ACTS[1] Radio Access Independent

---

[1]ACTS stands for the Advanced Communications Technologies and Services project, which is sponsored in Europe. One of its functions is to define the radio interface for UMTS.

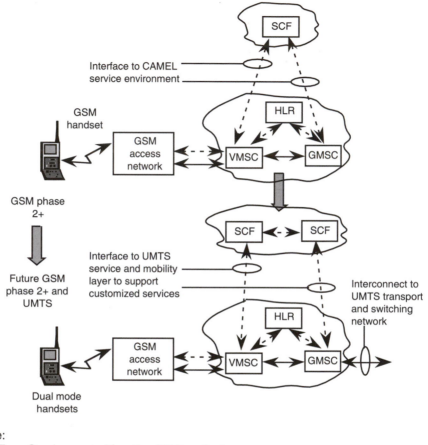

where:
  SCF   Service control function (IN Function)
  HLR   Home location register
  VLR   Visitor location register
  GMSC   Gateway mobile switching center
  VMSC   Visited mobile switching center

Figure 11–2 Migration from GSM to UMTS. (*Source*: BT Technology Journal, Vol. 14 No. 3, July 96, p. 130.)

Broadband on Wireless (RAINBOW). The objective of RAINBOW is to define a generic UMTS architecture with these functions:

- Mobile terminal (MT): The mobile station that connects with the network through the air interface.
- Base transceiver station (BTS): The base station that interworks with the MT on behalf of the network.

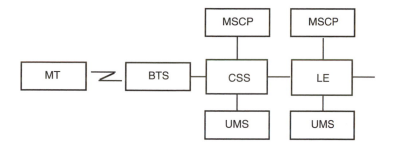

where:
BTS   Base transceiver station
CSS   Cell site switch
LE   Local exchange
MSCP   Mobile service control points
MT   Mobile terminal
UMS   UMTS mobility service

Figure 11–3   UMTS architecture.

- Cell site switch (CSS) and local exchange (LE): The core network machines that control the fixed part of the mobile wireless system.
- Mobile service control points (MSCP): Nodes that support hand-off, mobility management, location determination, etc.
- UMTS mobility service (UMS): Devices that provide access and core functions to support operations that are not performed readily by an ongoing backbone network (such as ATM).

A key concept of the UMTS work thus far is to allow second and third generation mobile stations to be supported by the same fixed network. Of course, this approach is embedded into the North American operation with the use of IS-41.

THE LAYERED ARCHITECTURE

Figure 11–4 shows the layered architecture of the third generation system from the standpoint of the MT, BTS, and UMS. Notice that the layers are classified as service dependent, mobility dependent, and basic transport categories. The dashed lines across the figure denote that these categories operate in the MT, BTS, and UMS. The radio dependent functions operate at the basic transport and are implemented with the radio

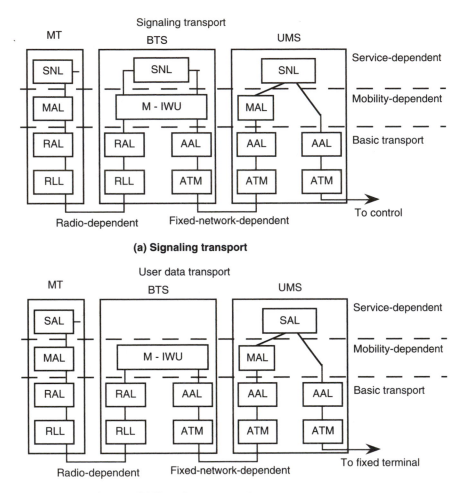

(a) Signaling transport

(b) User data transport

where:

BTS	Base transceiver station
CSS	Cell site switch
LE	Local exchange
MAL	Mobility adaptation layer
M-IWU	Mobility interworking unit
MSCP	Mobile service control points
MT	Mobile terminal
RAL	Radio adaptation layer
RLL	Radio lower layers
SAL	Service adaptation layer
SNL	Signaling network layer
UMS	UMTS mobility service

Figure 11–4 Third generation layers. (*Source: IEEE Personal Communications,* April 1998.)

adaptation layer (RAL) and the radio lower layers (RLL). The RLL is radio specific whereas the RAL is radio independent.

The second broad category, called mobility dependent, encompasses the mobility adaptation layer (MAL) and the mobility interworking unit (M-IWU). The MAL is responsibility for operations such as handoff, and the M-IWU (which is located only in the BTS) is responsibly for the interworking between the RAL and the transport mechanism in the fixed part of the network (such as AAL/ATM).

The service dependent category provides operations to allow the applications to use the underlying services of the radio interface or the fixed network operations. An example of a service dependent operation is a vocoder.

The service adaptation layer (SAL) in Figure 11–4b is designed to enhance the operations of the MAL and is service-specific to the application. It has the difficult job of mitigating the differences between the wireless services and the fixed services while keeping these mitigated operations transparent to the user application.

Finally, the signaling network layer (SNL) is used for the routing of signaling traffic.

THE FRAMES PROJECT

The FRAMES project is part of the ACTS research program. FRAMES is an acronym for Future Radio Wide-band Multiple Access System. During the initial investigations by the FRAMES working groups, the FRAMES multiple access (FMA), which consists of two access methods, was selected. The first method is called FMA1 and it includes wideband time division multiple access with and without spreading. The second FMA mode is FMA2 and it includes direct sequence wideband code division multiple access (CDMA). Table 11–1 provides a summary of the major aspects of FMA.

FEATURES AND OBJECTIVES OF TGMS

It is beyond this book to provide a detailed description of TGMS. However, we summarize some of the key aspects of the third generation system in Table 11–2 (Source: "IMT-2000: Service Provider's Perspective," by Ken Buhanan et al., *IEEE Personal Communications,* August 1997). For the reader who wishes a look ahead and examine this technol-

Table 11-1 The Main FMA Parameters

Multiple Access Method	TDMA	TDMA/CDMA	DS-CDMA
Duplexing method	FDD and TDD		FDD
Basic channel spacing	1.6 MHz		4.4–5 MHz with 200 kHz raster
Carrier chip/bit rte	2.6 Mbit/s–5.2 Mbit/s	2.167 Mchip/s	4.096 Mchips/s, also 8.192 and 16.384 Mchips/s
Time slot structure	16 or 64 slots/TDMA frame	8 slots/TDMA frame	—
Spreading	—	Orthogonal, 16 chips/symbol	Spreading factor 4 – 256, short codes for DL and UL; long code optional for UL
Frame length	4.615 ms		10 ms
Multirate concept	Multislot	Multislot and multicode	Variable rate spreading and multicode
FEC codes	Convolutional codes R = 1/4-to-1, puncturing/repetition		Convolutional codes; UL: R = 1/2; DL: R = 1/3, puncturing/repetition
Data modulation	BOQAM/QOQAM	QPSK/16QAM	QPSK
Spreading modulation	—	Linearized GMSK	Dual channel/Balanced QPSK or complex 4-phase spreading (UL)
Detection	Coherent, based on training sequence		Coherent detection, UL: reference-bit-based, DL: pilot/reference bit based
Other diversity means	Frequency/time hopping per frame or slot		Macrodiversity
Power control	Slow power control, 50 dB dynamic range		UL: open loop and fast closed loop (80 dB dynamic range); DL: fast closed loop (20 dB dynamic range)

Source: IEEE Personal Communications, April 1998.

Table 11–2   Key Features and Objectives of IMT-2000/FPLMTS

Global system	• A global standard promoting a high degree of commonality of design while incorporating a variety of systems and terminal types • Worldwide marketplace and off-the-shelf compatible equipment (leading to lower costs) • Worldwide common frequency band and roaming
New services and capabilities	• Provision of capabilities that enable new audio, video, and data services, including packet data and multimedia services, which are significantly more advanced than pre-IMT-2000 technologies • High service quality and integrity, comparable to the fixed network • Flexible radio bearers, leading to improved spectrum efficiency and lower cost • The capability to provide bandwidth-on-demand supporting a wide range of data rates, from simple low-rate paging messages through voice to the significantly higher rates needed for video or file transfer • Support for asymmetrical data capabilities that require high rates in one direction but much lower rates in the other • Improved security and ease of operation • Distributed control of service creation and service profile management based on the ITU-T Q.1200 series of Recommendations • Coherent systems management based on the ITU-T M3000 series of Recommendations
Evolution and migration	• Flexibility for evolution of systems, and migration of users, both from pre-IMT-2000 and within IMT-2000 • Compatibility of services within IMT-2000 and with the fixed telecommunications network (e.g., PSTN/ISDN) • Provision of a framework for the continuing expansion of mobile network services and access to services and facilities of the fixed network • An open architecture that will permit easy introduction of advances in technology and of different applications • The ability to coexist and interwork with pre-IMT-2000 systems
Flexibility: Multi-environment capabilities	• Accommodation of a maximum level of interworking between networks of different types to provide customers with greater coverage, seamless roaming, and consistency of services • Integrated satellite/terrestrial networks • Provision of services by more than one network in any coverage area • Provision of these services over a wide range of user densities and coverage areas • Provision of services to both mobile and fixed users in urban, rural, and remote regions • A wider range of operating environments, including aeronautical and maritime

Table 11–2 *Continued*

- A modular structure that will allow the system to start from as small and simple a configuration as possible and grow as needed, in size and complexity, and supporting evolution to meet emerging needs
- Caters to the needs of developing countries
- Flexibility to utilize adaptive software downloadable terminals to support multiband and Multi-environment capabilities
- Key parameters of bandwidth, transmission quality, and delay can be selected, negotiated, mixed, and matched by the requirements of the service according to the instantaneous capability of the radio channel
- Better use of the radio spectrum than pre-IMT-2000 consistent with providing services at acceptable costs, taking into account their differing demands for data rates, symmetry, channel quality, and delay

Source: IEEE Personal Communications, August 1997.

ogy, I refer you to two issues of *IEEE Personal Communications*: August 1997 and April 1998.

SUMMARY

TGMS represents a very ambitious plan for the next generation mobile wireless technology. In order to be backward compatible to DECT, GSM, and so on and to support multiple radio interfaces, CDMA, satellite, PCS, the mobile station and the network must have a great amount of intelligence.

It is obvious that such a plan requires a very long development time. It is likely that the second generation systems will be substantially upgraded in a evolutionary manner by the time UMTS becomes a reality. This likelihood, coupled with the massive deployment of satellite-based PCN/PCS systems, will likely necessitate altering the UMTS vision as time goes by.

Abbreviations/ Acronyms

AC or AUC Access Control or authentication center
ACKs positive acknowledgments
A/D analog-to-digital
AG guard time for abbreviated RACH burst
AGCH access grant channel
AMPS Advanced Mobile Phone System
ARQ authomatic retransmission request
ARCH access response channel
ARFCN absolute radio frequency channel number
ASE application service element
ASN.1 Abstract Syntax Notation One
AT access tandem
AUTHR & AUTHU authentication reponse
BCCH broadcast control channel
BCP basic call process
BER bit error rate
B-ISDN broadband ISDN
BRAT Basic Rate adapTation service
BS base station
BSC base station controller
BS-to-MS forward channel
BSIC base station information code
BSS base station system

BSSMAP base station subsystem management application part
BTA Basic Trading Areas
BTS base transceiver station
BTSM base transceiver station management
CAMEL Customized Application for Mobile Networks Enhanced Logic
CAVE Cellular authentication and voice encryption
CBS Cell Broadcast Service
CC country code
CC call control
CCH control channels
CDMA code division multiple access
CDPD Cellular Digital Packet Data
CDVCC coded digital verification color code
CGSA Cellular geographic service area
CHAN channel number
CICs Carrier Identification Codes
CISS Call independent supplementary services
CLMS Connectionless message service
CLNP Connectionless Network Layer Protocol
CLNS Connectionless netwrok service

CM connection management
CM communication management
CMIP Common Management Information Protocol
COTS Connection Oriented Transport Service
CRC cyclic redundance check
CPR call-processing logic
CRD Call rerouting distribution
CS capability set
CS-1 Capability Set 1
CS-1/R Capability Set 1/Refined
CS-2 Capability Set 2
CS-3 Capability Set 3
CSI channel stream identifier
CSFP coded super frame phase
CSS Cellular Subscriber Station
CSS Cell site switch
CSSINACT CSS inactive message
CT cordless telephony
D-AMPS digital AMPS
DCC digital color code
DCCH digital control channel
DCF data communications functions
DCN data communication network
DCR Destination call routing
DCS digital cellular system
DCS 1800 Digital Cellular System 1800
DDC data communications channel
DECT Digital European Cordless Telephone
DII dynamic invocation interface
DLC data link control layer
DLS data link switching
DMAC digital mobile attenuation code
DNS Domain Name System
DOC distributed object computing
DPC destination point code
DTAP direct transfer application part
DTC digital traffic channel
DTMF dual-tone multifrequency
DTX continuous/discontinuous transmission
DVCC digital verification color code
E-BCCH extended broadcast control channel
EC European Commission
EIR Equipment identity register

ERMES Eurpopean Radio Message System
ERP effective radiated power
ESH End system hello
ESN electronic serial number
E-TDMA extended TDMA
FA foreign accent
FAC final assembly code
FACCH fast associated control channel
FAS fast associated siganling
F-BCCH fast broadcast control channel
FCC Federal Communications Commission
FCCH frequency correction channel
FDD frequency division duplex
FDCCH forward DCCH
FDMA frequency division multiple access
FDTC forward digital traffic channel
FDX full duplex
FEC forward error correction
FES fixed earth station
FFD full-full duplex
FMA FRAMES multiple access
FOCC forward analog control channel
FSMM finite state machine modeling
FSWI Frame SWItching service
FT fixed terminal
FTP files transfer protocol
FVC Forward voice channel
G guard time
GEO Geosynchronous earth orbit
GGSN gateway GPRS support node
GMSC gateway mobile switching center
GP guard period
GPRS General Packet Radio Service
GSL global service logic
GSM Global System for MobileTechnology
GSM/DCS global system for mobile communication/digital cellular system
HA Home agent
HLR Home Location Register
HSCSD High Speed Circuit Switched Data
IAB Internet Activities Board
ICMP Internet Control Message Protocol
IMEI international mobile station equipment identity

IMSI international mobile subscriber number

IMTS Improved Mobile Telephone Service

IN intelligent Network

INA information network and architecture

IR interface repository

IS intermediate system

IS-41 Interim standard 41

ISC intermediate system hello confirm

ISDN Integrated Services Digital Network

ISG Internetwork Services Gateway

ISP Internet Service Provider

ISUP ISDN user part

IVDS interactive video and data area

IWF unterworking functions

LAC location area code

LAI location area identifier

LAP link access procedure

LAPB link access procedure, balanced

LAPDm link access procedure, d channel, for mobile

LCE link control entity

LCI local cell identifier

LE local exchange

LEOs low-earth orbit

LLC logical link control

LLME lower layer management entity

LMDS Local Multipoint Multichannel Distribution Service

LOCID location area ID

LOCREQ location request message

LPP lightweight presentation protocol

LSB least significant bit

LSAI local service area identifier

LU link user plane

MAC Mobile Attenuation Code

MAC medium access control

MACO mobile assisted channel allocation

MAHO mobile-assisted handoff

MAL mobility adaptation layer

MAP Mobile Application Part

MBDS mobile base data station

MC message center

MCC mobile country code

MCS Mobile Switching Center

MD-IS Mobile Data Intermediate System

MDLP mobile data link protocol

MEA message encryption algorithm

MEO medium earth orbit

ME-S mobile end system

MFR manufacturer's code

MHS Mobile Home Function

MIB management information base

MIN mobile identification number

MIP Mobile IP header

M-IWU mobility interworking unit

MON monitors

MM mobility management

MMDS Multipoint Multichannel Distribution Service

MN mobile network

MN mobile node

MNC mobile network code

MNLP Mobile Network Location Protocol

MS Mobile Station

MS-to-BS reverse traffic channel

MSC Mobile Switching Center

MSCP mobile service control points

MSF Mobile Serving Function

MSIC mobile subscriber identification code

MSISDN mobile station ISDN number

MTA Major Trading Areas

MTP message transfer part

MTP2 message transfer part 2

MT mobile termination

NAKs negative acknowledgments

NEI Network Entity Identifier

NID network identification

NPA numbering plan area

OAM operations, administration, and maintenance

ORDER order

ORDQ order qualification code

OSI Open Systems Interconnection

PACS Personal access communications system

PC protocol control

PCH paging channel

PCI protocol control information

PCN personal communications network

PCS personal communications system

PCS 1900 Personal Communications System 1900

PDU protocol data unit

PEA partial assign field

PHS Personal handyphone system
PIC point-in-call
PIN personal identification number
PL power level
PLMN public land mobile network
PLP packet layer procedure
PMSID permanent mobile station identity
PMRs private mobile radio networks
PN pseudonoise
POCSAG Post Office Code Standardization Advisory Group
PPP Point-to-Point Protocol
PRAT Paging channel
PREAM preamble
PROFREQ Service profile request message
PSID private system identification
PSTN Public Switched Telephone Network
PT portable terminal
PWT Personal Wireless Telecommunications
PWT/E PWT/Extended
QUALREQ qualification request
QPSK quadrature phase shift keying message
R ramp time field
RACH random access channel
RAINBOW Radio Access Independent Broadcast on Wireless
RAL radio adaptation layer
RAND random number
RAND random challenge
RANDSSD shared secret data random variable
RDCCH reverse DCCH
RDTC reverse digital traffic channel
RDC request redirect confirm
RDF redirect flush
RDR Request redirect request
RECC Reverse control channel
REDREQ redirection request message
REGCANC registration cancellation
REGNOT registration notification
REF reference
REL Release
RF radio frequency
RLL radio lower layers

ROSE Remote Operations Service Element
ROUTREQ routing request message
RPC remote procedure call
RR radio resource
RR receive ready
RSID residential system identification
RSSI received signal strength
RSVD reserved
RVC Reverse voice channel
RX receiving
S signaling or control bits
SABM Set Asynchronous Balanced Mode
SACCH slow associated control channel
SAL service adaptation layer
SAPs service access points
SAR segmentation and reassembly
SAT Supervisory audio tone
S-BCCH SMS broadcast control channel
SBI shortened burst indicator
SCC SAT color code
SCCP signaling connection control part
SCF shared channel feedback
SCF service control function
SCH ssynchronized channel
SCM station class mark
SDCCH stand-alone dedicated control channel
SGSN Serving GPRS support node
SIBs service independent building blocks
SID system identification number
SIM subscriber interface module
SMASE systems management application service element
SME short message entity
SMEKEY signaling message encryption key
SMF service management function
SMS short message service
SMSCH SMS channel
SNDCP subnetwork dependent convergence protocol
SNL signaling network layer
SNMP simple network management protocol
SNMP2 simple network management protocol , version 2
SNR serial number

SOR standard off-set reference
SPACH SMS point-to-point paging and access response channel
SPNI service provider network identifier
SRAT Secondary Rate adapTation service
SRES signed response
SRI security related information
SS signal strength
SS7 Signaling System Number 7
SSCP service switching and control point
SSD shared secret data
SSF service switching function
SSN subsystem number
SSP service switching point
ST signaling tone
STDM statistical TDM
STP signaling transfer point
SUS suspend
SYNC synchronization
SYNC+ additional synchronization
T tail bits
TA timing advance
TA terminal adaptation
TAC type approval code
TACS Total Access Communications System
TAF terminal adapter function
TCAP transaction capabilities application part
TCH traffic channels
TCP transmission control protocol
TDD time division duplexing
TDM time division multiplexed
TDMA time division multiple access
TDP trigger detection point
TE1 terminal equipment type 1
TE2 terminal equipment type 2
Telco Telephone company
TEI terminal end point identifier
TGMS third generation mobile wireless systems
TI transaction identifier
TIA/EIA Telecommunications Industries Association/Electronic Industries Assocaition

TIA Telecommunications Industry Association
TLDN temporary local directory number
TLV type-length-valve
TMN Telecommunications Management Network
TMSI temporary subscriber identifier
TMSIn new temporary subscriber identifier
TMSIo old temporary subscriber identifier
TNA telecommunication networking architecture
TP4 transport layer protocol class 4
TRANUMREQ number request message
TRUP Transport UnProtected service
TTP telephone twisted pair
TUP telephone user part
TX transmit
UAN Universal access number
UDP user datagram protocol
UDR User-defined routing
Um air interface
UMS UMTS mobility service
UMTS Universal Mobile Telecommunications System
UNRELDIR roamer data directive invoke message
UPT Universal personal telecomm
UTC Universal Coordinated Time
VLR Visitor Location Register
VLR Visitor location register
VMCS visited mobile switching center
VOT Televoting
VP-MASK voice privacy mask
VPNs Virtual private networks
VSLEP vector-sum excited linear predictive coding
V/UV voice/unvoiced
W-CDMA Wideband CDMA
WLL wireless local loop
WS workstation
WSF workstation function

Index